PSYCHOLOGY
AND
THE MEASURE
OF MAN

JOSEPH LYONS

PSYCHOLOGY
and the
MEASURE
of
MAN

A PHENOMENOLOGICAL APPROACH

The Free Press of Glencoe
Collier-Macmillan Limited, London

FOR
MILDRED
AND
RICKI

Think that this world against the wind of time
Perpetually falls the way a hawk
Falls at the wind's edge but is motionless—

Think that this silver snail the moon will climb
All night upon time's curving stalk
That as she climbs bends, bends beneath her—
                                                    Yes
And think that we remember the past time.

These live people,
These more
Than three dimensions?
By time protracted edgewise into heretofore
People,
How shall we bury all
These queer-shaped people,
In graves that have no more
Than three dimensional

        —ARCHIBALD MACLEISH
        "Signature for Tempo"

PREFACE

IN THIS BOOK I HAVE ATTEMPTED TO OUTLINE A PHENOMENOLOGICAL psychology of clinical problems. There are surprising difficulties which turn out to be connected with such a task; and perhaps for this reason all of us may understand, even excuse, the nearly complete absence of similar endeavors in all the recent rash of psychological writings in English. One has first to compose a kind of philosophy of psychology, touching on topics that are often fearfully avoided in scientific works. I am not sure whether this is because contemporary philosophy has abdicated from its traditional role, or, as is more likely, because at this moment in history, philosophy and psychology seem to be stumbling toward a convergence of sorts. It may well be that I might better have left the discussion of the topics to professional philosophers. But these are questions that the reader himself will have to answer as he considers the ways I have found to pose, and struggle with, the relevant issues.

In particular, a book that touches on phenomenology and existentialism runs into special difficulties of its own. The major sources for my approach are to be found, of course, in the writings of European thinkers whose works ought certainly to be consulted first hand. But the temper of American thought, especially in psychology, seems to run counter to the attempt, even when the need is apparent and the material available in translation. Perhaps a flanking maneuver will succeed where a frontal assault must surely fail—and so I try to emphasize in my discussion those problems of clinic and laboratory which are of direct concern to American workers in the clinical disciplines. For this reason, too, I usually choose not to drop the ac-customed roster of well-known names—Kierkegaard, Husserl, Hei-degger, Sartre, Merleau-Ponty, Jaspers, Straus, to mention them at least once—nor even to quote from them except in a few scattered and harmless instances. However, the knowledgeable reader will for-tunately recognize the kinship of many of my terms and notions to concepts already current in the European literature. If, then, one looks for a phenomenology, or an existentialism, or for whatever terminological amalgam is currently fashionable, it will not be im-mediately evident in these modest pages. As my subtitle indicates, what is offered here is the indefinite rather than the definite article.

Although this book is intended as a first contribution toward the re-evaluation of some basic clinical problems, it is not meant as a manual on what to do in the clinical situation. I have no new method to offer—but I hope that the criticisms as well as the positive sug-gestions offered here, many of which would seem to be long overdue, will begin to make possible an approach in which our main interest is recentered. If this were to happen, our emphasis as clinicians and scientists might shift from "Others" to "Persons"—to introduce at once a pair of terms which will carry the main burden of my argument. I will claim that a science of Others is basically different from a sci-ence of Persons, and that psychology as a science is therefore forced to conform to two very special requirements: Since it is the special discipline which is concerned with persons as observed by persons, there is required (1) that the perceived be a Person, not an impersonal Other, and (2) that the perceiver act as a full human being. If phe-nomenology, like any other method and approach, is understood as a stand that one takes in order to gather data about the world, it be-comes clear that only a phenomenological psychology, with its trick of freeing the person as perceiver, is able to serve as the basis for a true science of man.

These are surely matters that demand our earnest and extended discussion, and I hope that reopening some neglected topics, as I have tried to do—in particular, the topic of time, which is curiously neg-lected in psychology—will serve a constructive purpose in the hu-manistic science to which we devote our efforts as professionals and as citizens.

Ideas are the foundlings of our world; we are never quite sure of their parentage. I could not begin to track down the pervasive influences that are probably the real foundation for what I have written. Nevertheless, I ought at least to publicly announce my more recent intellectual debts, even though I will hardly be able to repay them. The ideas spelled out in this series of interconnected essays owe more than I can adequately express to Martin Scheerer, John Chotlos, Paul G. Smith, Alden Fisher, and most of all Erwin W. Straus. I have been most fortunate in my teachers and friends.

I would like to thank the following individuals and publishers for permission to reprint material: Samuel Beckett, *Endgame*. Translated from the French by the author. Copyright © 1958, by Grove Press, Inc., New York. Archibald MacLeish, "Signature for Tempo," in *Collected Poems*. Houghton Mifflin Company, Boston, 1933. Gilbert Ryle, *Dilemmas*. Cambridge University Press, New York, 1954.

JOSEPH LYONS

Lexington, Kentucky
May, 1963

CONTENTS

CONTENTS

PART III SITUATION AND ENCOUNTER

PART I

INTRODUCTION

HOW
TO
WRITE
THIS
BOOK

"But talk ain't nothin' till it ask," said Powell. "Man is a question
the beast ask itself."
—GEORGE LAMMING, *Season of Adventure*

THE SPECIAL NATURE OF THIS BOOK, AND PERHAPS MY PARTICULAR
approach to it, may explain why there is required at the outset an
introduction and summary: hence the title of this chapter. I have
chosen to meet this improbable dual requirement by discussing at
some length the various ways in which I might have written the
book, as well as the ways in which you, the reader, might undertake to
read it. You should then discover, as I now discover in writing these
pages, that the two roles of reading and writing do not simply stand
opposite one another in a complementary relation like the familiar

3

masks of comedy and tragedy or the sword and scale in the two hands of Justitia. Reading and writing do not only fill each other out, they also offer each other mutual support. They require and define each other, and chiefly, they feed upon one another. The writer, as he writes, learns to read; and the reader, as he reads, writes his own version of whatever occupies him. This is why an essay on how to read this book, which is what this chapter is, is also an exposition of its writing. My business is your business. In setting down these words I undertake a certain commitment to you, and in reading these pages you pick up the other end of the handle and follow along with me. I am entering into this discussion simply because I believe that writing and then reading a book is itself a perfect example of the very two-sided problems about which this work is concerned.

Are there many different ways in which I might say what I mean in this book? The obvious answer, perhaps delivered in a tone of mild surprise, is that of course there is only one way. I must express as clearly as possible what I have in mind so that you, the reader, may grasp it, agree or disagree in some measure, and either dismiss it or introduce it into your own thinking. If I have something to say, I should say it—not dogmatically, of course, but with certitude and firmness. If there are facts to present, I should marshal and present them in organized and, we may hope, palatable or memorable fashion. The organization of facts, especially when the organization arises out of my own convictions and is therefore interpretive to some degree, should be identified as such and logically developed. The conclusions ought to be relentlessly pursued and, hopefully, impaled at last on the point of the summary aphorism. Above all, opinions should be identified as such so that they may not be confused with facts nor with logically acceptable interpretations arising out of organizations of facts.

But does not this approach, satisfying and respectable though it undoubtedly is, almost demand our prior agreement on all of the essential material? Does it not imply that the reader is limited to being informed (which means *molded*) rather than stirred or aroused to action on his own? Does it not suggest that the facts *are* there to be discovered by one of us and then displayed to the other, that a book cannot in its writing change what is there but at best only organize it in palatable and memorable fashion? There is probably a very great need for books of this sort; I am sorry to say that most textbooks seem to aim at satisfying only this need. But are there not other needs that other kinds of writing may satisfy? There are many other ways of writing; let us consider them one at a time and see how they differ from what I will call the "textbook" approach.

Poems and Poets

I mean to use these terms, *poems* and *poets*, in the broadest possible sense, to include not only poetic verse as we usually understand it but also the whole range of poetic-like writing, such as fiction, drama, and even highly personalized essays. There is clearly something about a creative use of words that sets it apart from "textbook" talk, no matter how well organized or inspired the latter may be. Even the most passionately convinced of poets, even in his most didactic verse, does not lecture. The relationship between the poet and his reader is strange and singular. It resembles more the whispering of lovers than a talk between teacher and student. The poet does not offer facts, nor does the dramatist organize data. These may indeed be their own expressed aims, for writers are sometimes the most poorly equipped judges of the significance of what concerns them most deeply. But whatever their aims, however they choose to talk about themselves and their words, their reader, when he embarks on the work with them, begins a unique kind of journey. His goal cannot be that of the student who is bent on acquiring facts or their organization; if this were the case, he would do better to consult a textbook or a teacher. The reader may doubtless learn something by attending a drama or reading a poem, but what he learns will have come out of the time spent rather than from the data apprehended, even when these are novel or most apposite—just as the young man who looks back on his first love affair will have learned something (if he has learned something) that is not reducible to facts acquired concerning his love's preferences or practices. The term "learning" somehow falls short of describing these experiences in retrospect; but we psychologists have no other terms, unfortunately, to sum up an episode of growth and change.

Consider what happens when the reader "meets" the poet for the first time. He opens the page, he reads the title, he begins the first line. Is this similar to opening a textbook, looking over the title page, and then turning to the initial chapter? There is a similarity in the fact the both are books, that each is bound, that each may have a title, and that there may be a different title for the first poem or opening chapter than is found on the title page. However, these similarities are largely extrinsic; they depend on a similar process of manufacture, which in turn comes from the fact that both a textbook and a volume of verse are, as objects, man-made things. But here the similarity ends. The reader who "meets" the poet can expect something quite unique in the realm of the printed word. There might be a title for the volume as a whole—but how informative are titles of books of verse? How much information, indeed, is ever offered by the title of a work of art? Musicians, as a matter of convention, use the titles of their works primarily as a simple cataloguing system, usually identifying only the form of the composition and its position in the sequence of the author's finished efforts. The Beethoven symphony which is counted as the ninth in the sequence of this instrumental form, and as Opus 125 in the catalogue of the composer's works, is also called the Choral; but this is not a title so much as a convenient, identifying description. It is true that painters, at least those of former centuries, often title their works in a simply informative way, but even this custom has tended to disappear. The titles of works painted under the influence of modern schools tend to be either arbitrary or unconnected with the apparent meaning of the work, or else a catalogue-like listing, after the manner of serious music.

Thus the reader who comes to the book offered by a poet is not likely to receive much in the way of introduction. It will not be as it is with a textbook, in which the book is picked up because it fits in a certain way into the reader's interests and promises to provide him with a desideratum of knowledge or organization of data. To continue the analogy of the meeting between persons, the reader who begins a textbook is in the same position as someone who goes to a lecture or attends a teacher's class or drops into the office of a colleague in order to learn something. The reader of poetry is in the position of meeting a complete stranger. Even if the author is well known to his reader—in fact even if the reader has read these very poems before and is now going back to them to renew his pleasure—he will expect a fresh and new experience; his disappointment can lie only in not having this kind of experience, not in that, in the end, he knows no more about some area of knowledge. Further, each single poem in a book of poems will strike the reader in this same way. Each poem will be an independent episode to which he will have to find his own way and from which he can turn refreshed or disappointed, stirred or unmoved, but neither more nor less informed. This is not because, as is so often claimed, poetry is a matter of emotions rather than reason; for such a dichotomy is both naïve and psychologically ill founded. The book of poems differs from the textbook, not because one calls to the affective side of the reader and the other to his rational aspect (for the passionate lecture is as common as the cool and reasoned poem), but because they set up different relations with their readers. The reader of poetry meets someone new at each poem, helped along by no more than a title, as he might be helped by a conventional introduction to a stranger which includes the mention of the separate names. At best he may have some idea of what he and the poet intend to consider jointly in their meeting. But beyond this he will not, and indeed he ought not, know what will happen in the meeting, whether it will be moving or banal, or how and to what degree he will be enriched. He takes his chances with the poem, for there is nothing that could be stated *a priori* to help minimize the challenge and the risk that he undertakes. Unlike the textbook, there is no summary one can write, no explanatory introduction, no helpful preface to a poem or a book of poems. These helps, if they appear at all, can never be more than individual judgments by the poet; and when he stops to consider his own work in this way, he, too, gives up his special status as author and deserves no better consideration than any other reader and judge of the published work. A poem cannot be concluded with an explanation of itself or a statement about itself; nor can it contain a reference to another poem as a kind of invitation for two persons to meet again for the first time. The relationship of poet and reader is *sui generis;* collaboration between poets is almost unheard of, and indeed strikes us as somehow unpoetic. Only in this way, and for this reason, and on this basis, can a poem have value without factual meaning.

The Example of the Example

Writing by means of examples is, perhaps properly, not usually considered a method in itself, and certainly not an art form nor a mode of expression. At best it may be viewed as a technique. Gilbert Ryle has used it most effectively in recent years, particularly in his book of essays entitled *Dilemmas* (1954), but surprisingly it is far from common, even as a device in psychological writing. Yet it has an honorable history. It was the choice of William James, and we need only read again some of his most impressive passages to see that he delighted in making his point by means of an elaborated example. In discussing the continuity of personal consciousness, for instance, he remarks: "When Paul and Peter wake up in the same bed, and recognize that they have been asleep, each one of them mentally reaches back and makes connection with but one of the two streams of thought which were broken by the sleeping hours. As the current of an electrode buried in the ground unerringly finds its way to its own similarly buried mate, across no matter how much intervening earth; so Peter's present instantly finds out Peter's past, and never by mistake knits itself on to that of Paul" (1950, Vol. 1, p. 238). The approach is typical of James' style. He makes a point; he elaborates it; and then he clinches it with a telling example that brings it alive and makes the reader suddenly capture, or perhaps be captured by, a subtle and elusive, yet wonderfully apt, thought. It is not important that one agree or disagree with James. As a matter of fact, the number of psychologists who have disagreed profoundly with him on matters of basic orientation has been very large during the past half-century; yet it is not one bit larger than the number (often the same persons) who have been impressed and even excited by what he has presented in so catching a fashion.

The technique which stands opposed to a method of examples is the development of argument through a hierarchically interconnected series of propositions, much in the manner of a complex and elaborated syllogism. Such a method needs no examples. It depends for its force on the reader's acceptance of the power of a logically proper deduction. In this sense, but only in this sense, the conclusion of an argument when presented deductively is self-evident. One might quarrel with its premises or perhaps with the adequacy of some of the data proffered in support of various steps in the argument; but otherwise, if one accepts the first step one is forced to admit the conclusion. All that one could maintain, even if he were the most antagonistic and persistent of critics, would be that the conclusions have to be accepted, but that perhaps they are narrower in scope than their author has realized and are therefore limited in their application to a few special cases; or he may say that the conclusions are not in fact true. This may not be said of any *theoretical* proposition in science, but only of logically impeccable extensions of useful, if arbitrary, starting points, or quasi-arbitrary approximations to nature, or approximations that gain whatever truth value they have, not from any intrinsic content or appeal to reason but solely because empirical data can be shown to be consistent with them.

The method based on examples is, however, an alternative to the deductive method, and is worth considering. One would begin by proposing that there can be more than one way in which what seems true to one person is told to another and finally comes to be accepted by him as so. One of the ways I have already discussed under the general heading of *poetry;* it consists of the overriding experience we sometimes achieve when we share with a poet his grasp of some truth. A second method occurs when a point is made by means of an example—when it suddenly strikes home, as we say, and appears to the listener as certainly so. The great power of analogy, misused though it may often be, rests on this possibility. To use an example is not to provide information, for examples rarely tell us more facts than we already know from looking at what is exemplified; nor is it to build logically toward a conclusion, for the example is usually complete in one step. An example—which literally refers to taking one entity out of a group of many, to selecting—reminds us of what, as reasoning and often skeptical thinkers, we tend to forget or dismiss:

that very often the single instance is sufficient to clinch an argument or drive home a revealing truth.

The effect of the example resides in the fact that it is simply an apt version of the particular, and therefore living, instance. From the parables of the New Testament to the calculated anecdotes told by contemporary after-dinner speakers, we find evidence that an argument can be offered and a conviction shared when the listener suspends his insistence on a developed logical structure and permits himself to discover some truth in the impact of a single example. If it is a poor one for him, he will accept it as a more or less apt story and be no worse off than if the argument had not been made to him. But if he grasps the example as a telling one, he needs no further convincing. He accepts what the example points to, even though he himself might not be able to reason backward, nor restate it so that it will convince others, nor even fit his newfound conviction into a reasonable structure. Whatever is so for him will now appear to be self-evident—as, indeed, all truth must be to the one who holds it.

Under the influence of the natural sciences, which have for good reasons depended so fully on the method of logical deduction, we have tended in modern times to devalue opinions held or conclusions reached by way of the example. We have, in fact, devoted a great deal of sober thought to puzzling out the question of how it is that people who otherwise seem quite rational and sensible, ready to admit the overriding power of logically correct thinking, as well as its necessity in significant matters, should in many situations most central to their own thinking display a lamentable disdain for logic and reason. They will hold firmly to their ideas without being in the least able to defend them, to explain how they arrived at them, or to persuade others in a rational manner. Worse, they may even be unable to reconcile their own cherished convictions with the logic of the particular situation. They will be completely unable, and often unwilling as well, to adopt a dispassionate attitude, to examine their own positions coolly and reasonably, and to apply to themselves the very rules of argument that they will insist are otherwise basic to intelligent discourse in science. But to accuse these people of being emotional rather than rational can arise only from an overevaluation of the method of deductive logic. It is no part of wisdom to confuse the ways of thinking with the techniques for talking about thinking, yet this is what we do whenever we work backward in this way, applying to the processes of searching out the truth a set of methods that are at best sometimes useful for organizing the various aspects of truth once it has been discovered.

An example is a unique kind of evidence—although it is true that for many scientists it would never be admitted as a kind of evidence at all. In order to examine the example as evidence we will have to consider first what happens when a person arrives at that point in his thinking where he can nod his head in affirmation. This may occur when he has thought his way through to a reasoned conclusion; or when he has solved a problem and reached what seems to him a satisfactory answer; or when he hears or reads something offered by another person and learns something from it; or when he changes his mind because of a telling argument; or when someone else says something more clearly than he has been able to do and he therefore signifies his agreement; or sometimes when he merely apprehends a datum, such as a reading on a meter. One scientist has essayed a description of the process in these words: "Now, it is an interesting question, but one which is not easily answered—just at what point in the gradual accumulation of circumstantial evidence can the latter be accepted as adequate for demonstrating the truth of a proposition? Perhaps the most we can say is that, in practice, this point is mainly determined by the multiplicity of independent sources from which this evidence is derived; if several lines of argument based on apparently unrelated data converge on, and mutually support, the same general conclusion, the probability that this conclusion is correct may appear so high as to carry conviction to the mind of unbiased observers" (Clark, 1959, pp. 299–300). Certainly this rings true in regard to problem areas in which the limits are pretty well known and the major possible lines of attack fairly well established. But what of the issues about which the scientist feels less secure? What is his experience when he begins to reach out toward the boundaries of his own knowledge? Conventional scientific methodology does not provide us with much help, nor does formal deduction as a general method; for as Toulmin (1958) has remarked in the course of an intensive examination of the questions we are here discussing, it will not usually provide complete justification for our arguments.

In the act of affirmation, no matter what specifically occurs on the way, the person finally comes to a point where acceding either does or does not occur. Data may keep piling up, evidence may accumulate impressively, the logic may be honed to a finer and finer edge, but there must eventually come a moment in the argument at which the data are deemed sufficient, the evidence impressive enough, and the logic unanswerable. At this point the person stops reasoning, stops judging or weighing, and, indeed, even stops thinking. He either throws up his hands in full disbelief and turns aside, completely disavowing what he has just heard, or else he takes a plunge into belief. He accepts some proposition as so—and at this moment he knows full well, were he able to freeze all his thinking and examine it, that his acceptance is constituted of more than the sum of the data or the organization of the argument to which he has been attending. He knows that the step from attending to agreeing is of a different order than the steps from one level of an argument to another. Evidence does not add up to truth; it merely supplies one stable ground for it. And so, even in the simplest instance in which, let us say, we look at a meter and read it, taking in the datum, so to speak, and nodding acceptance of it, we either know that it is so or we do not; the alternative possibilities, such as that we are visually deceived or indulging in metaphysical heresy, are simply out of place. These are arguments that belong to the sequence which may lead up to the moment of conviction, but they do not belong to the act of acceptance itself. And the fact that *after* the moment of acceptance we can discuss the whole event—as I am doing now—is not to say that acceptance is other than I have described it. The distinction here is related to what has been called "validating" and "procedural" forms of evidence, the former referring to "observable consequences following a prescribed succession of events designed to test that principle," the latter to the belief in a "statement or principle because of its intelligibility, consistency with common-sense knowledge, or implicit self-evidence" (Rychlak, 1959, p. 645).

We may now see that the example is simply a common form— almost the prototype, in fact—of a datum that is accepted as knowledge. A datum that is *not* accepted as such may be treated by the listener, or potential recipient, in a number of ways. He may reject it completely; he may continue to consider it, weighing it or examining its various aspects and facets; he may hold it suspended in a fog of doubt; he may simply be fascinated by it, beyond its possibilities as knowledge; he may use it as the starting point for some idiosyncratic elaboration, either as threat or as challenge; or he may remove it from the field that he considers as belonging to himself and to his own functioning, continuing to recognize its existence, so to speak, but as something alien to himself. All of these alternatives are interesting, and each leads to its own form of knowing or not-knowing, from rigid partisanship in the first case to hysterical dissociation in the last. But if the datum is accepted as a bit of knowledge, with all that this implies, a unique kind of act takes place, an act that I have been describing in these pages as one of acceptance. The example is itself the best example of acceptance. Indeed, in no other way could we understand how it is that anyone can become convinced by means of an example. Suppose, to take an obvious example, that you do not believe that an adult who exercises power can possibly be kind and gentle toward those under him; and suppose that you are told that the boss of your department plans to give all his employees a Christmas bonus and an afternoon off. I need not repeat here all the possible alternatives to your acceptance of this datum as a piece of knowledge—but assuming that you do accept it, what have you done? One theory has it that you have generalized. You have in effect gone through a logically connected series of propositions, in more or less the following way: all adults are authoritarian; this particular adult is nonauthoritarian; therefore it is not true that all adults are authoritarian; well, then, if this is so, and if this adult is kindly, then some adults are probably kindly and I have been wrong.

The trouble is that there is no way to state this argument in such a way as to make it seem trenchant, for it clearly is not, or to eliminate the very phenomenon that I am describing. There is no way to reduce the phenomenon of acceptance-by-example to the phenomenon of generality, for the latter only describes rather vaguely one of the many aspects of the former. Whether or not the process of generalization—which is not a process in deductive logic at all, of course—is a possible route toward accepting a piece of knowledge, it would still be true that it is the example, not the logical process, which best describes, sums up, or serves as a prototype of the gaining of knowledge.

This is so most of all in regard to the kinds of knowledge that are important to us. It is always possible for reasonably broadminded persons to accept the most outré propositions on the basis of a kind of temporary loan, perhaps only to carry them around for a while and see how they feel. We refer to this phenomenon when we hear something small but remarkable and smile a little and shake our heads, amused but intrigued and interested, and then say, "Well let me think about it for a while." But usually we can do this only for those data that are peripheral to our basic concerns, never for what is most central or significant for our own values and beliefs. In matters that matter we will accept nothing short of acceptance; we demand the telling example; we want to know for sure. In his difficult, yet most fundamental, discussion of the nature of human dialogue, Martin Buber tells us at one point: "What I am here concerned with cannot be conveyed in ideas to a reader. But we may represent it by examples—provided that where the matter is important, we do not eschew taking examples from the inmost recesses of the personal life. For where else should the like be found?" (1958, p. 5). The point at which ideas and their necessarily logical interrelationships fail us, the point at which we either accept or reject and then find or do not find the truth, is the point at which the example resides. It is never to be judged solely as another datum, although of course it is that, but as the keystone of all the relevant data. This is why we reserve it for what counts.

Biography as History

The Freudian influence has revolutionized many aspects of clinical thinking and practice, but in no respect more than in regard to the patient's life history. In the psychoanalyst's hands biographical data have come to mean more than the factual details of previous illnesses or hereditary background; they tend to assume the importance of first causes. Adult character is said to be the inevitable result of certain kinds of childhood experience that have occurred at key points in the biologically determined stages of the individual's growth. Character is the ground against which the figures of specific behavioral acts appear; and these figures, in the form of symptoms, may also be equally determined by patterns of events in the patient's personal history.

The Freudian system, taken as a whole, is a continuous and puzzling paradox in science just because it seems to combine the most scintillating discoveries with the most atrociously simplistic organization of its data, the most brilliant of clinical insights with the most mechanical explanations—and most significantly because, even at its most foolish, simplistic, or mechanical, it appears to contain some germ of truth. As one instance out of many, one does not have to accept the theory's tortured constructions concerning a division of psychic territories and energy to recognize in the psychoanalytic conception of dynamic unconscious processes the glimpse of a profound and central problem—that human experience is somehow larger than human awareness, and, therefore, that the way in which one comes to know the truth may provide the key to how it is possible for each person to learn and report what is true for him.

By the same token, one need not agree with the Freudian conception of a specifically determined causal link between childhood experience and adult destiny to remark on the importance of the psychoanalytic conception of the significance of one's personal history. I do not mean by this statement that psychoanalysis is either the first or the only system to make use of the idea of meaningful personal development. We needed no metapsychology to tell us that life is a pattern, a sequence, an order through time; that it is marked out in special ways, and that the stoppings and startings, the turnings, and the wishes gained and the hopes unfulfilled tell a story that makes sense in terms of the individual person. But in the hands of the psychoanalytic practitioner the biography of a patient takes on a new significance, one that is related to the role the analyst plays in the patient's *present* life experiences. Recall that whatever else he does, when the patient comes for psychoanalytic treatment he brings with him everything that belongs intimately to his personal world and his life in it. The primary and basic rule is impressed on him from the outset: he must hold nothing back, no matter how small or trivial or mean, no matter how good or ill it seems to him, how important or insignificant. The patient brings all of his life into the analyst's office; specifically, he brings it in the form of a presently pressing problem which, together, they agree to regard as the inevitable end result of all the patient's previous history. And the course of the treatment itself involves either a careful tracing out of the lines of action and fantasy and emotion that have made up the patient's past, or else a detailed examination of the full meaning of today's hour as it reflects all the former hours of his life.

The link between the present hour, the hour of today in this office, and the tangled lines of cause and effect of all the former years, is to be found, according to this conception, in the patient's changing relation to the analyst himself, a relation known as the *transference.* We need not be concerned here with the theoretical structure by which this idea is bolstered and spelled out. For our purposes we need only point to a key discovery in placing the role of the analyst at the point of convergence of an ongoing present and a living past. This is the point that I wish to make about the role of the analyst, particularly as his role is expressed in the conception of the transference —that because the patient brings his whole life into the consulting-room, and because the analyst stands at the point where, dealing actively with the present hour, he can still scan that life and pass judgment on it in its totality, the case history takes on a new and fundamental significance in understanding the person. From his unique vantage point, both inside and outside the full meaning of another person's life, the analyst's overview, working within, yet standing outside, the history of the patient, thus provides him with an understanding on a new level. He is more than either the participant in today or the historian of yesterday; he becomes an active biographer of both.

I mean to suggest here that there is a difference between history, as a general approach to organized thinking about the past, and biography, as a method of constructing a life pattern or its analogue out of the materials of history. One can write the biography of a political movement, a plant, or a city, as well as of a person—

biography meaning, in this sense, a history that requires a special vantage point. The vantage point is one which is well within, and even caught up in, the contemporaneous significance of the phenomenon being examined. In turn, this requires that one have somehow achieved a comprehensive grasp of the phenomenon as a whole, and, equally important, that one have gained the position of being biased toward one kind of reconstruction rather than toward another or none at all. Faced with the task of writing the story of his own life, Mark Twain ruefully remarked, "Biographies are but the clothes and buttons of the man—the biography of the man himself cannot be written." But his may have been a unique problem which led to a special despair. Biography, as a visible judgment about a life lived, can be produced whenever the occasion calls it forth. The funeral oration is biography and so is the widow's grief—although both may be insincere and neither one profound nor lasting. We commit ourselves to a theory of history and demonstrate that biography is possible whenever we nod in proper judgment at the news that a full and rich life has ended peacefully.

Reading a biography, a reader hopes to share with the writer an experience that cannot be duplicated in the form of a deductively presented argument. His aim, if he could express it, may well be to gain that point of vantage from which he will be able to scan an entire phenomenon even as it retains for him the import of a situation which is still close and meaningful to him. He does not simply organize some data while keeping it at a distance, as he would, for example, if he were to memorize the list of names which identify the major periods of prehistoric cultural evolution. Although this, too, is a kind of overview of a phenomenon which has expressed itself through time, it lacks that tie to the intimate present which marks the special sort of history that is biography. Most of the textbook history with which students are afflicted—the history made up of chronologies, of battles and coronations, of laws passed or presidents elected—is of this distant and unreal sort. Toward this kind of history we can only direct our memory, whereas our *remembrance* works with that which retains its significance in the present moment. Because we enjoy a remembrance of our own pasts, we are capable of guilt and pride; but these experiences are out of place in regard to historical events which we only remember. Indeed, it is the pride we may have in our country's past, like the respect held by Oriental peoples for their ancestors long dead, which points to the fact that the past is still alive in the present. Between memory and remembrance is a gap in which there is expressed a vast difference between two kinds of knowing. *Knowing of facts* is one kind, and is organized and manipulated in the form of logically interrelated propositions with their proper supporting evidence. The other kind is, quite simply, a *knowing of what is so,* knowing which is approached in many ways—by the impact of poetry, or by the method of examples, or by the construction of biography as a form of history.

Biography is applicable to any material, from personal documents —as Allport (1942) has brilliantly demonstrated—to the story of a single life or a period of scientific development. Its technique, as distant from its sister methods of examples and poetry, is to cast light on a whole group of seemingly unrelated items which may have been known individually as facts or even have been tied together in terms of another biographical scheme. There is no more limit to the potential number of biographies of Lincoln than there can be limit to the number of possible poems about, or pointed examples of, human dignity and suffering. The biographical light which is cast, however, always has its source; it is not simply the lighting up of an area; it is not just light as opposed to darkness. It comes from a special place, which is the vantage point of the biographer and also, he hopes, of his readers who will go along with him to study the phenomenon when it is lit from this new angle. Biography as a method, then, as opposed even to the most exquisitely organized presentation of facts like that in a textbook, creates its own facts out of the whole of its phenomenon. It is in this way, I would guess, that psychoanalytic theory was able to create a whole new set of facts about childhood behavior. Without doubt there had been, long before Freud and his pupils, many observations of nursery behavior related to aggressiveness, to "mouthing" objects, and to sexual play. As facts they were known, for facts are easy enough to discover; and we may even now know almost all the raw facts we need for a reasonably complete clinical science of man. But the method of biography, by which the psychoanalytic theoretician was able to take a stand in relation to the meaning of a life's development, led to the recreation of these same facts. They were now seen from a new angle and in a new light.

It is sometimes argued that the facts were simply reinterpreted rather than discovered anew, that they were not recreated in any basic sense. But I would think that this both misses the point and obscures it, for a fact reinterpreted is not the old fact at all but a new entity all of its own. Those who assert the contrary seem to have fallen victim to the peculiar philosophy that the fact, like a little round ball hanging out in space, contains all its own significance like an inner core, a significance that we can only seek out and attempt to grasp as we fish in the void for this and other little round balls of knowledge. But as long as we believe that we as humans have something to do with the meaning of the facts in the world, that a basic distinction has to be made in our philosophy between a world of brute matter and a world of reality that is tied to human subjectivity, then we will perhaps go on to the idea that we do not reinterpret facts but create and recreate them constantly. We shift the angle of our regard, cast our light into different areas, light up new places and new combinations of old places, and find endlessly new and more stable positions from which we organize new chapters in the histories we write. This is the biography that I mean; it is not a product of memory but a dividend of remembrance.

A person's life span is the perfect manifestation of the organic persistence of an entity through time. It has its course of growth, broadly predictable in general outline but wonderfully unique and unpredictable in its individuality; and therefore it expresses fully the problem of the general versus the unique, the predictable versus the emergent. It has an enduring pattern that we call the *personality* yet it is in constant change, thereby demonstrating exquisitely the problem of constancy versus flux. Finally, in its presentation of both observable and inferable aspects it demonstrates perfectly the issue we call the *real* versus the *apparent,* the surface versus the depth, or the overt versus the hidden. Grasping in some sort of comprehensive totality this organic span, this representative marvel of the living entity, thus requires that we come to grips, even to a small degree, with all of these defining issues and problems. We have to find a way to fix this entity without transfixing it, to hold it in one piece without crushing it to a mass, to mark off its limits without constraining it, and to take a definable stand in reference to it without arbitrarily delimiting what it expresses for us. There is no way that this can be done without assimilating it to our own personal history; we cannot stand outside of it. Though we scan its entirety, we must do this from the inside. We must at least approximate the lived life whose meaning we wish to present to some other person—who must, himself, in turn undertake in part the same commitment if he is to grasp what we try to say. If we fail, we are left with a catalogue of facts.

Belonging and Independence

Many of us, I am sure, have been fortunate enough to know at least one teacher whose inspiration lay in the fact of his presence and his company rather than in his systematized views. Those who have had contact with such a person might have spent many hours with him, talking, discussing, or just listening, and have left him on each occasion with the sure feeling that he had more to contribute than most of his colleagues who had written volumes of articles or a shelf of books. His thinking was not in the least scattered; indeed, it often seemed to his students to possess a special rigor of its own. Each time one talked with him the thought occurred that what he had to say should be recorded and thus preserved, and there followed a resolve to program the ensuing sessions in such a way that they might trace out a theme that could later be put into permanent and, one hoped, publishable form. But each time, despite the best intentions, one was defeated in this aim, and each time defeated by the same characteristic of the sessions—that they were always new. The starting point was always unexpected and certainly never predictable; attempts to begin by picking up the thread of a previous meeting always fell flat. The point of beginning always belonged entirely to the session which it began; it arose only out of the moment at hand, out of the very situation in which the participants were engaged. No general propositions preceded the opening of a session, or if they did, they seemed forced and clumsy, like the speech of a poor actor as he delivers a carefully memorized line. Nor did any summary propositions ever issue from the separate sessions, to become the basis or starting point for other meetings in the future.

In short, in their interchanges the teacher and student seemed to have written a series of poems, or shared some examples, or fashioned a bit of their joint biography. This is what was done; but what was not done is equally significant. They were never able to develop a framework which would have been independent of their meetings and upon which they could have hung the content of their talks. This is not the same as to say that they could not have developed a coherent set of ideas or worked toward a systematically organized point of view. But whether they did or not—and this, as a fact, is irrelevant to the kind of situation we are considering—an organized set of ideas could have served only as a report about the sessions, a collection of elaborate minutes of the proceedings, not as a framework within which to place the talks, and certainly never as a means by which their continuing could have been assured or determined. An analogy with poetry will perhaps make this clearer: writing a précis of each poem in a volume, and later organizing these summaries into one outline that serves as a prose report of the volume's contents, is by no means the same accomplishment as developing some schema by which the poet could be helped to compose even one more poem. The former may be done by critics or scholars; but the latter defeats even lovers of poetry. A poem, we have said, is *sui generis*—and in an approximate way this is also the nature of the meetings that I am describing. Therefore such meetings provide excellent examples of both the good and the bad of the approach that I have been discussing in this chapter. An orientation bordering on the poetic, resting on shared examples and the living out of biography, is good if one comes to talk, to learn, to grow, and to feel that one belongs in situations of personal interchange. But it raises special problems if one wishes to transpose these meetings, in all their significance for the participants, into a medium of another sort. I mean here, specifically, the medium of a published book.

To write a book is to start with a problem, or at least an area, which is stated at the outset; to read a book is, for the reader, to bring an interest in that problem to the reading, or at least to agree to share it with the writer for a while. The common concern shared by writer and reader makes for a kind of meeting. But it differs importantly from the meetings I have been talking about. The writer, and the writer alone, has to state what the problem is that concerns him and, he hopes, will also concern his readers. There is no way at all that the writer could discover his own problem after a reader has picked up the book and turned the first page—that is, after the meeting between them has started. A book must be written in such a way that it is independent of the time, the place, or the situation in which the reader comes to it. It is not addressed, like a letter, from one person to one other person, but goes out from a single author to many readers. Therefore it must be an object, that is, a transferable item. Books are bound—they are sewed and glued and wrapped into a package—and their being bound quite well expresses their role in the process of sharing ideas. They are carriers which transcend the personal, the momentary, and the immediately shared. A book can be picked up and read by anyone; it can be duplicated endlessly, carried anywhere, read in whole or in part, and indeed in any order, at any time by any of its multiple and anonymous readers.

That this is not always completely true of books in general, and that volumes of poetry provide what seems to be an important exception, are phenomena worth examining in greater detail for what we may learn about the dichotomy I am posing: between the *belonging* of the poem, the example, the biography, or some meetings, and the *independence* of a schema which is exemplified in the printed book as a carrier. Of course, not every book necessarily presents for each reader a clearly stated problem which writer and reader can share for a while as a matter of their common concern. The reader must, for example, read the language and be familiar with the topic; he must be acquainted with the technical terms and possess whatever level or background in the subject the writer presupposes. This is to say that all meetings, of whatever sort, require a time, a place, and certain appropriate conditions in order to occur at all. But the volume of poetry, uniquely, must set up demands which are even more critical than these necessary conditions. If poetry does indeed belong fully to its given situation; if, as Emily Dickinson put it with plush contempt, "Publication is the auction of the mind," then the printed book of verse, if it is supposed to transcend a situation by virtue of its independent character, would seem to be a contradiction in terms.

However, there may be no contradiction here, but rather evidence and explanation for the changing historical status of published poetry. Quite possibly there has always been a kind of person who is attracted to the vaguely pleasing idea of reading poetry yet remains incapable of appreciating a poem as a work of art. He will look for, and relish, primarily those kinds of verse which clearly announce themselves as such. He will enjoy poems which are noble in theme, which clearly rhyme, have a definite meter, are divided into lines, and use a nicely exalted vocabulary and tone in dealing with specialized topics like love, nature, motherhood, or patriotism. These identifying character-istics, like a sequence of familiar street signs, group themselves into a crude but effective schema, a schema which is describable as such independently of any particular set of verses and which therefore notifies the reader that he is about to undertake a specific kind of encounter with the writer. In our day, when the packaging of com-modities threatens to crowd out of human existence the significance of original encounters between persons, when even the encounters themselves can be packaged and passed on from one person to another as a learned set of "skills" in interpersonal relations, as tricks in getting along on a date, as devices for being popular, or as rules for becom-ing a psychotherapist, it is small wonder that the arts, too, have been largely replaced by the carriers originally developed only to purvey them. In place of humor, our most successful comics depend on the gag line, an item purchased from craftsmen who are equipped to compose them on demand and at fixed rates. In place of popular music, there is the established "gimmick," as some entertainers call the trick which is used to make a selection sell. In place of genuine writing on even the superficial level, we have formulae for most of the stories that appear in slick-paper magazines. It is schemas of all sorts—gimmicks, gadgets, "tags," formulae—which, in increasing degree, have tended to substitute for the commercially uncertain results of original encounters between writer and reader. As a result, we are now faced with the tragic paradox that one can be taught how to produce popular art; all that is required, it appears, is a native skill which, like superior reflexes, is a kind of inherent characteristic that some lucky persons just happen to have. Having it like a possession, they require only sufficient practice with the schema as it applies in their chosen field; and the results of their artistic efforts will then depend entirely on the current state of the market.

Cultures that prize the technological above all else have usually neither the patience nor the taste to consider the relevance of art to nonartistic endeavors. For this reason it is worth our while to stress the difference between what belongs to a situation and what is extrinsic to it, between what arises out of a situation and what, being generally applicable, is imposed on it. In posing an apparent contradiction between the single poem as intrinsic to one encounter and the published volume of poetry as the carrier of an independent schema, I would emphasize that in poetry less than in any other kind of printed work there is very little of the carrier to help the reader along. Each poem in a book is an independent episode; the reader must find his way into it, then through it, and having done with it for the moment, he will have no guarantee that he thereby comes to the next poem with presuppositions or expectations different from those with which he opened the book. The total volume could not argue, though it might move; it could enthrall the reader but never convince him.

It will be clear by now that in this chapter, as in this book, I am engaged in making a case for the neglected orientation that might be called "poeticizing" (although I might just as well have named it "exemplarizing" or "historicizing"), and that I am proposing as its essential characteristic that none of the propositions that may arise out of it will attain the status of independence. One and all, they have the characteristic of belonging; they are like small bits of poetry, like apt examples, like key events in a biography, like moments of free encounter between persons—for they fit the situation giving rise to them; they are convincing though they make no argument that can be carried to another situation; they illuminate the moment but, providing light rather than the match and torch, they can never offer a guarantee that another situation, or even a succeeding moment in the present situation, will be lighted up or seen more clearly. They constantly leave the situation open, for no hinge is ever provided on which even the most certain and conclusive door could swing closed. Paul Tillich has given this strikingly similar summary of an analogous kind of endeavor: "The test of a phenomenological description is that the picture given by it is convincing, that it can be seen by anyone who is willing to look in the same direction, that the description illuminates other related ideas, and that it makes the reality which these ideas are supposed to reflect understandable" (1951, p. 118). Nothing here, note, about satisfying a set of independent and all-transcending canons; nothing about corresponding to procedures which have been spelled out for all time; nothing even about the supposed conflict between rational and nonrational modes of apprehending truths. Rather, we need only change a few adjectives, and Tillich's words might apply equally well to a poem as to a scientific description.

The Limits of This Book

The conclusion that must arise from the position that I am espousing, a conclusion that the critical reader may already have anticipated, is that a strict interpretation of the poeticizing orientation would preclude writing a book, or at least make improbable that the book be more than merely a diary. Certainly, it would seem, one could not use this orientation to organize a serious work on a scientific subject, even though presumably poets may do so in order to write each one of their poems. I have touched on the problem in a preceding section of this chapter, but now it will become evident that more than a passing difficulty is involved. A conclusion which seems to arise inevitably out of the argument I have been pursuing serves both to block my doing anything further and to contradict my very attempt. If what I have said thus far is acceptable to any degree, it would seem to follow that I should stop at this point, and further, that I should not even have gone as far as this. In short, the issue is more than whether poems can be written; they have, and they are. It is also more than whether they can be published; they will be, and perhaps consideration of the poeticizing orientation will help us understand some of the serious problems involved in the printing, publishing, and reading of poetry. The issue, in fact, strikes as deeply as the distinction between two orientations which cut across such endeavors as writing, reading, thinking, and meeting. It may be that for this reason no thorough answer can be offered; for to the extent that it is a real issue, and not a problem which arises out of a transitory lacuna in our thinking, to the extent that it is an issue in which we are embedded in what we do and, therefore, that it describes and transcends our condition rather than the converse—to this extent it may have to remain an issue seen and posed rather than grasped, contained, and finished off with an answer. I would not back away from problems that appear insoluble, for they are likely to be either improperly formulated, and therefore their restatement will help us along, or else signs of all-embracing concerns with which we ought at least to deal freely and humbly. Recognizing, then, that the problem may at least be stated although it encompasses our doings and thus surpasses our efforts at solution, we may note that we are here faced with a dilemma which is becoming increasingly familiar in our day. Many recent thinkers, perhaps beginning with Kierkegaard, who have chosen to pose their inquiry completely within the framework of the condition of man— refusing to accept that either a formulation or an answer will appear for them from somewhere out of the blue of science or magic or dogma—have by their very radicalism come face to face with what appears to be a similar issue. If one follows out the thinking of Sartre to any of its logical conclusions, one arrives at the simple proposition that this man has no right within his own system to erect a system, no basis within his own theory on which to expound a theory. As Jean Wahl has said, "Communication has consistently been one of the major problems in the philosophies of existence. Indirect in Kierkegaard, direct and striving in Jaspers, divided into 'authentic' and 'inauthentic' in Heidegger (the authentic sphere being reserved, it seems, for poetic expression), clumsy and failing in Sartre, communication is always there—at least as a problem. Even in the absence of communication, the idea obstinately persists" (1949, p. 11). Communication, we submit, is that aspect of a position in which is expressed its systematic, as opposed to its problematic character; for when the latter is made over into the former, communication becomes possible.

Let us state the issue in general terms. It seems to be the mark of problems that truly belong to a human history that their authors can nowhere turn to a transcendent or independent schema within which the problems might be restated in other, formal terms, and by means of which predetermined solutions for all possible questions might be easily sought and happily found. A philosophy which is fully grounded in human concerns gives us questions, not answers. Now, it turns out that it is the poeticizing orientation, as I have termed it, which appears to represent the human being in minuscule, catching him in one or another of his own moments—although he may often appear to transcend his humanness and step outside of the moments of his own history by the use of schemas which outreach him and will finally outlast him. My thesis is this, that without giving up these means of reaching beyond the given situation, we must also turn again to the situations themselves—concrete, of the moment, representative, *sui generis.* But to repeat, if we are able to achieve this we will seem to be trapped by the very solution that we find. The inescapable problem that will confront the writer of a book about persons, and eventually the reader too, is that he will have in hand a completed and packaged statement of just those issues which, on principle, would seem to transcend packaging and surpass completion by any one writer or reader. Communication will have overcome all obstacles, and the problematic will have been dissolved in the organized and systematic. The question of whether even a first chapter to such a book is possible, once its author has demonstrated that the writing of it is inconsistent with his own orientation, is in the immediate sense a practical question—for one ought not to produce a long essay explaining why he had written the essay but not the book to which the essay refers. In a larger sense, too, this is an appropriate question for books in general. Are we to have only books that in the opening pages of this chapter I called, disparagingly, textbooks? Is there no way in which a writer can, without being false to the principles he so movingly pronounces, apply the poeticizing orientation to matters of general scientific concern in psychology?

Fortunately for us all, readers and writers alike, science-minded poets and biographers as well as poeticizing scientists, the case is neither tragic nor completely desperate. There are many authors who have found their different ways out. In the work entitled *Being and*

Time, which represents his enduring contribution to contemporary philosophy, Heidegger (1962) resorted, perhaps of necessity, to coining a new terminology largely derived from new twists on old words, and in this way solved the problem of communication by going beyond existing modes of communicating. But for those whose choice is to remain within the structure of a language familiar to their readers, there is, first and most obviously, the approach in which one deals in generalities about the human condition. One makes statements which have the general form, "It is true of man that . . . " while recognizing, of course, the necessary limitations of all such statements. In adopting this approach, one hopes to transcend any given situation by reference to all possible situations, and therefore to compete with a "logicalizing" orientation on its own ground by presenting the opening propositions of what may culminate in a new—and hopefully, improved—independent schema. Whatever else philosophy is, philosophy does just this, thereby demonstrating that it is not the mother of the sciences but the elder sister of poetry.

A second and equally obvious way out of the dilemma is to deal deliberately with biographical data—not the biographies of persons, but rather the still living history of ideas, currents of thought, and collective movements. The sections of this book on the historical background of clinical psychology are an attempt in this direction. Third, there is a method of stepping outside an issue while still keeping touch with it; it consists simply in negative criticism. One handles a problem by means of an attack on the ways that other persons have found to handle it, thus standing, so to speak, at, but not beyond, a position which constitutes the problem's limits. The need for this approach will explain why so much of the present book is devoted to a thorough-going critique of contemporary theory in clinical psychology. Finally, to these three approaches may be added the attempt that I have made generally throughout this volume to begin and end with examples, to treat the material in other than formal, didactic, or textbook fashion, and to encourage the reader to go along with me on descriptions of the kind to which Tillich refers in the passage already quoted.

And now there remains a final point which is both the logical conclusion and the epitome of what has been discussed in this chapter.

I have noted that the issues dealt with here are not simply annoying little problems of technique—for example, how to say something well, how to argue forcefully and cogently—which confront a particular author who happens to have chosen to write a book about some aspects of psychology. Rather, with regard to the issue that I have raised in this chapter, in the form of a kind of dilemma confronting anyone who writes a serious work that emphasizes a poeticizing orientation, *this issue is the very problem with which this book itself is concerned.* The questions arising from it not only help to determine how this book is to be written, they define as well what I will write, for the content of this book is itself one version of just this issue. The logical circle is closed: the chapters that follow are concerned with what is in this chapter, as surely as (which is less commonly the case) the reverse. The reason is that this is a book about clinical situations, and specifically about the bases and uses of certain kinds of instruments and procedures in clinical psychology. The instruments and procedures, particularly in their common form as clinical tests, are avenues toward apprehending certain kinds of data which, I will maintain, can be dealt with satisfactorily only within a poeticizing orientation. What I have to say in the ensuing chapters, then, is in one sense a discussion of these problems in clinical psychology; but because the problems exemplify the issue I have dealt with in this opening chapter, I will be demonstrating, in the course of trying to resolve it, the dilemma that has been raised in these first pages. In brief, I will try to show that the data provided in certain clinical situations, when they are appropriately grasped, furnish us with a unique way out of the dilemma, in some ways like a poem but in other ways, surprisingly like the adumbration of a clinical science.

OTHERS

> It is other people's minds that are the odd thing; one's own is certain
> and necessary.
>
> —SIR GEORGE THOMSON

SOME FORTY YEARS AGO, IN THE HALCYON DAYS BEFORE INFORMATION
theory and teaching machines, Max Meyer (1922) published a textbook in psychology which amounted to a *tour de force*. Almost without exception, his every reference to a person, throughout the book,
was put in the form of "the Other-One." For example, one whole
chapter on human speech was entitled, "How the Other-One talks
and writes to himself." This form of address was, of course, no mere
trick. The author was seriously engaged in spelling out a thorough-
going behaviorism of the most mechanistic type. That it strikes us

now as a little on the simple-minded side is, perhaps, no credit to our wisdom; time heals many ills, even in science. But there was a logic to Meyer's position, then as well as now. He saw clearly that one kind of theory in psychology made demands on its basic concepts which could not be denied, at the risk of superficiality or—what may be more heinous in the view of the true scientist—of eclecticism. As Meyer put it uncompromisingly at the very beginning: "If I were a missionary and interested chiefly in the saving of a soul, the question, whether he has one or not, would be of the greatest importance to me. But I merely desire to know what use I can make of him benefiting me and also benefiting him so far as I can know thru [sic] sense organs what may be good for both of us. This I may be able to learn from the psychology of the Other-One" (p. 5). Rephrased in more elegant and familiar terms, Meyer was here stating that the psychologist's interest was not in the soul or mind, but rather was dominated by a purpose, which was to predict and control human behavior —and in order to do so, logic required that he treat the person as a special kind of object. For good reasons he referred to this object as "the Other-One." Here, in one phase, may be found as much of an underlying philosophy as contemporary psychology is usually willing to parade. It is therefore fitting that we begin our examination of basic concepts by discussing in some detail the significance of this expresssion.

A Science of "Others"

Psychology today, more than a generation after Meyer's book was published, may still be most succinctly defined as "the science of Others." Its subject matter is the comings and goings of people—in contemporary jargon, *human behavior*—but not of all possible people. True, psychology has come a long way since Titchener deliberately restricted its field of action to the description and analysis of specific activities perfomed by a select group of normal adults. Two wars, half a century, and three or four generations of psychologists have come and gone, and their combined influence has served to extend the boundaries of the field of permissible action. But at least one major restriction remains; and it is enforced by a fiat as high-handed and as peremptory as were any of Titchener's dicta. The contemporary psychologist, if he is to have his work accepted as scientific, must deal only with Others. He himself is always ruled out as a source of primary data.

At first sight it will appear that this is not so. It may be argued that psychology welcomes data which are called introspective; and, in fact, it is equipped to handle them in many different forms. There are Q-sorts in which subjects judge statements that refer to themselves, sentence completion items phrased in the first person, and experimental data in the form of subjects' perceptual judgments. In the final analysis, all these would seem to rest on the individual and even idiosyncratic response. Are they not instances of turning to the subject himself as a source of primary data? And could not the experimenter, too, serve as such a source?

These quesions are not easily answered. There is always an intrinsic connection between content and method; and for this reason we cannot take for granted that the mere utilization of one kind of subject will guarantee one and only one kind of datum. A method dedicated single-mindedly to a search for the Other might use even introspective, subjective, and self-reporting data, not to depict what some authors have called "inner worlds," but simply for the purpose of advancing an established method. In order to answer our questions, we must consider first what happens when a person provides data about himself.

When the test subject is asked for such data, he is required to think about himself—but clearly, he may well do this while maintaining an impersonal and objective attitude toward himself and his doings. Whether he will do so, in fact, depends on the form of the question put to him and on the situation in which, for his purposes, he finds himself. If he is asked whether and how much he smokes, he has to search his store of information about one person—in this case, the person about whom he has a great deal of factual information—and then choose whether or not to provide the datum requested. He can, if he likes, keep certain facts about himself private; but he might also do the same in regard to someone else—let us say his wife or his best friend. So far, then, there is little difference to be seen between the two situations: the one in which he reports about himself, and the one in which he tells about another person. That most persons can quite easily make of themselves an object of study and report is itself a most remarkable phenomenon, one worthy of extensive investigation and central to any theory of cognition. However, the circumstance that this occurrence is intriguing and psychologically significant should not obscure the fact that it is in essence simply a variant of Other-directed perception or cognition.

But as we are all aware, there are many other kinds of responses in which it is by no means as clear that the subject maintains an Other-directed attitude. When he tells us what he sees in an inkblot, for example, he appears to be responding in a special way, and we are pretty sure, even if we cannot quite explain our hunch, that his perception in this instance is determined in ways which differ from his ordinary perception and report of the things in his environment. And even in the kind of test situation which is calculated and arranged to produce specifically delimited responses—the test in this case being referred to as "structured"—the subject will often respond, in reference to himself, in terms not explainable simply as Other-directed cognition. The most common example is malingering, but a limitless variety of others, now generally lumped under the heading of *response set,* are becoming familiar to clinicians who construct and administer tests. Now the curious thing is this: that the overwhelming tendency in contemporary psychological theory is to attempt, with an almost desperate fervor, to fit even this special kind of test response into a framework based on a theory of Others. Rather than accept the ink-blot response or the instance of malingering for what it is, psychology insists on viewing it as a complex variant of the kinds of perception and cognition studied under the artifical conditions of laboratory experiments. Laudable though this may be as an effort to make one science out of what appears to be a sprawling array of disparate events, it need not be accepted as inevitable. Instead, I propose to examine it further, for it will lead us straight to the heart and the history of clinical theory.

One way of putting the matter is to say that for most American psychologists the role of citizen is nonexistent. This is not to say that although psychologists vote, or fail to vote, they are not aware of their own actions. They own homes, they mow their lawns, they send their children to school—and in these respects they are, and know they are, indistinguishable from most middle-class American voters, home-owners, and parents. But this does not solve the issue we are examining; strangely, it complicates it even further. For while psychologists do all the things that other Americans who are outwardly similar to them also do, they insist on making a careful distinction and an impassable gap between the person who acts as voter and parent and the person who acts as psychologist—both persons, in this case, being the same and both being themselves, which facts they also know quite well. The situation is clearly outrageous enough to require restatement in more formal terms. Put in this way, we might say that psychologists insist that matters of professional concern to them, broadly defined as constituting the subject matter of their discipline, are distinct from, and in no way overlap with, other matters that they might deal with as citizens. As psychologists, they insist, they have no role but that of scientist; and even if as scientists they interest themselves in human activities, their interest is always pointed out as though toward other persons. They may in the course of their scientific endeavors undertake to study the behavior of adults who vote or mow lawns, but the persons who become targets for study are, according to the most rigid of protocol, special objects which are specified in strict terms. The first and most important of the specifications is that the target is not the same entity as the scientist himself—even when they are, in actual fact, one and the same person.

That these are not matters to be taken lightly is evidenced by the attention devoted to them by some of our most distinguished philosophers of the behavioral sciences. Bergmann and Spence (1944), facing directly the issue that we are examining, begin by agreeing that "scientific empiricism holds to the position that all sciences, including psychology, deal with the same events, namely, the experiences or perceptions of the scientist himself. The behavior scientist who claims to study such perceptual behavior in his subjects is thus asked to start uncritically from his own perceptions; a piece of advice, the apparent circularity of which has continued to puzzle many of the more philosophically-minded psychologists" (p. 3). Here, then, is the problem, and it is stated as unequivocally as we could wish. The scientist who is interested in understanding perception must use his own perceptual processes, which he does not understand, in order to gather his data. He is in the position of a man who, possessing no tools but lead weights, has the task of determining the relation between the size and weight of pieces of lead.

Undaunted, however, Bergmann and Spence continue: "In the schema outlined by the scientific empiricist, the experiences of the observing scientist do indeed have a privileged, even unique position. If pressed too far and without the necessary epistemological sophistication, this account of the scientist's position can very easily lead to a metaphysical thesis of the solipsistic type" (p. 3).

A horrible metaphysical fate seems to threaten the psychologist who, lacking a certain "sophistication" about a philosophic theory of knowledge, draws the obvious conclusion from the situation in which he finds himself. At this point, then, one would hope that Bergmann and Spence will provide us with the epistemological underpinning that our psychology desperately needs. But they do not. "The fact of the matter," they add, "is that science is always epistemologically dogmatic" (p. 3). The issue is settled by resort to the unexamined dogma of another discipline. But this, of course, does not help us at all. It implies that pure scientists had better leave these tricky issues to their philosophic betters.

At this point, however, Bergmann and Spence offer at least a crumb to those of us who might still be disposed to concern ourselves with the metaphysical and epistemological aspects of our psychological question. The approach which they term *scientific empiricism* has, they say, provided a "re-examination of the mind-body issue—" thus notifying us, in this roundabout way, that what we had thought was a problem in contemporary psychological method is in reality an old, though perhaps not too welcome, friend from the arena of philosophic speculation. "This reëxamination tries, on the one hand, to overcome the dogmatism of *epistemological* physicalism, and on the other, to justify the *methodological* solipsism and physicalism of science. . . . The empiricist scientist should realize that his behavior, symbolic or otherwise, does not lie on the same methodological level as the responses of his subjects, and consequently that he should not in reporting the latter use any mentalistic terms which have not been introduced from a physicalistic meaning basis" (p. 4).

And now we are back again at the same point. For the advice that we are finally offered appears to consist of nothing but the warning that we should always bypass the problem by dealing with our own experiences as though they were facts observed in regard to the Other. Stevens (1939), in dealing with the same bedeviling issue, concludes with essentially identical advice, stated perhaps even more dogmatically:

What becomes acceptable psychology accrues only when all observations, including those which a psychologist makes upon himself, are treated as though made upon "the other one." Thus, we make explicit the distinction between the experimenter and the thing observed. This distinction is obvious in physics; in psychology it is equally valid. . . . Although a particular experimenter may himself become the object of study by another experimenter, and he in turn by still another, at some stage of such a regress an independent experimenter *must be* (i.e., is always) assumed. The recognition of this "experimenter-regress" unravels many knots in psychology (p. 228).

At the risk of finding or creating more knots, however, we will have to conclude that the problem is far from solved—as, indeed, few problems are ever solved by fiat. For what has Stevens said here except that this is a fundamental methodological problem and that he chooses to settle it by insisting on introducing an "independent experimenter"? If the latter is only the original psychologist under a new name, the problem is not resolved but merely restated; and equally, if he is a totally new kind of entity, the issue has been bypassed and not faced at all (Lyons, 1963). But in any case, when we are proffered this hollow little metaphysical tidbit as a sop for our most pressing concerns, we may take some satisfaction in knowing that all of us, as psychologists, are caught up in the same dilemma. When some psychologists then follow the dicta of the empiricists and maintain a peculiarly two-sided relation to their own roles as citizens, they are simply being consistent with an entire, if largely unspoken, orientation. Thus they will insist, even when the claim seems either superfluous or self-contradictory, that their obvious role as citizens is ruled out as a possible object of study. Even when it is studied as such—or rather, even when those persons who occupy the role of citizen are studied—the psychologist's interest is expressed in the third person rather than in the first person. It is *He* who interests me, says the psychologist, never bothering with the peculiar dilemma he has created whereby a scientifically nonexistent *Me* sustains one half of the situation of being interested.

Admittedly, it is difficult to put this paradoxical, almost self-defeating misconception in sensible terms, at least if you start by assuming that a living, thinking psychologist undertakes an investigation. On the other hand, if you do not start from this point but consider only the kinds of problems that interest the psychologist—that is, if you lop off the beginning of the situation in which the psychologist himself displays this interest—you will have no trouble constructing what is nowadays called an objective science of behavior. If you will always remember to forget who it is that does any of the scientist's work or displays the scientist's interests or thinks up the scientist's problems or writes or reads the scientist's treatises on methodology and research design, then you will never run afoul of the dilemma I have stated. But once it occurs to you that the one target who never appears on the psychologist's horizon is the psychologist himself as a person, that he has created a science of Others, then you will begin to be troubled by the feeling that something is amiss.

This is not to say that all your doubts will be resolved by the simple process of bringing the scientist back as a possible object of his own observations, for the issue is not to be settled as simply as all that. In fact, as Bergmann and Spence take pains to tell us, the issue is one that has troubled serious thinkers, usually in the guise of the "mind-body" problem, since the time of the pre-Socratic philosophers. But your doubts, if you have any, will at least be productive, for they may serve to start you on a study of history; and in this endeavor you will be constantly reminded that these are not issues to be settled by a fiat which is born of arrogance. For the attempt by some psychologists to resolve the question of subjectivity —which is one other way of describing our problem—by looking the other way is simply to assume that to care little about methodology is sufficient excuse for dismissing it. Indeed, even the current usage of the term *methodology* suggests the straits to which we have come —for a word that refers to a branch of logic and should properly be defined as "the science of scientific method" has been attenuated in meaning, concomitant with a pervasive loss of interest in the philosophy of science, to the point where it is used casually to signify a procedure or technique in the experimental laboratory.

The Independent Schema

Consider what happens when, as scientists, we engage in a continuing relation with a single other person and attempt to encompass our experience of him within some prearranged schema. We will usually discover that this experience is in important ways a unique and special phenomenon. He reminds us of a friend, for example; or unaccountably, we dislike him at sight; or after a time we become familiar with some of his gestures and they seem to fit him in a uniquely integrated way. In other words, as we begin to collect enough data about him to be in a position to utilize a schema, we find that he is no longer the pure object which he was at the beginning of our task. He is now a known and familiar part of our own history; if he were to be suddenly removed from our life, we would experience the change, perhaps as a loss or perhaps with a sense of relief, but in any case as a reaction which has its clearly defined place in our ongoing history. There appears to be no way in which we can encounter him often and yet have him still remain the human cipher which originally made him the target for our explanatory activities. In short, in regard to the single other person we could not possibly construct a schema which is totally independent of our own experience—as Newtonian mechanics is, for the purposes of science, independent of Newton's history and experience as an individual. It is true that we might write a description of him and that this could then become the basis for an explanatory schema by someone else; or a person might write a diary in which he reports on his own continuing experience, and this too might later be used for developing some explanatory schema. But even though, as Allport (1942) has argued, the data obtainable from such personal documents may be most useful as data for a science of psychology, they are obviously data of a special sort. They are, indeed, often suspect in the eyes of scientists who would like to develop a set of quantitative, general laws applicable to the activities of all human subjects.

By the very nature of his professional stance, the scientist very soon discovers that his individual relationship to a single other person provides data which are hopelessly self-contradictory. This may be the reason that with rare exceptions psychologists will turn to using data derived from the performance of groups. But interestingly, these groups are not conceived, in turn, as aggregates of those individuals with whom one-to-one relations are untenable; the groups—or, as experimentalists call them, *populations*—do not consist of a number of single persons. In fact, they do not appear to be made up of persons at all. The individual member of a population is, rather, one of the Others who are the only permissible targets of interest in an explanatory science of psychology. By definition, this Other is a completely loyal member of the group to which he belongs. The schema by which the psychologist orders his observations is applicable first to the group and only later, by a deductive argument, to the component parts of the group. On the principle that everyone is made uncomfortable by deviates, whether they be individuals in a social gathering or units in a distribution, the only findings which are now considered relevant are those which refer to central tendencies in the group when it is taken as a whole. In sum, inescapably a science of Others leads its practitioners toward a distrust of the unique or deviant individual person and, as a natural reaction or substitute, toward a faith—never admitted and frantically denied—in the truth to be discovered in the performance of artificially concocted populations of equivalent and anonymous ciphers.

Whatever else may be said of these data which are necessarily discovered by a science of Others, they are clearly not the primary data of human experience. By the latter I do not mean a sort of vague mental stuff lying on the fringes of conscious and rational processes, such as dreams, reveries, unspoken wishes, fantasies, unconscious and preconscious streams of thought, psychotic imagery, or hallucinatory experiences. Data that are primary are such simply because they are the constitution of the human world, and because they are apprehended in the course of ongoing, spontaneous experience. Such organization as they attain is given by the nature of the experience itself and is comprehended only upon reflective consideration at a later time. In direct contrast, there may be many kinds of second-order data which are grasped in one or another kind of organizing schemata. As Wild (1958) has put it, primary data are found within an "ultimate horizon . . . of concrete experience," whereas second-order kinds of data are found, for example, within "the objective horizons of science which attend exclusively to objects via perspectives that are partial and abstract" (p. 460). The former are given to all persons who will accede to the pursuit of meaningful acts within the human community; whereas the latter demand the prior construction in each case of an independent schema—a partial and abstract perspective, as Wild calls it—to serve as framework and carrier for the data.

But—it may be objected—is not all of this self-evident, and superfluous as well? Surely—the objector may continue—there can be no alternative within the realm of scientific endeavor. It would appear incontrovertible that the scientist must have at his disposal some schema or structure by which to order his observations and into which he can fit his results. And of course such a schema is characteristically independent of the scientist himself, in the sense that it does not depend on his activities as an individual. The schema is transferable from one scientist to another; if one dies, another may use the same schema in regard to the same problems; the schema may be referred to, described, taught, developed, or changed, all without reference to a specific set of observations or to any particular array of data; and finally, each time that a scientist uses it for the purposes of ordering and reporting his observations, he is aware that the schema was there, waiting for his call, as it were, before he arrived on the scene with the intention of pursuing his activities.

This kind of independent schema, as a scientist might describe it, would surely seem to be an essential requirement for all sensible reporting of scientific observations; indeed, in a general sense, for all communication of any sort. I cannot tell you what I know unless we two have a language in common and unless we use the language in roughly similar ways—and we cannot invent the language as we proceed but must have it available before we meet. But a schema need not be only a language, although this is its most common example. The adult who counts eleven pieces of candy in a bowl when there are twelve children present cannot discuss the matter with the child who apprehends simply a-lot-of-candy. There is no schema that will order both these observations; and communication is bound to break down unless the adult establishes by fiat the means by which the candy will be divided rather than talked about. Similarly, if I sigh at a sunset I can only hope that my companion will of her own accord sigh for the same reason; but if she grasps the event rather as an indicator of time passing, my attempted report of my experience will meet up with her prosaic, "Well, it's late; we'd better be going." Only love—or that incomplete passion we call *sharing*—can make possible a complete joining of experience without a report between the two persons. In every other instance either there will be a conflict, or the situation will bog down in misunderstanding, or the two will part—or else they will demand a schema. In short, the significance as well as the power of a schema rests on the fact that by means of it an experience is determined; and in addition, the one who has or shares the experience is able to state the way in which it is determined. In turn, this *way* may itself be conceived as separate from the experience to which it refers; and in this sense it is independent. Therefore anyone else who learns the way is entitled to apply it to the content of his own spontaneous experiencing—although fulfillment, of course, is never guaranteed.

It is clear that independent schemas have a very great value in our lives. But all questions of attractiveness aside, certain consequences are bound to follow on their use in science. Their proponent tends to arrive naturally at certain distinctive techniques. Objects rather than events come to fill the field of his action. Synthesis, he will say, follows after analysis, for in the hierarchy which seems appropriate to him the former is seen as logically dependent on the latter. Differentiation and dissection become his major goals, and his aim the elucidation of units which can then be compounded—in this way, he proudly hopes, ingeniously bypassing the immediate wholeness of spontaneous experience. But in the long run much more than this is bypassed when a science of Others adopts the independent schema as its first absolute. Its practitioners are led inevitably toward the contemplation of a set of meaningless integers which have value primarily as elements in a kind of combinatory play.

That kind of data we have termed *primary,* and which Sartre has
properly called *concrete* (1953, pp. 54–55), needs no determining
schema. It is gathered by each person in the course of spontaneously
organizing his own world, or else it is given in the course of perceiving
another person as subject rather than as object, as a fellow human
rather than as an impersonal Other. To offer these propositions, however, in the rather dogmatic manner that I have done, is to do no
more than state a possible alternative to a science which boasts of a
total reliance on second-order data in the form of independent
schemata. Many issues are immediately raised—for example, the
question of behavior as a topic for psychological science; the difficult
problems of social perception; questions of method as well as
methodology; the danger of an infinite regress if one utilizes perception by, and of, the person as the foundation of a science purporting
to explain perception; and many other issues that will, hopefully, be
raised in this and subsequent chapters. First, however, something
ought to be said, if only to clear the air, about an issue which is not
part of psychology proper but of its metaphysical underpinnings—the
matter of an order that may be presumed to reside in the scientist's
universe.

A real fear, I believe, lies behind the insistent claim by psychologists
today that their science must bypass the primary data of human experience in favor of that gathered by second-order schemata which
are imitative of the natural sciences. The fear may be expressed in
this way: that to say anything at all about human life in general
without having founded the statement on some schematic ordering of
organized and reportable data amounts to admitting as *a priori* and
axiomatic certain commitments about people, and it is just such commitments that a true science endeavors to avoid. An illicit philosophiz-
ing, an uncalled for religious dogma, a nonscientific set of guiding
and determining values—these are the dangers that lie ahead for the
psychologist who is soft-headed enough to start with primary rather
than second-order data. The shock of discovering these fearful con-
tingencies in a branch of science which up to now has been kept clear
of them—except perhaps in such undisciplined areas as aesthetics
or the practice of psychotherapy—is on a par with the crisis that
would ensue were the statisticians to find original sin in the response

repertory of a digital computer. And it is on the ground of this continuing fear, I would guess, that no serious attempt has been made in modern psychology—at least since William James defected to the camp of the religious-minded philosophers—to explore the methods and results of an orientation that, without basing itself on religious dogma, presupposes an order in human existence that is logically antecedent to all second-order schemata.

It is the possibility of this order which is denied whenever the scientist constructs a schema within which he hopes to organize *all* of his data. Whether such an approach is necessary in the case of the physical sciences, in particular physics and chemistry, is a question that I would not presume to discuss in these pages. But even if one accepts its necessity in some of the other sciences, the issue remains open in the special case of psychology—unless, of course, one slams shut the door in the questioner's face by means of a fiat couched as an inquiry into the methodological problems of psychology. I mean to show in the following pages that the problem is not solved this easily, that because it is the first of our concerns as psychologists it will have to be the last of our questions answered as scientists.

Explanation and Understanding

Psychology is both blessed and cursed with its special problem: that in attempting to study the person, it must always begin with a person who is already there and functioning. Unlike some of its sister disciplines, psychology dares not find its origins outside the realm of persons; and therefore all of its data must lie within a world of human existence. However, there are a number of modes of ordering the range of possible data, and two of these, commonly referred to as *explanation* and *understanding,* require our consideration here, for they will serve to indicate the strengths as well as weaknesses of a science of Others, at least insofar as it rests upon the unremitting use of independent schemata.

Both explanation and understanding are human endeavors. Therefore, their limits and their possibilities, their advantages as well as their disadvantages, are bound to conform to the human world. Granting this common ground, however, there are also fundamental differences between the two modes which will determine their range of applicability in science. Both require the person to bind his experience temporally and to construct some organization within its limits as they appear to him. In the mode of understanding, this organization arises out of an order intrinsic to human existence and revealed to him through the data of his experience. In explanation, on the other hand, the person attains an organization that suits his purposes by imposing on the data of his experience some order derived from sources external to him; these may be the unacknowledged history of his subculture, the product of a logically developed argument, or even a series of accidents. The prototype of understanding is the perception of the expressive behavior of a single, other person, whereas the prototype of explanation in science is a mathematical proof. This distinction between the intuitive-like knowledge with which we behold a smile on a child's face and the probabilistic knowledge with which we entertain a datum that has been mathematically demonstrated in science points up most sharply the possibilities as well as the inherent limitations of each of the two modes. Our knowledge in understanding is immediate and complete, and so, in this way, we manage to grasp phenomena of great complexity with only a bare minimum of definable techniques. It is obvious that biologically this gift is most advantageous; with it the creature who utterly lacks a developed talent for discriminating and analyzing complex patterns of his environment is enabled to act appropriately toward elaborately articulated phenomena. As one example, the infant will respond with a gurgle or smile to the adult's expression of love, yet analysis of the stimulus pattern of a smiling face reveals how tremedously complex is this configuration. It is, in fact, far more complex than a seemingly simple visual structure like a blue spot on a yellow ground, although the latter is a stimulus pattern which an infant of the same age is not usually able to discriminate. Thus, human interrelationships are grasped very early through the mode of understanding, as they well nigh have to be in order for stable conditions to be achieved for development. A rational explanation of human relations, however, is as yet only a dimly visualized goal for even the most sophisticated of adult scientists, whose explanations after the fact often sound trivial by comparison with the intuitive understanding of a layman of no more than average sensitivity.

On the other hand, the limits of understanding are of equal significance for a psychological science, although they have been outrageously overemphasized by protagonists of a pure science of Others. Understanding is primarily a mode of individual organization of reality. Moreover, it is often private as well. As Falk (1956) has noted in summarizing the good and the bad of *idiographers,* as he terms those whose endeavors are based chiefly on understanding, "Like venturing virgins, idiographers do not usually meet the mark in an exacting test of performance, but are capable of making interesting discoveries" (p. 61). Those who have attempted to do any teaching in the clinical area are well aware of the immense difficulty in passing understanding from one person to another. We say that it depends upon a skill, and this may be so; but whether or not there is a special talent that underlies the process of understanding, the fact remains that even when two communicants each possess a reasonable measure of clinical skill, they may still encounter great difficulty in passing the results of understanding from one to the other. It is precisely here that the explanatory mode is most valuable, and where, in fact, it appears to have no limits. Whatever can be explained may also, by the nature of the case, be perfectly communicated. The person himself is often no more than an agent in this transaction; and good agents, though they may be hard to find, are never irreplaceable. The existence of an independent schema by which the explanation proceeds serves to guarantee that someone else, at some time or in some place, will ultimately be able to use it for the same purpose to produce an equivalent result. Whether the result is in fact the same is a question that can, of course, be resolved only by means of an additional explanatory schema which encompasses both sets of results in their similarities as well as their differences.

However, the mode of explanation has its own limits in regard to completeness even though full communication is at least theoretically possible. What is communicated may in practice be either barren or very incomplete, as we see, for example, whenever some rational explanatory schema is called upon to encompass the data of a subtle and complex area such as literary artistry. The Freudian schema by which the unconscious motivations of the writer are culled from the content of his writings and the "case history" of his life serves as an excellent example of both the possibilities and the limits imposed by an explanatory mode. A great deal of diagnostic information is often revealed in this way, but the characteristics of the writing which led to the investigation in the first place and without which the writing would have no importance as an object of study—that is, its qualities of literary excellence—are usually quite completely lost. A further explanatory schema, utilized independently of the original content analysis, is then required in order to elucidate and demonstrate the psychological processes involved in the production of literary artistry, as opposed, say, to run-of-the-mill amateur efforts. But to the extent that this second schema comes closer to the problem that prompted the investigation, it begins to resemble all schemes of broad explanatory power; it covers so much territory that it loses all the details and differences which distinguish one literary artist from another. Thus, in one way or another the scientist who resorts to the mode of explanation will be limited in the completeness of his efforts. Only his schema is ideal; but the human world will defeat his best attempts to utilize it totally.

We have no way of knowing, at least at present, whether a psychological science can successfully balance between the two modes of explanation and understanding, appreciating both without succumbing to either. For the fact is that the narrow science of Others which has pre-empted the scene in America appears to allow very little room for the possible uses of understanding. This may be because, in ruling out the person as target, it must unequivocally banish the individual as a possible source of data. To fill the epistemological vacuum, it must then engage in a reconstruction, with momentous consequences for a science of human behavior. Moreover, in basing itself on an independent schema, it tends naturally toward a system couched as a series of purely formal mathematical statements; and the mode that it must prefer for apprehending the data generated in this way is explanation. There is a third characteristic, concerning the way such a science defines its own field, and to this neglected topic we turn now.

The Defining of Behavior

None of these points will you usually find discussed in a text-book of psychology. The reason for this is not simply that general agreement prevails among the members of the profession who are most likely to be concerned with these problems, for the fact is that neither side of the argument appears in textbooks at all. What has happened is that the entire field of psychology has been defined so as to lay claim to dealing with some subject matter other than individual persons. In this way it has been possible to avoid completely the problem of whether it is individuals or groups, persons or units, in whom the psychologist is interested. The chosen subject matter that substitutes for persons is, as we all know, *behavior*. It is therefore a central term in any psychological system, and we will have to consider at this point what it is supposed to mean, how it is defined, and whether its use solves or merely glosses over the issues we have been examining thus far.

A definition of behavior would seem at first sight to pose no problem. A person's behavior is simply what he does. Thus, in one dictionary of psychological terms (Harriman, 1947), we find that behavior refers to "anything whatsoever that is done by a living organism. Human behavior includes mental activities, consciousness, muscular functions, and the like." Undoubtedly this is comprehensive; but it is a moot question whether the sweeping nature of the reference adds to our understanding. For if all of this constitutes behavior, how is the concept to be distinguished from a term such as *life?* A more rigorous definition can be found in an older dictionary (Warren, 1934), where a distinction is made between behavior as "a generic name for all modes of muscular or glandular response of the organism to stimulation," which is a purely physiological conception, and behavior as the "portions of the organism's responses as are open for observation," which stresses the viewpoint of the psychologist. According to the latter definition, which is closer to our interests, behavior is understood simply as that which the psychologist observes. But this, although it may appear to be the most innocent of statements, conceals the very problem we are examining. What is in question here is, in fact, just this point: what is it that the psychologist observes?

Strangely, the circularity of most definitions of behavior has not been noted by system builders who are otherwise most insistent on rigor in their presentations. As a result, textbooks that offer properly attenuated versions of psychological systems for the beginning student have defined behavior in terms which are either redundant or empty. Currently, the author who begins his text with the stern reminder that the true psychological scientist concerns himself only with responses, or activity, or observable behavior, need offer no explanation for having left out the very issues which make his science worth pursuing in the first place. For this reason we will have to turn to older sources if we wish to find the relevant issues discussed at all. One of these sources, and perhaps most significant because his unique contributions and great influence have found no permanent place in the history of American psychology, is William MacDougall. In one of his earliest works, in 1908, he made behavior synonymous with *conduct*—itself a term that seems peculiarly out of place in today's scientific psychology. A few years later (1912), he stated that the behavior we study in psychology is a certain "characteristic of living things . . . striving to achieve an end" (p. 20). Note the way in which his definition differs from all those referred to above. MacDougall made no pretense of a systematic neutrality; he began his whole system with a title and a definition which contained in capsule form the argument that he intended to pursue in spelling out the system. Consequently, by the time he had worked out his system and was engaged largely in refining it, he was able to say in regard to behavior, "Practically, we all understand and use the word in pretty much the same sense. . . . By 'behavior' we commonly mean the action or actions of some living thing" (1926, p. 43). At this point his definition had turned into a statement concerning the common-sense vantage point of the psychologist insofar as he resembled the average person.

A comparison of MacDougall's definition of behavior with that offered by the strict empiricist of our day will indicate the difference between an approach not inconsistent with the phenomenological and a view that specifically rules it out. In his earlier works MacDougall had stressed what he called the *marks* of human behavior: it involves the active pursuit of an end, and it is both persistent and variable. Today the hardheaded scientist would ask, with righteous justification, how MacDougall would propose to measure the variables—persistence, variability—which for him define behavior, and further, why he would not agree that these variables, and not their combination as a vague construct called human behavior, constitute the subject matter of psychology. MacDougall's answer to these questions, expressed some fifteen years later, might be even less satisfying to the empiricist. For these he proposed, in effect, that one go back to the experiencing observer in order to have him, as a person rather than as a scientist, tell psychologists how to define the area which they as scientists propose to investigate. With an insight not inconsistent with the viewpoint of the phenomenologist, MacDougall proposed that naïve social perception be viewed as methodologically prior to scientific psychology—even though, as the phenomenologist fully recognizes, it is a science of psychology which hopes finally to provide a rigorous and organized method for understanding social perception.

In the convolutions of this paradox or dilemma—what we call it depends on where we stand in relation to it—lies the unique problem, and, in the long run, the significant contribution of a psychological science. A science of Others, I have said, chooses not to deal with individual persons. Instead, it substitutes for the person that formal reconstruction called *behavior* which distracts us because it seems a plausible way of defining our field of possible interest. But *behavior* is only a synonym for *person* under the special condition that it is naïvely apprehended as constituting the full meaning of another person's presence to the observer. This, in turn, implies that, unless we are to lose the *person* as the subject matter for psychology, we are committed to defining psychology's field in a special way. Not the behavior of a person but the person himself is to be our target. Therefore not simply the person as target but the person as apprehended in social perception must constitute our field of inquiry. In short, the definition of psychology will have to be enlarged to read: *the science of persons as they are apprehended by other persons.* A science which truly concerns itself with the human being need have no way out of the consequent dilemma.

Phenomenology and Psychology

It is only fitting that a criticism of one's respected contemporaries be followed by the guiding ideas, the orientation, and the basic concepts which are offered as an alternative. To put the matter initially in the broadest possible terms, psychology today may be described as positivist and empiricist in its bases, behaviorist in its origin, and physicalistic and quantitative in its emphases. Its proclaimed model is an objective natural science like physics or chemistry. Though it has often been difficult to reconcile the experimentalist branch of psychological thought with the much more elusive data obtained in the clinical area, many members of both wings agree that positivist and empiricist characteristics are the basic requisites for a scientific psychology.

By contrast, what I have to present in this work belongs largely within a phenomenological orientation. The origins of this view are not in recent experimental studies of reinforcement theory in American academic laboratories but in clinical and philosophical investigations in Europe; and more remotely, not in the philosophy of science developed in accordance with the burgeoning disciplines of physics and thermodynamics, but in Husserl's studies in the methods of logic and in Heidegger's essays in the history of Western philosophy. My greatest debt is therefore to these two figures and, in addition, to Sartre, Buber, and Straus rather than to Mach, Freud, and Hull.

One embarrassment, however, has to be faced at this point. Within the past decade a fad of phenomenology, so called, and of existentialism, in various palatable versions, has swept over this country. Contemporary literature, art, and science, as well as the more superficial aspects of our culture, seem to have been profoundly influenced by such ideas as becomingness, dread, and the self. Publicized by the popular magazines—fashion leaders in a society in which all too often new ideas are marketed, like dresses, when they are in season—a movement seeming to be based on existentialism has spread even as far as the profession of psychotherapy (May, Angel, and Ellenberger, 1958; Lyons, 1961; Nelson, 1961). In the thinking of many serious-minded persons, the term *phenomenology* is now quite familiar and respectable, though perhaps often vaguely or superficially defined. It has been applied, with some justification, by Combs and Snygg (1959) to a "perceptual" approach to a general psychology, and quite properly by MacLeod (1947) to problems in social psychology; but more remote conceptions, such as the emphasis by Gestalt psychologists on personal perceptual fields and by some clinicians on "private worlds," have also been linked in a slapdash but satisfying theoretical miscellany. The claim is made that the data of personal reports, private experiences, and subjective apprehension may all be termed phenomenological. Any therapist who professes an interest in his clients' viewpoints or is intrigued by processes of change or creativeness is praised or cursed, as the case may be, for his existentialist orientation. It might therefore seem that one more work claiming a place on the current bandwagon of phenomenology and existentialism is entitled to no more than cursory interest on this score alone. It will be necessary for me to state explicitly the way in which phenomenology is and is not understood in this book, even though a full exposition of the method of phenomenological inquiry is, for reasons of space as well as its author's competence, far beyond its scope. The excursion that follows must at least be attempted, for even a sketchy account of psychology's dilemma is hardly to be found in writings in English. The two volumes by Spiegelberg (1960), invaluable though they are in other respects, admit to this "shortcoming" (p. xxxi); and otherwise excellent papers on related topics, for example by Strasser (1957), Wellek (1957), Gurwitsch (1955), or McGill (1947), provide only a start on these problems. The reader of the present work, then, is entitled to know, if not whether the coin is genuine, at least the place of its manufacture.

Recently the Swiss psychiatrist Binswanger (1957) published a collection of five cases to which he had devoted a method and an approach that he called *Daseinsanalyse,* a term that has been translated as *Existential Analysis.* He meant by this, not a system of psychotherapy nor even a theoretical framework, but rather the application of Heidegger's ideas, although with some significant changes, to the understanding of the life histories and productions of psychiatric patients. Whatever else may be said about Binswanger's views, they bear only the remotest relation to a phenomenological approach to

purely psychological issues. Somewhat closer is the discipline to
which Buber (1955) has given the name *philosophical anthropology*.
His hope was that a philosophy which was in the grandest sense
existential might provide the insights for a new and more comprehensive *anthropology*—the latter term meaning, as it customarily does
in Europe, a science of man as the human animal. Still closer, perhaps,
to the phenomenology espoused in this book is the phenomenological
psychiatry of Straus (1960), in which the attempt is made to construct
a "psychology of the human world." To this aim I would add, for
my own part, the necessity for that specific orientation toward human
concerns which has its roots in the thinking of Kierkegaard and its
modern expression in the writings of Sartre. The result of this amalgam-
ation might best be termed an *anthropological psychology,* which
presupposes phenomenology as a method and takes as its subject
matter the hyphenated creature: the-whole-man-as-an-experiencing-
being-caught-in-a-human-world.

This is a very general statement of principle which will have to be
spelled out, particularly in respect to the kind of phenomenology that
will carry it along and define its scope. It is also a definition of the
task of psychology as this writer conceives it. It may be that the
question of definition is not as easily answered in psychology as in
the other sciences, whose practitioners rarely excite themselves
publicly over the matter; thus, even the currently accepted definition
of psychology in terms of observable behavior leaves much to be
desired when one tries to spell out the definition as a guide for activity.
Though they have continued to concern themselves with questions of
boundary and content, psychologists have on the whole tended to
bypass the issue of how the psychologist is to approach his task.
Stevens (1939) has, as usual, stated the problem very clearly. At-
tributing the gains made by the school of logical positivism to the
fact that its adherents have not been averse to "an empirical study
of the actual doings of science-makers," he adds, "Furthermore, these
studies investigating the science-makers are the beginnings of a
Science of Science" (p. 243). Psychology, in short, is not merely one
science among others, but because of its unique position as the science
which explains the doings of the makers of the other sciences, it is itself a
unique discipline, a science of sciences. "Does it not appear," he asks,

"that the Science of Science must go directly to psychology for an answer to many of its problems? . . . If there is a sense in which psychology
is the propadeutic science . . . it is undoubtedly in its ability to study the
behavior, *qua* behavior, of the science-makers" (p. 250).

Unfortunately, having stated the problem so well, Stevens now
offers us little comfort in our methodological extremity. What he fails
to tell us, once we have completed the propadeutic task, is where we
are to turn and on what we are to base our activities in order to
undertake an empirical study of the actual doings of the logical
positivists themselves. Indeed, we appear to need more than a science
of science; we need a science of science of science—and so on and
on. We seem here to be staring straight down into the emptiness of
an infinite regress; but this should not keep us from trying again and
again to restate the problem so as to resolve it anew for our own
stage of development. Bakan (1953), for one, has made a start
in the direction that we propose to pursue in these pages. Picking up
the clues that he offers, we may pose the issue in these terms: that
in order to define completely the field of psychology, one has to
define the defining and for good measure the definer as well. For the
act of defining a science is only another instance of the kind of
phenomenon which falls within the scope of psychology itself. And
since every possible phenomenon arising within this scope is grist
for the psychologist's mill, he finds that in defining his own field he
must include in the definition the presuppositions that any other
science can afford to ignore, as well as the very process of making
those presuppositions, and the activities that make the presuppositions possible in the first place. Does the philosopher begin with sense
data and go on from there? If so, then the psychologist must take
account of such data, and in addition he must be able to deal with
the philosopher himself who in gathering his own sense data provides
the underpinnings for just that philosophy of science upon which
the psychologist's methods are to be based. No discipline in all the
history of ideas has ever had to face such a vicious circle. Psychology
cannot hand its axioms over to any other field, for their content as
well as their mode of apprehension form just one more set of problems
in psychological theory; nor can it merely state the axioms and ignore
them, for psychology is not an abstract, formal discipline like symbolic

logic or arithmetic but a concrete set of scientific endeavors which exists by virtue of dealing with real problems.

There are, then, two questions with which psychology, uniquely among the sciences, must initially concern itself. The first concerns the nature of its data, the second their source. The latter is the more significant of the two questions, for in each case it must be faced and dealt with before the former can be properly handled. Thus, it will not do to define psychology simply in terms of certain categories of data, such as human behavior as opposed to the "behavior" of flowers or cell nuclei. The source of all the data in psychology is—as in all the other sciences—the observing person, but, as we have just noted, psychology cannot take this source for granted, accept it without further examination, and then proceed to dealing with some second-order data based upon this primary source. Psychology is literally stuck with the unique task of identifying and defining its own primary data. But what schema shall it use for *this* task? How shall the definer define the defining definer?

One of the most persuasive of recent answers to this question proposes a seeming phenomenology which is based on perceptual data. In brief, proponents of this view argue that the basic data for psychology consist, not of collectively achieved measurements of externally observable behavior, but of persons' reports concerning the contents of their own psychological fields. The trick is to be turned, apparently, by assigning a kind of theoretical priority to one set of second-order data, such as communicable reports about one's own perceptions, rather than to another, such as an experimenter's observations of his subjects. But when the solution is stated in this way, we see that the fundamental problem has not been resolved nor even attacked, but only turned to be seen from a new angle. For as far as the task of a science is concerned, the place in which one's data are found is irrelevant. Any experiment is as good as any other experiment, in this regard at least. What counts is how the data are gathered—and by this criterion, data gathered in experiments on perception are not, simply for this reason and no other, any more "phenomenological" than are data gathered in experiments on rote learning or even maze behavior in rats. In order to see why this is so, we may summarily review some recent history.

The thesis that has been most influential in organizing clinical theory along phenomenological lines, so called, is the one advanced by Frank (1948) in his influential essay on projective techniques. He proposed the term *private world* as a way of conceptualizing the special kind of data available by means of these techniques. The distinction he made was tripartite—between "the geographical world of nature," "the human world of . . . cultural traditions," and the "learned way of investing the world and people with these traditional meanings and imputed relations as [the person] interprets them and feels toward them" (pp. 13–14). To the last of these, an "individual-ized way of organizing and interpreting all experience," a "personal frame of reference," a "curious personalized version of cultural traditions" (p. 13), to mention a few of his many definitions, Frank gave the name of the individual's *private world*. At a time when clinical psychology was striving to become an accepted professional discipline, these impressive words, in which the use of projective methods was linked with the most advanced techniques in the physical sciences, from the use of the mass spectrograph to the transplantation of bodily organs, were very soon adopted as a basis for clinical theory. It was clear that the adjective *subjective* was applicable to the noun *world* in Frank's conception, if by subjective one meant the individual's report about his own, possibly unique, view. The distinc-tion between subjective and objective, in the overly simple sense of a difference between what the single person perceives and what may be simultaneously apprehended by a population of perceivers, was further emphasized by writers who undertook to build psychological proto-systems utilizing exclusively subjective data—or, as it now came to be called, phenomenological data. Snygg (1941), for one, argued very cogently that subjective and objective facts simply lead to two different kinds of psychology: "the facts derived from these two points of view are nonidentical and are often completely contradictory" (p. 406). As one instance, in the area of learning it is the objective view that the task stays the same while the learner changes, so that there is developed a system of teaching by the use of frequency, drill, reward, and punishment. In the phenomenological view, how-ever, it is the situation that changes while the learner remains the same, so that learning is seen as taking place by virtue of understanding the individual learner, fitting the material to his pace, and presenting it clearly.

In this manner the technical term *phenomenological* came to mean substantially the same as the familiar word *subjective,* and thus a painless revolution took place in psychological thought—or so it was supposed. But I would submit that change that comes about this easily may well be no change at all. Recall that the distinction between subjective and objective is itself the product of a deliberately engineered split which was inaugurated some centuries ago by Descartes and later promulgated by Hobbes. Its status in metaphysics is shaky at best, as Husserl demonstrated by founding a wholly new philosophical discipline which, in effect, eliminated the split by undercutting it. Although in his later development of "transcendental phenomenology" Husserl may have reintroduced just the split he had been at such pains to cast out, it would still be a distortion of the term *phenomenological* to substitute it, merely as a popular euphemism, for the scientifically discredited word *subjective.* When the philosopher who espouses the former speaks of a "disciplined phenomenological description" (Wild, 1954), he has reference to a method and an orientation which at this point has behind it a literature and a school as impressive as any learning theorist has ever commanded.

A phenomenological approach in psychology, then, will not just represent an active sympathy toward the clinical, in which one chooses as preferable those data which have to do with "inner" processes or which consist of "subjective" reports. For in principle these are no different from any other kind of data. They are second-order data in the sense that they are built upon data of another sort. These latter are conceptually primary, but they are more difficult to describe; they take the form of the individual constructions by which one's organized thinking is generally made possible. An effort of will and of attitude is required in order to "have" such an experience, in which the accumulated results of one's own prior constructions are held in abeyance and, by a series of "reductions," the world's appearance is revealed. Therefore the phenomenologist who would base his task on such an act, addresses himself first of all to the question of the ways in which the data of psychology are to be gathered. He does not differ from the empiricist in respect to the kinds of data he prefers—as though the scientist really had this choice—but rather in terms of his starting point. The empiricist presupposes a Hobbesian metaphysics based on a sharp and un-bridgeable chasm between the hard, real, and certain things of the physical world and that insubstantial content of the mind which, he supposes, reflects the world's real objects. Thus, for the empiricist there is no question about how the data for psychology—which admittedly consist of psychologists' perceptions—are to be gathered. They will accumulate whenever the psychologist arranges conditions so that only certain kinds of relations appear among the objects of the world. It is understandable, therefore, that in the view of some extreme empiricists—the radical behaviorists who follow Skinner, for example—the accumulation of scientific data is self-sufficient, and theory construction, at least for purposes of gathering data, is largely supernumerary. However, as we noted above, the empiricist who pursues this course must arrive finally at an unmanageable dilemma when he comes to consider the place of the psychologist himself in his own scheme—or, as we restated the problem, when he attempts to define the defining definer. He can handle every contingency except the one on which all the others are based.

By contrast, the phenomenologist takes as his primary task the elucidation of the very situation that binds and encompasses the empiricist. The phenomenologist does not insist that he merely looks out (as though through a window in the casing of his body) at an "outer" world which he can touch but never really know, can move in but have no part of, or can apprehend but never really grasp. Instead, the phenomenologist assumes from the start that the person's world is his own, and that it is all the world that he can ever know; that he is inseparably in it by virtue of his every reflective act, and that he can have no other way of knowing it, even if he is an empiricist in psychology, than to live in it. The world is not a separated thing or collection of things. As Wild (1958) has put it, "without a world there can be no man, and without man there can be no world. Far from containing us within a special, mental region, it is precisely our lived subjectivity that opens us to an ultimate world horizon, and it is precisely this last objective horizon that requires a subjective center" (p. 475).

The data for psychology, in this view, will consist of all the ways in which the person expresses his world, from the limiting case of an individual's silent wonder at one extreme, to the equally limiting and special case of impersonal and communicable cognitions in science at the other. And varied though these ways may be, they do not differ because one appears to refer to "mental" things and the other to repeatable operations performed on tangible objects. Rather, they are essentially one in that they are all meaningful acts; and they differ in the degree to which the person will rest upon known or given constructions. At the impersonal extreme of science the individual's act is almost wholly determined in this way and is therefore out of contact with the sensible and the macroscopic; at the other extreme he is caught up in the purely sensible, perhaps even in the immediately felt, because he has put aside every possible prior construction of the event.

Phenomenology and the Positive Approach

The propositions we have offered about phenomenology are not, properly speaking, statements in psychology but rather axioms provided by a philosophy when it is made overt and allowed to be uncompromising. They will provide the underpinning for an anthropological psychology, and in so doing they will give us a first answer to the paradox that though each of us is uniquely in the world, there is a common human world to which we are all directed by being meaningfully in it. Our task now is to begin resolving this paradox.

Our initial example will start, as it ought to, from a problem in clinical observation. If we consider the pathological symptom known as *withdrawal*—which is supposed to be evidenced by a decreasing contact with other persons and an increasing degree of solitary and autistic behavior—we note that it is defined in terms of a fixed reality somewhere out there on the other side of one's skin. It is this tangible entity from which the person is assumed to withdraw. The description of the symptom constitutes a positive statement about the reality that serves as a point of reference—but at the same time it is a negative statement about the experiencing person himself. This is a most curious state of affairs in a science that claims to find its data in persons rather than in the objects toward which their behavior is directed.

How would one phrase a positive statement concerning the symptom of withdrawal? It would not state merely that the person is withdrawing from a something which is positively described, but would have to tell something of the experiences of the person in the course of his withdrawal. This would require in turn that one go to the person himself to find out how things seemed to him during the occurrence of the symptom. In essence, this is what the clinician tries to do with the help of all the tests and methods in his armamentarium. But because the observation that is required and the understanding that may result are never finished, he finds himself engaged endlessly in probing his own methods, refining them, and searching for new ways of looking at his activities in relation to new clinical problems.

A preliminary example will demonstrate the issues involved in a positive approach. A patient of above average intelligence fails most of the arithmetic problems on the WAIS. When we look more closely at the way in which he failed, we see that his typical approach was to respond with a fast guess which, as it turned out, was usually wrong. Like many patients who are diagnosed as having a character disorder, he tended to dismiss a problem hastily rather than face the frustration or tension which would necessarily be involved in coping with it. A negative statement concerning him, then, is that this patient dismissed the problem and did not really attend to it. In order, now, to arrive at a positive statement about his experience—the goal that determines our testing him in the first place—we must begin by asking: if he has really dismissed the problem, what is there left to which he can attend? Surely a man does not attend to nothing. As usual, the negative statement tells us only what he did not do: he did not hold to a given "reality"—in this case, the reality of the problem presented to him by the examiner.

If we attempt to arrive at a positive statement about the patient's performance, we might trace out his experience in the following fashion: When he was presented with a problem, he glimpsed it, as it were, for only an instant, and at the end of that time he saw an answer. It is not that he dismissed the problem, but rather that he barely managed to see it at all. He saw through it immediately to an answer. Note that he did not see *the* answer—for this would have required that he apprehend the problem with some seriousness and then fit one of a number of possible answers to it—but rather, he saw a kind of answer *within* the problem itself. For him, we may say, a problem is only a way of stating an answer; it has no existence or demand-quality of itself, and therefore holds no possibility of challenging or frustrating him. A problem is never more than a transparent and disposable container for a presently apprehended goal, precisely like the cellophane wrapper around a piece of candy. It holds the answer to a present tension, but it is itself all in the present; it does not pull one toward a future point.

Our positive statement about the patient's performance, then, would be that when the examiner presents a problem, the patient in effect rephrases the situation. He offers in return his own version of the task, and this is his solution. He is hardly either challenged or frustrated, for in fact he has never entered into that situation in which the examiner is already present. But now what will happen when the examiner refuses to accept the patient's version of the situation—that is, when the examiner says that the patient's "answer" is wrong? This kind of patient will usually have no recourse, a fact which becomes evident if the examiner asks him to try the problem again. Were such a patient sufficiently capable of offering a reflective comment on his own performance, he might well tell the examiner at this point that there is simply no sense in his trying again. He would say that there are no alternative routes for arriving at an answer, no ways of making an error, and no methods for changing his answer. All these possibilities could arise only in a situation in which a given problem is posed by an examiner and is taken seriously by the subject, and where its most probable answer is sought—none of which is true for the patient we are considering. As far as he is concerned, he has simply read back to the examiner that version of the problem which appeared to him immediately and unreflectively, and therefore he takes it as a foolish demand that he be asked to repeat his work and correct an error. Usually the character disorder will treat such a request as a foolish demand, often with a certain irritability or impatience as well.

It is the heart of the clinician's professional task that he is usually unable to check immediately with the patient in regard to reconstructions of the sort we have just developed. This would require that the patient attain a degree of reflective understanding of his own situation—yet if he were capable of such reflectiveness he would in all likelihood not be in the position of a patient in relation to our efforts as examiners. We are therefore compelled to look in other directions for support or disproof of our constructions. This is the structure of the properly conducted interview, that patient and interviewer together explore every possible direction in which a reasonable and consistent construction of the patient's present situation may be achieved. However, it does occasionally happen that clinical data independently obtained enable us to test out the formulations arrived at by consideration of the test material alone. The example of William, a 22-year-old man who had very recently had a brief psychotic episode, may be considered in this light.

William's answers to test questions on which he had to organize his thinking can only be described as loose, roundabout, and inexact. He was not disorganized nor deviant in any other way which might have suggested that he was still psychotic. Rather, he tended to talk around a topic without ever arriving at a precise answer. This was particularly evident on the questions of the Comprehension subtest of the WAIS, as we might expect, for in contrast to items on other subtests the Comprehension questions allow innumerable subtle variations around a proper answer. There is not really a "correct" answer to the Marriage item, for example, in the sense that the only correct answer to the first item on the Arithmetic subtest is "nine dollars"; an acceptable answer to the former is, rather, one that expresses the essence of a central idea. It would follow, then, that the Comprehension subtest is peculiarly susceptible to variations and deviations in the organization of ideas; it will point to the ways in which given content is molded into a functioning whole.

A positive statement concerning William's experiences, when he was faced with such a question, might be that he did not apprehend the question as a full or whole entity but as a kind of hollow shell.

As far as he was concerned, the question as phrased served primarily to demarcate an area for his consideration. It did not demand that he pull together and focus his thinking in a specifically stated fashion; this he left to some other person, most probably to the questioner himself. In his view the situation consisted of an organized act on the examiner's part; then an account by the examiner of the general area with which his own act was concerned; and finally a request that the patient in his turn take a stab at dealing with the same area or topic. If we are reminded here, not of the interchange between two adults, but of a situation in which the child grasps only the bare outline of what an adult is talking about, we should not therefore be led to conclude that William relives in each such session a specific relationship with adults which is still alive for him. It would be more useful to view the two situations—of adult and child on the one hand, and examiner and William on the other—as analogous in structure. They resemble each other in that both point to a basic possibility in a listener's experience, that he hear the outline rather than the contents of a statement.

An approximation to William's experience might be found in the situation of a person who is given the task: "Talk for five minutes about baseball." Faced with this task, the normal adult might well appear to wander around in the area demarcated for him. He may perhaps state specifically that in the season of 1927 Babe Ruth set a record of sixty home-runs; or explain how the players are chosen each year for the All-Star games; or offer a discourse on the place of baseball in American life. However, if an observer had understood the original question as, "How are championships decided in baseball?" he might then perceive the respondent as wandering all around the topic without ever producing a specific answer—the same perception, indeed, that an examiner has about William's performance on the Comprehension questions. Like our hypothetical baseball fan, William apprehends questions as topic headings, not as goal-directed demands; and his response is therefore to areas of interest that attract him rather than to delimited issues which have their own internal logic and a significance independent of the time and person involved in the questioning.

Shortly after his admission, William was interviewed at some length to get his version of the events leading to his arrest, his incarceration for about twenty-four hours, and his transfer to the hospital. The following excerpts from the recorded interview are concerned with his references to the various persons who tried to talk to him during the evening he spent in jail.

PATIENT: I also remember going up to this Lutheran minister who had a Bible there and he wanted me to swear to something but I don't know what it was, and I said I don't believe in the Bible, and he said this is a Lutheran Bible. I said who wrote it and he said well, maybe I wrote it myself. I said what difference does it make, anybody can write a Bible. I said anybody can take a book and write Holy Bible across it. But it wasn't any good as far as taking an oath on it. I said you can't put all that man says in a book that thick. And then I think he got a little mad about that time and he said I'm sorry, and I said that's O.K.

DOCTOR: What did this man look like?

PT.: Well, I don't recall what this guy looked like. He was shorter than I am. I couldn't see his face. Every time I'd start to look in some guy's face every once in awhile and I'd raise myself and it would be as though the center would be blotted out and all the saints I could see them, all the good people, but all the dirty sinners were blurred.

DR.: You say when you looked at someone's face you saw a blur?

PT.: That is part of—when I thought he was a sinner—every time I looked. Like this minister when I looked at him, I thought he was a piece of falsehood and I wouldn't see his face then.

DR.: Then you saw the blur?

PT.: It wasn't a blur, it was a white spot.

DR.: A blank?

PT.: No, it had color to it—like a halo—you know, pictures with a halo around it.

*　　*　　*

DR.: Did it strike you in any way that a voice would come from this sort of just bright area and you couldn't see anyone's features?

PT.: It wasn't that so much.

DR.: How about when the Lutheran minister spoke to you?

PT.: Oh, well, you see at the time he spoke to me I could see him then.

DR.: When did it change back?

PT.: I didn't see this all the time.

DR.: Oh, but you never saw it this way when you spoke to him?

PT.: No, I didn't see it then.

Dr.: I see. It seems to me that maybe what it might have been like was like a halo going on and off.

Pt.: Well, it did just blink on and off. I mean I'd sit there and I'd say to myself, I'd say God you better get me out of this trouble, I want to know who these saints are and who these devils are, and I'd keep thinking that and thinking that and pretty soon I'd look around for people and I wouldn't see anything and then when I'd be least expecting it you know, I'd look out and there I'd see that halo.

*   *   *

Dr.: When you were still in the jail and your family doctor was there and the Lutheran minister, you talked to them on Tuesday, you were talking to them, did you have any trouble hearing or understanding what they said?

Pt.: Well, I'd hear part of it and when they'd make a mistake I'd correct them. Like the time the minister started to ask me to take an oath on the Bible and I said what difference did it make and from then on I took over. I didn't seem to have any difficulty but I never did know what he wanted me to swear to. He wanted me to take an oath on a Bible and I didn't know what he wanted me to take an oath on the Bible about.

Dr.: Did you hear him ask you to do this for any reason?

Pt.: No, he didn't ask me for any reason, he said something about lying, I might have heard that too. He asked me, Will you take an oath on this Bible? I think he thought I was lying. I didn't know what I would be lying about.

Dr.: Were you puzzled?

Pt.: Well, I just kept feeling like they were trying to trap me into something, as if I'd done something and I didn't know what I'd done.

Dr.: How far from them were you sitting?

Pt.: I was standing.

Dr.: How far was that?

Pt.: I'd say about three feet—pretty close. And when he stood there I was pretty close to him. When I was talking to him I was standing face to face with him.

Here, in the patient's own words, is a description of just the kind of experience we have constructed from the answers he gave to certain test questions—that he was addressed by other persons, he knew in general what they were talking about, he wanted earnestly to accede to the request that he do something in relation to a topic which was not unfamiliar to him, yet within this vaguely apprehended whole he grasped no inner details, either cognitively or perceptually. His experience was not one of confusion following on clearly grasping an articulated whole, but rather one in which the inner organization of an entity was felt to be missing. In thus arriving at the same kind of statement from two different sources—one constructed from his test productions and the other given spontaneously by the patient himself—we have made both statements appear more plausible. In addition, we have lent some support to that kind of approach that we called positive—beginning and ending within the experience of a test subject, insofar as we are able to capture and organize his experience.

Phenomenology and the Unconscious

We have just considered some related clinical examples as they might be treated by a method of phenomenological inquiry. Fortunately for all of us as scientists, the method need not be confined to the clinic but is applicable as well to theoretical questions. Of all the questions that we might tackle, one of the most vexing and intriguing is that mare's nest of dogma and construct which the psychoanalysts have made their own under the hypostatized rubric *the unconscious*. We may therefore essay a discussion of this topic, not in order to provide an "answer" to it, as though it were a neat little puzzle, but with the hope of providing some useful notions about it, hints that could guide us at another time toward the systematic ordering of our ideas.

Let us begin, again, by remarking on how the phenomenon appears to the person himself. It is evident that in order to do so we must suspend all commitments, pro or con, to the "existential" character of the phenomenon of the unconscious—that is, to whether it does or does not really exist, or to what its status might be in logic or theory or the real world. We are prepared to do no more than look at what its appearance might be like. Curiously enough, such an approach is only rarely to be found in all the voluminous literature which purports to describe the clinical manifestations of the phenomenon. The degree to which the client's view of the matter is ignored and the therapist's view proclaimed and endlessly discussed might even make one suspect that the unconscious, in our contemporary clinical science, does not refer to the inward workings of the client but to the outward extensions of the therapist.

One difficulty presents itself immediately—that it would appear to be a contradiction in terms to state the mode of appearance of a phenomenon which, on principle, does not appear as such. But in point of fact the contradiction itself points directly to a most significant finding. It suggests that both the conception of the unconscious and the very method that we have here adopted to investigate the conception bear upon the same issue, at it were. Our chosen method of inquiry presupposes a set of psychological activities; and it is just these activities which are theoretically called into question by a notion such as the unconscious. In one sense this finding serves as a limiting factor in regard to the value of a phenomenological method, and indeed some such criticism is at least implied in the writings of many contemporary Freudians. But in a more important sense our finding serves to direct us toward an unsuspected source of phenomenal data. We are now led to consider the workings of a set of activities which might form the natural counterpart of forces that are termed unconscious. We begin to see—because the contradiction referred to above forces us either to see it, or else to abandon our inquiry—that phenomena called unconscious do not constitute the whole of the matter we are discussing. From the point of view of the person whose unconscious is under discussion, so to speak, there can be nothing at all by way of a reality which is coherently organized and tied to his current activities; and this, in fact, is our definition of the phenomena as unconscious. But our acceptance of the unconscious as a topic of inquiry forces us to explore further; we must look for those phenomena whose accessibility by our inquiry is guaranteed but which are also and at the same time the counterpart of unconscious activities—that is, the other side of the unconscious coin.

What might such accessible phenomena be? Clearly, they are to be discovered in the circumstances invariably associated with our target activities—assuming that such invariability can be discovered at all. When we consider the matter in this light, it is not difficult to see that every observable instance of the phenomenon of the unconscious, insofar as it makes clinical sense, calls for and is therefore invariably tied to the presence of a very special type of situational partner. The latter, summarily described, is a reflective observer. He is not just any observer; the phenomenon we call the unconscious could not appear as conceptual reality simply by virtue of the presence of a second person. Beyond offering his presence, he is required to act in a certain way, to take on a certain stance, in regard to his own history and its engagement with that of the person observed. These terms—*history, engagement,* even *person*—will call for a thorough exposition in the chapters that follow, but they are introduced at this point in order to tie them to the specific example we are exploring here. We may now make a first attempt to utilize them in relation to Freud's great discovery concerning the phenomenon of the unconscious.

Our exposition here, you will note, does not follow the usual course, in which Freud is credited with a discovery analogous to that of the scientist who finds evidence for a new chemical element. The concept of the independent schema, introduced in a preceding section, will serve us here: the scientist who finds a new element has at his command a schema that is independent of his personal history; therefore, the approach that he adopts, the kinds of data that he finds useful, and the very character of the facts that represent his contribution will partake of the independent nature of the schema that directs his activities. But by the nature of the case—and this proposition, too, will have to be spelled out in the following pages—this situation cannot hold for the scientist whose field of activity comprises the meaningful behavior and experiences of persons, including himself. For this reason we will affirm that Freud did not follow the procedure of the natural scientist, fitting a new set of impersonally known facts into a preexisting framework of logically interconnected propositions. Rather, he made a discovery, first of all, about himself. But again, his discovery about himself is not to be understood as an impersonally apprehended datum. To take a rather trivial example, a man might one day discover that all his life he had had, without knowing it, a mole in the middle of his back; and this new fact would have, for him, precisely the status of any other new fact which he might come across in science. But Freud's discovery was in a different realm entirely. In making it, he put at stake his total understanding of himself and of his own history as a sensible being.

Faced with those famous first patients who could neither resort to open expression nor straightforwardly act on their own wishes, Freud might have merely come to know some things about them—for ordinary diagnostic formulations, as such, are easy enough to achieve without training, as the performance of any amateur psychoanalyst will testify. However, if he had proceeded in this way, he might never have asked himself the critical question: What, then, can be the experience of the patient himself under the circumstances in which I know something with certainty about him yet he does not know it about himself? The amateur diagnostician in psychology does not ask himself this question, for the answer, if it were forthcoming, would have to be: clearly, the patient had no "experience" at all in regard to these matters; there was for him merely an absence of relevant factual data under circumstances in which the data should have been present. The very asking of this question concerning the patient's possible experience presupposes a totally new attitude on the part of the diagnostician or therapist. He must be able to grasp that phenomenon which in its dual presence expresses both aspects of the historic being —that he is on the one side capable of a reflective awareness of his acts in their significance for him, but equally, that on the other side it is possible for him to act in terms of the very absence of this awareness; in short, that he may manifest either a reflective consciousness or a dynamic unconscious. And the grasp of this phenomenon represents the basis for Freud's conception, and perhaps as well the basis for his subsequent exploration of his own self-awareness in the course of his famous self-analysis.

The way in which typical "insight" into one's unconsciously determined acts (as it occurs in therapeutic treatment) may be reformulated as an instance of a change in reflective awareness can be demonstrated in an example from psychotherapy. Let us suppose that a patient, in his usual unreflective manner—that is, without considering his act as though it had any significance for his own life pattern— has done what he always does at the beginning of a session: instead of hanging his coat on the clothes-tree in the outer office, he has brought it in with him and folded it neatly on a chair next to his own. The therapist chooses one particular hour to bring up this matter; he asks the patient why he does this with his coat. There follows an interchange in which the patient offers, and they discuss, a number of transparently improbable reasons for this practice. Finally, during this session or perhaps at a later one, patient and therapist come to the point where they confront each other across this question, as it were. It is the patient's unexpressed claim that his habitual action with his coat has no significance in terms of other than the impulse of the moment ("I don't know why I put the coat there. I just did it without thinking, that's all"), or perhaps an extraneous necessity ("The clothes-tree outside is always filled, so I just bring the coat in here")—and indeed, this may not only be unexpressed but unexpressible; the whole character of the patient, and his entire status as a patient, may rest upon the unreflective nature of his acts and upon his inability to attain a level of reflective awareness of them. Facing him over the issue he has chosen, the therapist claims that reflectiveness is possible, that the patient should begin at this point, and that his reflective awareness ought to take a specific direction in regard to the issue at hand. Theory-oriented therapies would seem to differ from those which are nondirective chiefly on the necessity for carrying out this last demand.

It is not that therapist and patient are here engaged in a simple disagreement, nor is it that error of a more subtle sort in which it is supposed that the therapist is possessed of some knowledge that the patient must manage to grasp in an acceptably emotion-laden moment of insight. The critical factor in this moment in which they stand poised is that in regard to the fact under question—the patient's way of keeping his coat during the therapy hour—one of them, the therapist, has a position which has required that he be reflective, whereas the other, the patient, as yet has not. The therapist's position centers around a statement which goes something like this: "Your opening act in every session with me is to arrange your outdoor clothing so that it is close to you and immediately available for your rapid departure; you never fully come in from the outdoors, or in other words you have not yet completely entered my office except as a transient and not fully committed visitor." Every part of this statement mirrors the reflective awareness with which the therapist must necessarily conduct his own professional activities. He must constantly find intimate relationships between what he sees and learns of his patients' lives and his own conduct with them as therapist. None of the patient's statements, however, are reflective in this sense. They exemplify the transient, the impulsive, the emotionally charged, the habitual, or the extraneous—all of which are ways in which we can, and often must, avoid a position of reflectiveness. Agreement between the two will come, not when the patient accedes to the therapist's superior knowledge or "learns" something which just happens to concern himself as an indentifiable person, but when the patient becomes as reflective about himself in this situation as the therapist is about *him*self in the same situation. Then, because they are in the situation together and because finally they will be confronting each other as persons—or, in the terms we will introduce later, because the perceptions of each will have the characteristic of social rather than nonsocial data—some resolution will be possible, and perhaps even inevitable, which will change both of them, the patient in all likelihood more than the therapist.

A CLINICAL
SCIENCE
OF MAN

THE HUMAN
DIMENSION

A line is a line in its minutest subdivisions, straight or crooked. It is itself, not intermeasurable by anything else. Such is Job. But since the French Revolution Englishmen are all intermeasurable by one another: certainly a happy state of agreement, in which I for one do not agree. God keep you and me from the divinity of yes and no too—the yea, nay, creeping Jesus—from supposing up and down to be the same thing, as all experimentalists must suppose.

—WILLIAM BLAKE

IN THE COURSE OF A SESSION OF GROUP THERAPY, THE THERAPIST suggests that the group do some role playing. To this one of the patients objects: "What's the use? Let's just figure out by talking what we would do if we played the roles. That way we won't have to go through the business of playing them."

We will propose at the outset that the difference between patient and therapist in our example revolves around a matter more fundamental than the merits of a therapeutic technique. In order to make the example most useful, we will assume that the patient is here expressing a basic attitude. To put it immediately in the terms with which the present chapter is concerned—and which we will try to spell out in the following sections—we may say that the patient and his therapist have parted company in respect to the distinction between process and terminus. The therapist proposes dealing with a situation by beginning it, whereas the patient prefers a device that would imitate a session already concluded. Now, it is not a lack of awareness on the part of either which splits them in this way. Both of them are well aware that a situation, unless it is still under way, is at any moment either at its beginning or at its conclusion; and both are probably aware that if either were the case, they would not be likely to discuss whether they should act as though the situation were one rather than the other. Rather, it is their differing orientations which set them apart from each other.

Approaches to Role Playing

Just what was the patient demonstrating as he tried to persuade the group? It might be, of course, that his insistence had something to do with his motives—his attitude toward the therapeutic procedure of role playing, for example, or his feelings about what might occur in such a session. A complete discussion of the clinical aspects of the exchange between patient and therapist would air all the possibilities in the light of what was known about the patient's personality, his usual behavior and place in the group, his relationship with the therapist and with the other group members, and so on. But let us bypass this valuable material and restrict the example to the question of the distinction between process and terminus. Considering the exchange in these terms only, what the patient was avoiding, and also trying to get the others in the group to side with him in avoiding, was the opportunity of beginning a situation. In its place he offered the alternative that the group proceed as though this situation were already over and done with.

This distinction sounds simple, but it may not be. On the face of it, the patient, too, seemed to proffer a way of plunging into issues that might be raised by a role-playing session, and his method might seem potentially as evocative as the one suggested by the therapist. Might it not be argued that even if the group members only talked about what would happen if they played the roles, they would produce a session just as valuable for therapeutic purposes as one in which they actually went through the procedure of assigning and taking roles? Granted that the two approaches are not identical, and that as we all know, the approach which rests upon "as if" can never be as rich nor as complete as one that involves direct action. But is this really all that divides the patient and the therapist in this instance? Further examination will, I believe, reveal that it is not. If, as we agreed, this is taken as a critical example, the point which is involved touches on matters more significant than a contrast between pale speculation and a vividly real thing. Consider, for example, that the therapist was proposing a kind of situation in which the group members could not know where the session would lead or what its outcome might be. He was suggesting that the patients as a group embark on an enterprise the conclusion of which would remain unknown to them until the very end. Whether this conclusion could be known by the therapist himself is a difficult and—let us admit it—delicate issue which will have to be passed over in the present discussion.

To repeat, if the group were to act on the therapist's suggestion, the members could not know what the outcome of their session would be. Individually they might guess or suspect, fear or hope, concerning specific outcomes; but this is not the same as knowing what is going to happen. To say that a patient suspects he might express anger toward a figure of authority in a role-playing session is to put together a number of separate propositions: that for this patient the act in question is at least a possibility, something which he knows might be done; that it is not an act which is part of his repertory of unthinking and ordinary habits; that he has definite feelings, though they may be mixed, concerning the possibility; that he entertains certain private estimates about the likelihood that he will indulge in the act; and many other propositions as well. But not a single proposition which is pertinent here is of the absolute sort which states: this is an act which he is certain he will do, or which he is driven inescapably to do, or which he sees himself as having already done. In general, this is true of all the feelings and attitudes that the group members might hold concerning anticipated outcomes of a role-playing session. All of the outcomes are possibilities, neither more nor less. None of them is a conclusion. They qualify as statements about the future, it is true, and in this sense they might almost pass as predictions. But they are all in the subjunctive mode. They do not declare facts, even nonexistent facts, but rather are subjoined to and depend upon other occurrences, most of which have not yet come about. In proposing that the group act as though the role-playing session had already been completed and could be looked back on and discussed, the patient in our example was in effect asking that the members give up the subjunctive mode in favor of the declarative. He proposed that in place of their feelings and attitudes about the possibilities in an impending set of events they substitute a conclusively known set of facts about past events.

Suppose that some of the group members knew—in the sense in which I am using the term here, to refer to grasping a set of conclusive facts—just what would happen, at least in part, if they began the session. To carry the example a bit farther in fantasy, suppose that they knew without any doubt that one of the other members would leave the session in the middle of it, that another would erupt in anger, or a third refuse to take part in a scene under certain circumstances. What basis could any of the members have for a flawless conviction that these demonstrations might occur? Short of an unlikely ability to foretell the future, their knowledge would have to come from a very few sources: the memory of repeated instances of similar behavior in the past, or their construction of likely events by some process of weighing interrelated probabilities. Viewed in this way, their knowledge would not refer to how the session would conclude but rather to some of the most probable tracks on which it would run. But then the knowledge would not be of the role playing itself but of the fixed and predetermined grooves which would at best restrict the uses of the role-playing technique and at worst stymie it completely. This sort of knowledge about role-playing sessions must therefore be limited because it is knowledge only of restrictive habits or else ancillary to a procedure the usefulness of which depends on the members' capabilities for transcending fixed and unthinking habits. Conclusive and factual knowledge, such as this would be, runs counter to the purpose of the session or else is minor and perhaps even irrelevant. In fact, perfectly complete knowledge of this sort—for example, if one member knew in exhaustive detail what everyone else was certain to do—would have to preclude that anyone but the most foolish optimist would enter a proposed session. The member who possessed knowledge to this degree could never hope to gain anything from the session except just one more weary instance of verifying what he already knew. The role playing could not have the significance of a therapeutic technique, a challenge, or a danger, but simply and inevitably a chore. It is the essence of a chore that nothing new can happen to it, that its beginning and end and all that takes place between are more or less fixed, that its bypaths and ramifications have already been explored, and that the situation does not offer enough scope to provide even the germ of new possibilities; yet one must still go through with it. No more deadening prospect can be imagined, and no more unlikely attitude with which to enter a session supposedly organized for purposes of change.

To return to the patient in the role-playing session, we may now extract from his proposal a lesson to be applied to similar situations. His approach, when examined, has revealed one of the two ways in which any situation may appear to the person involved in it. The session may seem to him, even though in actual fact it has not yet started, as *over-and-done-with;* therefore all of his dealing with it will be as though it were in the past—just finished, an hour or a week ago, last century, or remotely distant in time and space. He will know its contents as facts, he will have dissected it into its logically interrelated parts, and he will be able to deduce one of its parts on the basis of given information about some other parts. It is in this light, we reasoned, that the session must have appeared to the patient at its actual beginning. But to his therapist it appeared in a different light. It seemed to him that he was at its beginning and that all he could ever do was go forward into it. It had as yet no determinate shape, vague limits at best, and no content that was assuredly known. Not that it seemed to him empty—for he most probably did not have at this moment the experience of facing an abyss. Rather, its character must have been what can best be termed *to-be-filled.*

But we know—as, indeed, patient and therapist also knew—that this was the very same session to which both of them referred. The situation which appeared to one of them as over-and-done-with appeared to the other, at precisely the same time, as to-be-filled. More than this, we can now see that this apparent anomaly was not a unique or unexpected circumstance. It was, in fact, precisely for this reason that the two of them found themselves together in the same situation. The expectation was that just this division would occur; and its occurrence defines and therefore provides the starting point for those changes which such a situation will, it is hoped, finally bring about.

What may we now say about the situation itself? We may proceed from this point to define the role-playing session in terms of its specific character of appearing in two such diametrically opposed ways to its several participants. The role-playing situation, we now see, is one in which the choice is open to its participants as to which of the two poles of its appearance he wishes to declare for himself. This is not true of most situations, even many in which its participants become deeply involved. In regard to situations that we usually encounter, the kind of grasp of it which seems to fit is determined immediately and naturally by the structure of the situation itself. Indeed, for most of our ordinary and unthinking behavior we are in a neutral, "factual" world; if we sense its reverberating possibilities, it is only as a faint undertone to the fully grasped array of sense data. Our behavior is therefore easy, habitual, practically automatized, and ethically almost neutral. In this everyday situation there are few problems solved, few chances taken or decisions faced. Things are just about as they seem, and where and in what shape they seem, as a set of nonladen givens. Occasionally, although perhaps not very often, we are caught up by the urgency of a moment, and though we cannot sustain this feeling for very long, we have the experience of passing through a memorable or decisive time. But in this instance, too, the situation is just what it is, no more. In both the neutral and the critical situation there is lacking that specific structure which allows us a choice as to how it may appear to us and therefore how we will grasp it and make our individual use of it. This, we may conclude, is the way in which the role-playing session is unique; and for obvious reasons it has to be contrived; for if it were to occur naturally as a type of situation, it would be ignored by all but those whose gift—of creative artistry, of profoundly self-reflective insight, or of saintliness—has prepared them to step into it.

The role-playing session, therefore, is one example of a special kind of situation: in it the persons involved are offered a choice between beginning and ending, between process and terminus. Other examples will immediately occur to anyone familiar with the clinical setting—the therapy hour, the psychodrama technique, and of course the projective test. This is, in fact, the basic structure of the clinical situation, that the special choice we have discussed here is presented to its participants: it appears to them as the self-evident way in which such a situation ought to appear; the participants express and therefore share with each other their separate ways of grasping; and if they continue to act conjointly in the same situation and do not break apart on the issues, they must finally effect between them some resolution of the divergence with which they began their meeting.

Beginning and Ending

The clinical example we have just discussed centered around a distinction between yet-to-be (or to-be-filled) and over-and-done-with. Fortunately for our expository purposes, the example is not restricted in its significance to the matter of approaches in psychotherapy. The pair of phenomena to which it refers have been discussed, in one guise or another, since the time of Aristotle; and luckily, they have recently been the subject of a chapter in the remarkable little volume of essays which Gilbert Ryle (1954) has with scholarly humility entitled *Dilemmas*. Although the issues that he treats have to do mainly with perception, and particularly with the verbs we use for our different perceptual acts, I think his argument may justifiably be extended to a whole range of behavioral data.

To begin with [says Ryle], seeing and hearing are not processes. Aristotle points out, quite correctly (*Met.* ix, vi. 7–10), that I can say "I have seen it" as soon as I can say "I see it." To generalize the point that I think he is making, there are many verbs part of the business of which is to declare a terminus. To find something puts "Finis" to searching for it;

to win a race brings the race to an end. Other verbs are verbs of starting. To launch a boat is to inaugurate its career on the water; to found a college is to get it to exist from then on. . . . It will, I think, be apparent why, with certain reservations, verbs which in this way declare termini cannot be used and are in fact not used in the continuous present or past tenses. The judge may say that he has been trying a man all the morning but not that he has spent the morning or any stretch of the morning in convicting him. I can say that I am occupied in searching for a pencil or trying to solve an anagram, but not that I am occupied in finding the pencil or getting the solution of the anagram. In the same way I can be looking for or looking at something, but I cannot be seeing it. At any given moment either I have not yet seen it or I have now seen it. The verb "to see" does not signify an experience, i.e., something that I go through, am engaged in. It does not signify a sub-stretch of my life story" (pp. 102–103).

The distinction is clear. There are words which refer to process, the general term that Ryle uses being *experience,* and there are other words which refer to terminus, the latter including, among others, all of the phenomena we ordinarily call perception. Properly speaking, one should not refer to perceptual processes but to perceptual termini. To perceive is to have done, not to be doing. Note that this is not, as some critics might immediately assume, a semantic issue, a mere matter of words, of verbal qualifications. The phenomena that are under discussion here are very real. To say, as Ryle does in example after example, that verbs having to do with perception tell of the completion of the situation, not to an ongoing, process-like phenomenon, is not simply to offer a generalization concerning the uses of language. More important, and this is his main point as well as his reason for dealing seriously with these matters, the generalization about some verbs clarifies a distinction that is basic for systematic ordering of the phenomena that the verbs refer to.

In some respects [Ryle continues], though certainly not in very many, the verbs "see" and "hear" function like the verb "win." They do not stand for bodily or psychological states, processes or conditions. They do not stand for anything that goes on, i.e. has a beginning, a middle and an end. The assertion that a subject has seen a misprint carries with it the assertion that there was a misprint for him to see, somewhat as the assertion that a runner has been victorious or defeated carries with it the assertion that there was at least one other runner. The fact that he has seen a misprint has a great deal to do with facts about the light, the condition and position of his eyes and their distance from the page and the absence of screens, the conditions of his retina, nerves, etc., the nature of his early education and his present interests, mood and so on. But his seeing or missing the misprint is not itself among the facts about him which can be established in the ways in which these physiological and psychological facts are established. It is not a fact of any of these sorts. None the less, it is not a mysterious fact, any more than winning or losing a race is rendered a mysterious fact by the failure of experiments upon the runner to establish it (p. 106).

I have quoted these passages at some length for a number of reasons. They are clearly and even elegantly written, which immediately commends them in a discipline in which barrenness often substitutes for simplicity and pedestrian rigidity has come to be mistaken for scholarly rigor. But more important than stylistic merit, which might after all be found as well in the most meretricious journalism, they demonstrate quite neatly that a nonexperimentalist, even a nonpsychologist, can get hold of a central issue and literally think his way toward a conclusion that teaches us something. We have tended too often to deny the value of any conclusions but those that are forced on us by the logic of an experiment; and it is time that we turned again to the worth of a finely reasoning mind. We can learn from the thinker here that we have to keep constantly in mind two kinds of facts (though this may not be the best possible term to encompass both) which are available to us whenever we deal with psychological issues. The first is the familiar phenomenon of the observable. It includes, as Ryle puts it, "anything that goes on, i.e. has a beginning, a middle and an end." Processes, conditions, states, situations, events, all these fall into this first class. They happen; they happen through some stretch of time; and their happening, as a temporally extended phenomenon, does not consist solely of the instantaneous moment when they are observed. Though observation of them must, of course, take place at one specific time rather than another, and may even stretch over only a very brief interval, this does not change their character as things that go on. They are not points in time but passages.

Understandably, phenomena of this sort gain much of their meaning as a consequence of their changing aspects at different times. What they have been is often significant, as is what they might become, and especially how these are related to what they are now. We are always interested in studying the history or the prospects of this kind of phenomenon. It makes sense to talk about causes and consequences in regard to them, and when the subject in question has to do with persons, it makes sense also to discuss motive and purpose or to try to predict. All of these issues are appropriate because phenomena of this first sort take place in time. To use some of Ryle's examples, acts like searching, looking, solving, are of a specific kind, all manifesting the temporal characteristic of referring to some passage through time.

Phenomena of the second kind clearly differ in respect to their temporality. They do not take place in time at all. Not that they take place in a very short time, nor in a flash; for this would be only a process-phenomenon with a limited span for its operation. Rather, this second sort of phenomenon has no relation to time except in a negative sense. It is never anything but "it was." To talk about it at all is to have it over and done with. It is not really an observable, for what is observed must be in some way there to be seen; that is, it must be going on. But the nonprocess phenomenon, which Ryle refers to as the *terminus,* is never observed as something that is; and as a consequence, it can never be talked about as something that has been or will be. It is not observed but referred to, and the reference only calls it up without changing its nontemporal status. "At any given moment either I have not yet seen it or I have now seen it"; this is the way Ryle puts it. If I have not yet seen it, it cannot be said that my *seeing* of it is now beginning but has not yet been completed—for this is patently not what is meant. I may, it is true, be expecting it, which is itself an ongoing experience, a kind of process; or I may be thinking about it. But my seeing, as such, is an act which must, for its existence as an act at all, take place once and for all. When my seeing does take place, it takes place all of a piece. I cannot at any point in time be in the process of seeing it. All of the evidence we have at our disposal serves to verify this, for no matter how many times we try to stop the seeing in mid-act and catch ourselves in the course of the seeing, we discover that either we have seen it or we have not yet seen it. Although we can always distinguish sensibly between, "I am eating," and "I have eaten," and can make the distinction at any point during the act, there is no way at all to make the same distinction about seeing—as Aristotle clearly realized. Seeing, in short, cannot be an experience that we have. The nature of an experience is that it is had by someone's consciousness; and the nature of consciousness is that it is always at least potentially capable of turning on its own processes and grasping them. Within the limits set by the kind of person I am, I can as a conscious being always contemplate my acts. But I cannot contemplate my seeing. It eludes me; even as my consciousness turns, it is gone. I can only refer to it, knowing that I have seen or that I will see. And because my consciousness, and therefore my experience, is always in a human time—in a present, remolding a past, unfolding a future—the phenomenon that eludes me is not in time at all. The two can never meet, any more than the fish and the bird could mate.

This second kind of phenomenon, the terminal phenomenon, is not a part of human time, but this is not to say that it cannot be located in some temporal order. It has its appropriate place, and reference to that place will tell us a great deal more about it. I say that I cannot experience my own seeing, that if I were able to bring it into my own experience it would already be, not something going on, but something that has happened. But all of us can quite easily experience someone else's seeing. Seeing is one of those phenomena which cannot be experienced in the first person but can often, and quite easily, form the content of experiences when they take place in the third person. Unless we are so confused as to fail to distinguish between our own experience and what it is an experience *of,* however, we will recognize that to put the phenomenon in the third person in this way does not change it from "terminus" to "process." All that can be said about seeing is that it can be referred to, that it can be established as having taken place, or that it can be overlooked, but not that it can itself be the experience that takes place in the first person.

The consequence that follows immediately from this is that reference to my own seeing is in no way different from reference to someone else's seeing. When I grasp this fact about myself, as when I say, "I see it," meaning that I have already seen it, then I am referring to myself just as though I were some third person. I am declaring a fact about myself, in the same way that I customarily declare facts about other persons. And I can order this fact in some temporal sequence, just as I can order any or all the facts gained about other persons, about objects, or about the world in general. The temporality appropriate to terminal phenomena is familiar to all of us, and we have come across it in a number of guises in preceding chapters. It is the time of clocks; it is chronology. It has its units, which are equal and interchangeable. It has as its basis some scheme which is independent of the preferences, hopes, or experiences of any individual person. It is the temporal order which enables us to deal efficiently and appropriately with all the facts that science and technology have enabled us to accumulate, as well as with all the factual data that we gather in our everyday activities.

But the temporality appropriate to process phenomena is not the same at all. It is in some measure personal time, but more fundamentally, human time. It is the time of the living person, the fabric of his world, and it changes as his world changes. There are no equal units in it, and there is no possible scheme that could be devised and stated independently of it except in the mind of God; for although any human being may deny human time, he can never live outside it without giving up that humanness which would enable him to tell us about the alternative he has chosen. He would not be a part of our human world but confused, out of contact, or comatose.

Since we have now restated Ryle's distinction between process and terminus in terms of temporality, we are ready to examine its correlative pair of alternatives, beginning and ending. Just as we considered process and terminus, not as physical events which happen to be open to our observation, but as aspects of the human world that we all share because we act in it, so we will look at the beginning and ending also as aspects of action situations which have meaning for us.

If I know the end of something, I can encompass it wholly. I grasp its totality, even though I may not know many of the details making up the whole. To take an example, I may know only that a certain horse won the Kentucky Derby but not that he ran last around the first turn. But it is clear that knowledge of this detail, of one of the things that go to make up the total situation, is not required in order to encompass the whole. If I know the conclusion and nothing else, I have grasped the whole matter. Knowing that a certain horse won the Derby, I also know that a Derby was run, and I know that at least one other horse finished and that the horse I know about came in ahead. In this way I know *of* the whole race. Indeed, it makes no sense to state that I know about an ending—that a certain colt won the Derby—without also knowing these other facts, that is, without also knowing of the whole race. To know the end is in this way to encompass the whole. It may be that my knowledge, even of the whole, is far from complete; factual knowledge may be partial, or it may be inaccurate. But whether or not it is accurate and full knowledge, as long as it concerns a concluding fact it is all that I need in order to grasp in some manner the total situation or event of which the fact forms a conclusion.

Compare this, now, with the knowing of a beginning fact. Suppose that I know that a certain horse started the Kentucky Derby. What do I now know of the whole race? At this point, clearly, I know nothing. I do not even know whether this particular horse shied as he left the starting gate and threw his rider; nor could I know that the stands collapsed and that the race itself was interrupted at the halfway mark. Knowing nothing beyond the beginning fact, I can either participate in the situation *as it unfolds* or I cannot, just as I choose. I can decide to remain aloof, or I can indulge in hope, wish, and cheering. I can follow the race, or I can have nothing more to do with it at this point. But whatever I do, I will in any event be associated with the situation in terms of my unique experience with it; the relation between me and the race-situation will not consist in my having access to certain public and observable facts about it, as would be true if my knowledge were of its conclusion rather than of its beginning.

This, then, is the essential difference between knowledge of the beginning and knowledge of the ending: in the first we experience a situation on the basis of some knowledge of it, and in the second we encompass the situation by virtue of owning some facts about it. In the latter we "have" the situation, to deal with it mentally, as though it were an entity temporarily in our hands; indeed, this is just the expression we customarily use, that we "have the matter in hand."

In the former, however, we "are had" by the situation, and only the degree and nature of our reflective awareness determines whether we are totally and unthinkingly caught up by it or maintain our idiosyncratic distance from it.

Notice that wherever we turn in considering these issues we find that we are also dealing with *temporality*. I use this word in place of the more customary *time* because its use frees us to take a fresh look at a matter that is perpetually obscured by the obvious. In no phenomenon more than in temporality are we so unthinkingly bound to a structure which is built into our organized life; and therefore in no other aspect of our lives are we so blind to the elementary character of our own experiences. Just because all of civilized life rests upon a kind of grid of time units, and because life as we know it is unthinkable without this obtrusive substructure, we find ourselves unable to break loose from it. Children have some trouble learning it, as witness their exasperating inability to reckon their and our actions in terms of an orderly scheme of time units; but once accomplished, they become like the rest of us and have no resources to give it up. Therefore the task before us in this chapter, to work toward a re-evaluation of temporality and then to apply our findings to some aspects of the clinical situation, presents obstacles more impenetrable than they might be solely on the basis of their complexity or logical difficulty. It calls on us to think quite simply but in new ways; and one or both of these demands is likely to be considered an insult to the scholar or scientist.

We have seen in Ryle's examples that process and terminus are different kinds of events and therefore have to be referred to by different groups of verbs. Following this, we noted that the beginning and the ending, though they may seem to be simply the boundaries of one event taking place in time, are also phenomena which differ qualitatively. If we restrict ourselves to the way of thinking about these matters that is second nature to us, we will accept without further concern a phrase like "takes place," with its implication that the event has been assigned a definable locus in a temporal space of which we know the dimension and its units. But if we suspend our usual acceptance of this scheme, we may be free to try to envisage the two phenomena, beginning and ending, as themselves events which in their concurrence organize time into a meaningful entity—in this case, a race we call the Derby. Moreover, we will see that they can provide this organization only because to us they appear as one and the other—as a beginning fact and an ending fact, with all the differences between these two kinds of fact that were discussed above. If, finally, we are willing to continue looking at the matter in this light, we will come to grasp a significant reversal—that *it is beginnings and endings as phenomenal entities which make possible what we know as past and present, not the reverse.*

At this point we begin to come closer to grasping the temporality which, as we all somehow feel without being able to express it, engenders the very texture of our lives. We also begin to see the critical difference between temporality, conceived in this way, and time, conceived as is required by science. We all think that we understand time, even though there is no way that we can talk about our understanding: we mean by time that uni-dimensional passage through which events move irreversibly. It is a passage with three compartments, the middle one containing the events within our ken, the one in back of it those which were once in the middle but have retreated so as to enter the past, and the one in front of it meant to contain events that have not yet occurred. We all know, too, because we have learned it well, that the passage is marked off in equal units which are related in a final analysis to the movements of the stars or the energy changes within atomic nuclei. But temporality must be conceived in a different way. We cannot easily think of it in terms of a spatial analogy; rather, it may turn out that the reverse is more probably true, and that we will truly understand space once we have a way of thinking about temporality. The starting point for this conception will have to be two orders of events; their prototypes are the beginning and the ending event.

Because it is more familiar to our usual way of thinking, let us consider now the kind of event of which the ending is a prototype. We always stand in a certain relation to this order of event; to put it another way, the event always appears to us in a certain way. As an event, we know *about* it; that is, we are not engaged in knowing it. Some distinction can always be made between the known event, as such, and wherever it is that we happen to be at the time of knowing about it. There is a distance, a space, let us say, as though we had pushed the event away. It does not occupy a spot in the structure of our present reflective experience—by which I mean that when we stop to contemplate what it is we are at the moment, in all its significance, we do not find the event within our contemplated situation. Nor can such an event be discovered as the set of limiting conditions for our present situation—which would be an alternative possibility. The kind of event of which the known ending is a prototype is neither within our situation nor are we within it. It is outside our present insofar as the present can appear to us in its historical significance; and by the same token, we are outside it.

Because of this relation to us, the terminal event, that which we know about, has the character of a package. It is, in relation to us, an entity that keeps its own boundaries just as a package does. We can take it, handle it, or let it go; yet it will retain its integral and separated character—just as though, in fact, we had not come close to it at all. The concept may be pushed one step farther. The event known about, as the ending is, resembles an object or thing. This is its basic characteristic, that it is a thing, and things are for us always integral entities that keep their distance. They are no part of us; we contact them, but they never become part of us. Our range of actions in regard to them is limited by their thing-ness, for it consists of destroying their boundaries while preserving our own; and in the end it either reduces them to smaller entities which are still things or else combines them into larger, changed things. It is the package, wrapped and bounded, which we can dissect; whereas something like the weather, which gathers us in while we incorporate it into our situation, is an example of the alternative phenomenon which eludes both analysis and synthesis. Aspects of nature are distinguishable from the things of the world in other important respects as well. Nature is impenetrable, whereas the thing preserves its boundaries. This is by no means the same quality, for nature, in presenting to us its face marked by reserve, holds a mystery which is never completely revealed; but the thing, although it may have many sides, is in its essence knowable. The thing but dimly reminds us of nature. Indeed, it would not be inappropriate to call it a caricature of nature—and perhaps this is why our contemporary civilization, which has almost lost touch with nature, has been so busy at providing an artificial substitute in the form of an endless collection of things.

A terminal phenomenon, we said, has all the characteristics of a thing. This tells us why it is that to state a terminal proposition, as we did above in the example of the Kentucky Derby, has the effect of removing it, of wrapping it up, as it were, so that it can be dealt with as a separated thing. The event which we handle in this way, when we assign it to a locus in our familiar space-like time, we customarily call a *past event*. We refer to our own contemplated situation as the *present,* and we usually think of ourselves as somehow standing in a present and having reference to a past which is removed along the axis of time. In our everyday dealings in the world, this is a useful scheme—though its value when directly translated as a scientific scheme may be quite questionable—but we have to break loose from it completely, as we have just done in the paragraphs above, to be able to grasp the essential nature of the event we call *past*. If we do so, we will have the beginning of a structure by which we can fit together many aspects of experience.

Mr. God and Mr. Kinnebrook

The story of science has to do with man's understanding of nature and, on occasion, his control over it. Therefore it is fitting that we find in two widely separated natural scenes a pair of human expressions to start us on a brief survey of the historical antecedents of the ideas we are discussing. One of these scenes is the grounds and gardens of the palace of Versailles, designed for Louis XIV by André Lenôtre, the greatest of European landscape artists. They are a vast, magnificent array of formally clipped and pruned and tended trees and hedges. From the window of his apartments, the monarch could survey a stunning avenue which stretched, straight and tree-lined, all the way to the gates of Paris, thirty kilometers away. Each time that he looked out, he saw displayed for his benefit the full fruits of Renaissance civilization: it had brought nature under man's control, enduringly and concretely, as a secular servant for man's earthly pleasures. Here is the pure apogee of that civilization which underlies the Western world as we know it. By contrast, and in order to under-stand fully what the gardens of Versailles have to tell us about science in the twentieth century, we may turn to another garden, equally famous. Constructed in 1499, it is in the Buddhist temple of Ryoan-Ji in Kyoto, in central Japan. It consists of a small courtyard of smoothed sand on which are arranged in a few groups a total of fifteen moss-covered rocks. That is all. In its perfection it fully and serenely expresses the Oriental view that true knowledge of nature is best reached through symbols, that man's place is not to trespass on reality but only to attain to contemplation of it.

Between these two attitudes there stretches more than a few thousand miles. The range is all of man's awareness of the world and all that he has gained in the hundred or more centuries since he first became man by creating art in some caves in the southern tip of Europe. The contrast is between the man of the Renaissance, first in all history to be able to say, "The world is no mystery but something known; by means of my knowledge I can control Nature—" and the Zen Master, whose credo is: "I am a bit of the encompassing Nothing. I own nothing; the world is not mine. At best I may grasp my own destiny in discovering how it is possible for me to have a place in this world." The first of this contrasting pair is recognizable as modern, Western man who boasts of his clear mastery over all of nature on which he can get his grip. The other is like the Eskimo, who makes his dog sled without nails, by lashing wood pieces together flexibly; or like the primitive South Americans de-scribed by Thor Heyerdahl (1950), who made their rafts in the same manner, not fighting nature but adapting themselves to it. They typify the spirit of timeless Oriental man and his awareness that to come to grips with nature at all, to construct a world rather than to experience oneself at a position in it, is not to have reached an in-evitable goal, but simply to have chosen to intrude on the world.

It was God who troubled man in the years when the Middle Ages had come to an end and the modern age was still being born; God had become a bothersome problem. Recall that Galileo, admittedly the most original and important thinker of his day, came finally to his downfall on the question of whether his discoveries were acceptable to God and to His agency on earth, the Church. God was no longer to be held in awe or in fear, or even to be taken for granted, but had now to come, like any other solvable problem, within the purview of man's inquiry. For the ancient Hebrews, God had been a punishing Father and the source of that moral law which sustained the universe but in every case was beyond the reach of mere man. For the Greeks, the gods (now no longer capitalized) were on Olympus, and though they may have consorted with mortals, they were beyond the limits of man's knowing or man's rebellion, as both Prometheus and Icarus could have testified. Even for the secular-minded Romans, who brought their gods to their very hearthstones as lares and penates, the divine represented the limit of the human and could never be encompassed within merely human endeavor. Restated and reinforced as early Christianity, which emphasized the vast gap between the temporal and the godlike nature of things, this abiding view of God's utter inaccessibility pervaded the thinking of all men for centuries. Such a view both stated and supported men's conviction that the firmament of heaven was meant to be a severely restricting pall over mortal attempts to probe beyond an existing state of affairs. During the Dark Ages the inhabitants of Europe, the most gifted of them included, by and large acceded to this arrangement in which through innocence or by divine fiat they were condemned to a life of thought which was rigidly bounded by the dicta of God's agents on earth. They could not imagine themselves free of their bonds, and above all they could hardly conceive that this was to be accomplished "from the light of reason alone," as Descartes clearly advised in his *Rules for the Direction of the Mind.* Even in the teachings of Aquinas, where human reason was exalted as never before, it was wholly within the service of God, man being blessed with reason in order to enable him to fulfill his destiny as one of the children of God. To be told now—and by a professedly devout Catholic at that—to apply oneself in a competition with powers of comprehension previously attributed only to the divine, was a challenge heady enough to shake the very foundations of the intellectual life of a continent.

By the middle of the eighteenth century the science of mathematics was established as the new vernacular of the educated European man, assuming for the scientist the role which medieval Latin had once played as the universal language of culture. As national boundaries were crossed with the new lingua franca and its scheme of observation, experimentation, and prediction, the whole of the natural universe came under the controlled scrutiny of the scientific method. One grand, all-embracing intellectual endeavor was needed to cap these two centuries of progress—and fittingly it came in the form of a mathematical and mechanical scheme which reached out to the very nebulae of the heavens to explain the origins of the entire solar system. From 1799 to 1825 Pierre Simon de Laplace published the five volumes of his *Celestial Mechanics,* a climax to the work of the French Encyclopedists and the age of enlightenment, and a most fitting introduction to our own times. All of the perquisites of the age in which we live and struggle had been laid down unequivocally by the time of this work—the major discoveries in each of the sciences, many of the encompassing schemes, the faith in democracy and in the common man, the worship of material achievements, the belief in infinite progress, the delight in reason, and the complete lack of faith in any significant power beyond that of man himself. There is a famous story told of Laplace which epitomizes his role as the first citizen of the modern world. Napoleon, when he had finished looking through the work, said half-teasingly to the overly serious astronomer, "But I find no mention here of God." To this Laplace replied with great and stern conviction, "Sir, I have no need of that hypothesis."

Here we have the end of a road that had been traveled, in almost arrow-flight fashion, from 1543 to 1799. The direction was clear—from the shadow of a wall behind which an arbitrary and incomprehensible deity ruled the affairs of men, to a palace of light within which God was construed as just one among many possible hypotheses, and not a very useful one at that. The world had become a secular one, in which the might of the universal church could be successfully challenged, as in the Reformation, or pridefully dismissed, as with Laplace. So now man was no longer a mere creature or one among many created beings who stayed in his assigned place in the scheme of things, but the only possible source of knowledge and of wisdom. These were bold adventures at the outermost reaches of human responsibility—for let us make no mistake about it, this was the true significance of the stakes for which these thinkers were playing. They had John Locke's "rational religion" as a more or less workable substitute for St. Thomas' all-embracing rational synthesis. In his *Essay Concerning Human Understanding* in 1690, Locke had outlined a system which proclaimed that all we can apprehend of anything, even the most tangible of substances, are certain attributes gained from minimal sense impressions combined and repeated. Aside from the "primary ideas" of extension, motion, sound, and color, which lead in turn to abstract ideas, we have no contact with any order in the universe, even if there were such an order. Words, which we might have trusted, are only arbitrary signs. Man is left as a kind of primitive calculator in a world he could not make and will not comprehend; and the universe itself begins to take on the shape and significance of a cosmos of arbitrarily whirling dust. In this rational hell, Man had now to depend on nothing but the light of reason alone—but not a light which was part of a divine spark. It was a cold new light which was given off by the physical sciences, with mathematics as their tool. Responsibility, indeed; the Greek tragedists would have delighted in the high drama here being played out with Fate, and perhaps shuddered privately at the potential consequences.

Here was an awful burden to assume, as Kierkegaard was one of the first to point out only a half-century later and as modern writers are prone to remind us today. But when it was first achieved, this position became the clear and ringing expression of a proposition which remains today the credo of our own civilization: that beyond the world of man there is nothing, no knowledge beyond what he can attain and no forces beyond what he is able to muster for his own purposes. The logical end result of this proposition, when it is applied in the realm of ethics, is Sartre's pronouncement that "man being condemned to be free carries the weight of the whole world on his shoulders; he is responsible for the world and for himself as a way of being" (1957, p. 52). Nature may be in some degree unknown but in principle it is completely knowable. And that which is left over, when all of man's conceptualizing work is done, is not an unknowable mystery but rather the part that cannot be ordered at all; we call it the *random*. For this reason it is no coincidence that the eighteenth century, which was the age when all the foundations of the modern world were laid, is also when probability was first established as an organized branch of mathematics.

Fittingly, in the Introduction to his *Analytic Theory of Probability,* Laplace stated the possibility of the case for an anthropocentric cosmos. "Given for one instant," he mused, "an intelligence which could comprehend all the forces by which nature is animated and the respective positions of the beings which comprise it, if moreover this intelligence were vast enough to submit these data to analysis, it would embrace in the same formula both the movements of the largest bodies in the universe and those of the lightest atom: to it nothing would be uncertain, and the future, like the past, would be present to its eyes."

If any reader were still naïve enough, in this age of post-Revolutionary Enlightenment, to suppose that the author of this passage was here referring to an immortal and omniscient God, he was to be rudely shaken. The human mind unaided, said Laplace, could approximate this state of intelligence. It could "comprehend in the same analytical expressions the past and future states of the world system." An order was becoming apparent to scientists of that day, and it was to take the place of the world-order by which divine power had always made itself evident in the affairs of men. The first characteristic of the new order was that it was centered in man and his doings—and his newborn passion for a reasonable structure of things was very soon apparent, for example, in the fact that for the first time in the history of scholarship books were indexed efficiently and subjects in a compendium of knowledge began to be arranged alphabetically. A second and far more significant characteristic of the emerging order was that it was completely materialistic and deterministic. It assumed no history and needed none; history was replaced by an ahistorical sequence of states in which each changed from its successor in accordance with natural laws. If one knew the laws and had access to a reasonable amount of relevant data, he could then with a high degree of confidence—or significantly more often than not, a qualification that was supposed to amount to the same thing—say what the state would be like at a certain point in the future or calculate what it had been like at a point in the past. In dealing in this way with future and past as nothing but points on a line of continuous and orderly change, the familiar tenses had of course been eliminated in their accustomed human meaning. The future was no longer a special realm with such characteristics as unknowability or mystery, challenge or threat; and the past was no longer a repository, a comfort, or a shadow from behind. Both were now only places on an abscissa, defined simply as being so many units of time on either side of the location known as the present. Therefore prediction could now become possible as well as understandable. To know the future was no longer magic but only the application of known laws, directing them one way along the abscissa rather than another; and it made exactly the same sense to talk of "predicting" the past.

We can see now, even in the light of this brief survey, how much of the orientation and method of the modern scientific temper is contained in these few sentences from Laplace. Looking back in this way, attempting to trace out the very beginnings of an attitude totally new in history, we can also see more clearly what it was that was replaced. The new human mind, as Laplace saw it with its tools of mechanics and geometry like shiny new thunderbolts, was an unabashed substitute for a pre-Renaissance God in his heaven. All space and all time were open to its survey; the possibility of omniscience was clearly in the offing. In place of the mind of God—"an allegory of Kings and nothing else," as Blake said—there was now proposed the mind of the educated citizen; the one was dethroned precisely as the other was exalted. And as the all-powerful deity of pre-Renaissance ages was transformed into Mr. God of the Enlightenment, the medieval natural philosopher was just as surely changed into the modern scientist. Man was now to grasp the whole universe as his own; and the scientist was commissioned by history to develop the means to obtain it for him.

The great adventure began, not with a bang but a whimper. At about the time that John Dalton, in England, was establishing a science of individual differences by his observations on the color vision of himself and his brother—a fascinating and neglected chapter in science's history, if only because of the startling fact that no one before him, apparently, had ever discovered the defect in himself—an assistant in the astronomical observatory at Greenwich became an unwitting footnote to the history of psychology by getting himself dismissed from his position. In a rapidly expanding commercial and naval power such as England had become, it was more and more necessary that time be kept accurately; and the basis for all reckoning of time was in those days the data supplied by an observatory such as Greenwich. These in turn were obtained by a method which, though admittedly neither elegant nor precise to a fine degree, had at least the solid English virtue of dependability. That this characteristic itself rested on the capabilities of observers was hardly even guessed at—though perhaps the discovery might not even have bothered scientists who could not grasp the significance of built-in differences in individual response to the raw material of sensation. The method in use for establishing certain constants for the reckoning of time was to record, to the nearest tenth of a second, the time at which specified heavenly bodies were seen to cross the hairline of an eyepiece. Known as Bradley's "eye and ear" method, it required the observer to count the passage of seconds as the star appeared to come toward the wire; to note down the second completed just before the star crossed the wire, and the position of the star in relation to the wire at this instant as well as at the instant when the next second ended; and finally to make a rapid calculation in tenths of a second to determine the time to be added to the full second already counted.

The incident in question was reported, in Vol. 3 of the *Observations* of the Greenwich institution, by Maskelyne, the head of the observatory. These are his words, as quoted by Sanford (1888):

I think it necessary to mention that my assistant, Mr. David Kinnebrook, who had observed the transits of stars and planets very well in agreement with me all the year 1794, and for a great part of the present year, began from the beginning of August last to set them down one-half a second of time later that he should do according to my observations; and, in January of the succeeding year, 1796, he increased his error to eight tenths of a second. As he had unfortunately continued a considerable time in this error before I noticed it, and did not seem to me likely ever to get over it and return to a right method of observing, therefore, though with reluctance, as he was a diligent and useful assistant to me in other respects, I parted with him. . . . The error was discovered from the daily rate of the clock deduced from a star observed on one of two days by him and on the other by myself, coming out different to what it did from another star observed both days by the same person, either by him or by myself. . . . I cannot persuade myself that my late assistant continued in the use of this excellent method (Bradley's) of observing, but rather suppose he fell into some irregular and confused method of his own, as I do not see how he could have otherwise committed such gross errors (p. 8).

There is at this distance no way of solving the fascinating puzzle of just what it was that caused Kinnebrook's sudden lapse from the status of "diligent and useful assistant." Maskelyne's account tells us very little about this, except to suggest rather plaintively that his assistant somehow chanced on an incorrect method. On the other hand, though it is rather sparse, Maskelyne's report tells us a very great deal about the thinking of the scientist of that time, and from it we may draw some significant conclusions. To repeat the description of the task that observers at Greenwich were supposed to perform with accuracy, they were required to check the rate of a clock by following a set procedure. Pointing a telescope either due north or due south, they marked the exact time a certain star passed the hairline on their eyepiece on one day, and then again on the next day. If the times were the same on the two days, within the limits of accuracy of the "Bradley method," the clock was assumed to be running true. From this it would follow that as long as Mr. Kinnebrook was constant in his personal response time—either by displaying the same objective accuracy each day or by committing the same objective error each day—no one could have had any cause to be dissatisfied with his observations. To take an extreme example, if by some physiological quirk it always took him precisely one half a second to call out the instant of the star's crossing the line, thereby invariably adding exactly one half a second to his reading, he would still have been a perfectly valuable assistant, for he would have done no harm in regard to the task he performed. The rate of the clock could still be exactly determined from his daily readings.

We may therefore note in passing that Kinnebrook has passed into the textbooks of science as the perpetrator of a dereliction of which he was actually innocent. Today we understand the situation well enough to be able to state that in regard to the task confronting the observers at Greenwich, no one at all is error-free. In this situation, either the term *error* is synonymous with the term *reaction,* or the term *error* is simply meaningless. By error we mean nothing more than the individual's personal rate of response to a specific triggering percept. It is the possibility of Kinnebrook's variability, not the fact of his "error," which should have offended Maskelyne. Therefore the hapless assistant was dismissed, not for the variability which he did display, but for the presumed error which in fact he shared with all other observers. If Maskelyne had been able to deduce that Kinnebrook's deviation was the result of uncontrolled variability of response, he would have displayed a proper scientific insight; but instead he merely judged his assistant's constancy, found it different from his own, and in authoritarian fashion exercised his disiplinary powers. Of such accidents is history made.

What is revealed here is the simple fact that Maskelyne seemed to have no way of testing for variability. It is even probable that neither he nor his contemporaries entertained such a conception, assuming that he had given more than passing thought to the whole problem of observation. For nineteen years later, in 1816, von Lindenau, writing a history of the Greenwich Observatory, duly reported the incident in the *Zeitschrift für Astronomie;* there it was seen by Bessel, the astronomer at Königsberg, who was sufficiently intrigued to make some tests on his colleagues; and only then was it discovered, to everyone's surprise, that the "relative personal equation," as Sanford (1888) later called it, the comparison of one person with another, was a most complex matter and not a simple function of the two persons themselves. We may therefore assume that since the conception of variability remained untested for another two decades it was not a part of Maskelyne's thinking.

How would one go about making such a test? Clearly there is required some known and fixed standard to which the person's repeated performance may be compared so as to chart the precise way in which he varies around it. Maskelyne did not have access to an apparatus to enable him to do this, even if he had been able to envision it, for its development depended on a long series of technical steps in accurate and reliable instrumentation. Indeed, by the circularity which prescribes the relation between science and technology, the instruments were not likely to be developed until a need for them was felt in theory and expressed in experiment. It was actually not until 1856 that the first complete apparatus for establishing one's "absolute personal equation," in Sanford's phrase—that is, his relation to a known, objective standard—was perfected by the American astronomer, O. M. Mitchel. Measuring what he vividly termed "the personality of the eye," he obtained the first data on what are now called reaction times. But Maskelyne, lacking these objective standards, could not measure absolute reaction time and did not even conceive of measuring the related phenomenon of sequential variation around the mean of one's absolute reaction time.

But this is not to say that no measurements at all were made at Greenwich. They were, and quite usefully, but they were of a special kind—for they were directed toward a unique sort of event. The thing to be measured was not the absolute time of the clock—a datum which, incidentally, we have since learned is unreal—nor even the absolute reaction time of the observer of the clock, but rather a second-order phenomenon: the difference between two measurements of the clock. Interestingly, it was a fact of just this sort that was occupying John Dalton in another area of science at about the same time in science's development. Dalton had begun his observations on color vision because he noted certain characteristics about a difference between two perceptions; and Maskelyne had more or less inadvertently begun the experimental study of the individual by chancing on the same kind of happening, a characteristic of the difference between two observations. In Dalton's case the "absolute" or presumably objective standard, which was established in the case of color vision by Newton's discoveries about the constituent rays of light, only seemed to settle the basic psychological issue: the relation between the presumed objective and the presumed subjective data in regard to color. And in much the same way the development of the experimental problem of reaction time subsequent to Maskelyne's contribution only seemed to resolve the question of the relation between absolute and relative personal equations.

Here was the fundamental issue, then, the basis for a psychological science. The Greenwich incident is perhaps most apposite for the purposes of a historical survey, for we can easily trace a development from Greenwich to Königsberg to Leipzig, from Maskelyne to Bessel to Wundt and then on to Cattell and modern psychology. No experimental psychology of color vision arose to match the exciting programs and achievements of the German experimental laboratories in the last half of the nineteenth century. But the situation that produced Dalton's discoveries was just the same as the one that resulted in a century of scientific concern with the problem raised by Maskelyne and Bessel; the difference is only that the former was not subjected to later experimental tests and therefore has never been recognized as one of the two founding incidents representing a whole new turn in the history of ideas. The problem itself was wholly new. Aristotle would not have understood it; Galileo would have been stirred by its implications without grasping its full import; even Newton might have been sincerely puzzled. In the rest of this chapter we shall see whether we can arrive at a satisfactory statement of just what the problem was—for the fact is that although it is now 150 years old we have not yet learned to state it clearly. We are still arguing, though in the past decade or so only in faint whispers, over how to define psychology. To do this we need to spell out its *Problematik*.

The Line of Time

For a discipline of psychology, the first fruits of the Enlightenment were in the form of a unique attitude which enabled scientists with nonpsychological interests to take notice of the human factors that affected their particular data. Guiding ideas do not come to birth easily but by fits and starts, so to speak. The grand scheme of Laplace, in which man as a reasoning intelligence was to take over the omniscient powers of God, took a century or more to establish in anything like the explicit form in which students are taught it today. And so the work of Dalton seems rather naïve, the puzzlement of Maskelyne somewhat dated. We find it difficult to conceive, for example, why the latter, who was a gifted scientist, could not grasp immediately the rather obvious idea that many different factors might affect the time required for a person to respond to a situation. The magnitude of a star, its rate and direction of motion, even the fact that it was a star being viewed rather than the sun or the moon, all tended to condition the observer's speed of response, his absolute personal equation. Yet even Sanford, who used this descriptive term, and even Wundt, who built a laboratory around a kind of experimental situation which seems to be only a variant of the Maskelyne-Kinnebrook task, were never completely clear as to the relation between the personal equation and reaction time. Clearly, the situation is by no means simple; even at this vast distance in the progress of science, it merits re-examination.

In a series of papers in which the problem of the personal equation was most thoroughly surveyed and discussed, Sanford (1888, 1889a, 1889b) finally came around to a kind of grudging admission that the personal equation was a special form of the reaction time experiment. Conversely, the RT experiment was the general form of the situation in which the specific problem of the personal equation was first studied. And this was one reason, perhaps the chief one, for the hesitancy with which both Sanford as well as Wundt himself approached the issue of definition. Boring refers to their difficulty, although he uses the terms within which he prefers to constrain the history of psychology from Aristarchus to Köhler: "There was in the '60's some psychological experimenting going on, mostly in the hands of physiologists. The philosophers, however, owned psychology; they believed that philosophy and thus psychology must depend upon scientific method, but for all of this conviction they could not make themselves into experimentalists" (1929, p. 362). A distinction between the proponent of scientific method and the experimentalist seems almost a contradiction in terms; yet it was real and present to the men who were founding a science on the basis of a wholly new and incompletely grasped problem. It was this distinction, and not the fact that they were philosophers—rather than what? one may ask—which stymied them. For the experimental method, which seems to our modern eyes the only possible way of subjecting a problem to test, came to fruition quite painfully. William James, for all his grasp of basic issues in psychology and for all his sympathy toward a naturalistic science, could never bring himself to perform a real experiment as we would now define it. He helped to found a laboratory, but that is all.

To try to puzzle out wherein lay the difficulty, we may go back to the events which followed on Bessel's rediscovery of the Greenwich incident. During the ensuing half-century, the necessary instruments were developed to enable satisfyingly exact measurements to be made of events distributed in time. The scientists and engineers of the U.S. Coast Guard Survey, under their superintendent Bache, developed the first successful chronograph about 1850. Wheatstone invented a chronoscope in about 1840, and Matthias Hipp another and better one in 1843. Mitchel's contribution was an apparatus to introduce the initial event in the temporal sequence, a momentary flash or sound— now known as the *stimulus*—to which the observer was required to attend.

For the first time one part of the problem of the personal equation had been wrested free of its embodiment in an individual's perception —in just the way that Newton's conception of color as a function of the wave length of constituent rays took a statement about color out of the mind of the person perceiving and put it into the physicist's instrument. A new sphere of events was in process of construction, its methodology based on the Cartesian insistence that mind-stuff, including perceptions of colors and stars, was in its own realm, eternally separated from the matter-stuff of the world; and given this insistence, the devices and procedures were being constructed which would enable scientists to order the events to which perception seemed to be directed. Redefining was the order of the day. Color was now a measurable wavelength. The stimulus was a point on an axis of time. Therefore there was needed only another event at a later point in time, a reliable measure of the temporal difference between the two points, and a theory to account for the relation of such differences to relevant conditions. The RT experiment was about to be born—or at least so it seemed. Yet Mitchel's very first discovery was not, as we might expect, that the human reaction time to visual or auditory stimuli was of a certain duration. On the contrary, he found that without exception his subjects, including himself and his assistant Twitchell, anticipated the stimulus instant whenever they were asked to respond to a controlled, artificial transit. We would now say that their reaction times were negative. But this way of expressing his results tells us less than nothing; for it makes no sense to say that a person requires less than zero milliseconds to respond to a certain kind of stimulus. A peculiar new phenomenon was coming into view, made possible by the development of devices by means of which the passing of an artificial star across a hairline could be plotted as an event on an axis of time. The achievement has received less recognition than it deserves, although in some ways it is comparable to Newton's contribution to the physics of color.

The central difficulty has already been noted, in Mitchel's discovery that subjects anticipated, producing what could only be called negative reaction times. It was this sort of knowledge that Wundt carried with him when he first conceived of laying out a sequence of human actions as points along a time axis. The phenomenon of relative personal equation, or the comparison of one observer with another, had been known for half a century. Then, about 1850, Helmholtz began to experiment with frogs' legs and later with human subjects, attempting to determine the speed with which nerve impulses travel within the body. In the 1860s the astronomer Hirsch used the Hipp chronoscope to obtain figures, which he called "physiological times," expressing the latency of the various sensory receptors. At about the same time Wundt devised his "complication" experiments to test the speed with which mental processes of varying degrees of complexity took place. It was not until 1873 that Exner, an Austrian investigator who had little influence on the early psychological laboratories, coined the term "reaction time" to refer to the kind of event which had already been studied in such great detail. And when we think about the term we can see that it describes a phenomenon quite different from the one with which previous workers had been concerned. The word *reaction* clearly implied a movement of a certain kind—an act against or toward, an act in answer to some precipitating circumstance, or as we would now say, a *response*. No such implication was contained in the work of Helmholtz, for his interest was entirely in the time between one physiological event and another. Nor did Hirsch imply, in his "physiological times," anything more than the fact of differing latencies. Wundt on his part was interested in patterning a theory of the mental processes after the known facts of physiology, and in fact this is the reason for the name he gave to his new experimental discipline. To all of this, however, Exner added something new. He brought into the open the issue which had been created as a problem by Dalton and Maskelyne—the relation, if one can properly call it that, between the event which occupies one position on a time axis, now called the stimulus, and the event, now called the response, which seems to occupy a position farther along the same axis. In fact, for proof that the issue is by no means simple and the problem not at all solved by making both events points which are marked out in temporal sequence, we need only point to how difficult it was for Maskelyne, Mitchel, Hirsch, and Wundt, among many others, to see the situation in this light.

When we use the term *reaction time,* we refer, without thinking further about it, to an answer which the person offers to a stimulating situation. If his instructions are to call out, or press a key, at the precise instant he sees an artificial star cross a hairline in an eyepiece, he will wait until the moving light comes to the appropriate position, perceive this as his invitation for action, so to speak, and make his movement as rapidly as he can. But if he does this, how can he possibly make his response before the star reaches the hairline? We question the subject, but in all sincerity he denies that he "jumped the gun." His experience has been that he made his response at about the last possible instant, or perhaps a shade later; yet when we make accurate measurements of the time intervals, we find that he may have been as much as a tenth of a second ahead of the target. This ought to give us the first hint that there are really two kinds of events occurring here. One is reported by the subject as his spontaneous experience; the other is measured and evaluated by the experimenter. Because of his understandable bias, of course, the experimenter will not usually recognize the existence of the "nonexperimental" event, for what is required for such recognition is to break in on the problem at a pre-Cartesian level. In terms of the experimenter's view, a negative reaction time makes no sense, whereas in terms of a subject-oriented—or, as we may now say, a phenomenological—approach, it is the idea of reaction time itself which makes no sense; and if what occurs is not a reaction, and what is measured is therefore not a reaction time, then it hardly matters whether we call it positive or negative.

What in fact does the difference between positive and negative in this term refer to? The answer comes easily. It is a distance along a time axis; and it is made possible, first, by the fact that the separate events have been arrayed in a line along this axis, and second, by the further fact that they are assumed to display a fixed logical progression. The subject's response—pressing a key, for example —occurs at a point further along this axis than does the event which is supposed to be the trigger for the response. But this is exactly where the sincere and cooperative subject crosses us up. His response occurs a tenth of a second in advance of the triggering event, at least as measured by the time of a clock. One might maintain, of course, that his response is unrelated to the event which calls it forth—but anyone who has seen a cooperative subject poised to make his response in such an experiment will know that this is hardly an acceptable way of getting out of the dilemma. The simple, stunning fact is that, in this case at least, the time sequence is reversed: the response to an event occurs before the event itself. To call it a negative reaction time helps us not at all; this only makes its alternative expression, positive reaction time, useless for experimental purposes.

Time, Facts, and Things

We must now look a little more closely at the aspect of time which has run through our account, counterpoint to the historical survey. The chief actor in the unfolding drama of science was to be, not simply the Other, but a figure who might more aptly be called the *Generalized Other*—the supposed person, necessarily nonexistent, who was assumed as the active agent in the procedures of science. To put it in terms more immediately practical, there was a role which the very human scientist took on when he adopted the scientific method as his approach to the apprehension of natural phenomena. The role required that he act as though he represented within himself in generalized form all of the grasp which could be achieved by any impersonal, other-centered eye. To do this he had to give up very much—his own prejudicial view, his sense of his own position and of his stake in the situation, his idiosyncrasies, and most of all the way in which as a functioning human being he made his own life in time. He had to act as though another kind of time were not only possible but preferable as well. In this new order of time the model object was a clock, the scheme was a giant, endless ruler laid out in limitless space, and the concrete embodiment of the whole was that celestial mechanism which the genius of Newton had discovered and reduced to a series of understandable laws.

Time was here equivalent to what Barrett (1959) calls "the indifferent eternal chronometrical cycling of the fixed stars" (p. 44). The clock was the great invention of the eighteenth century—a role which the steam engine played in the nineteenth century and the electronic computer seems about to do in the twentieth—expressing at once the needs, the faith, and the genius of an entire era. The clock is indeed an instrument of time—but of a certain kind of time only. Basic to its activity is its mechanical heartbeat, some device by which a constant, unchanging, ever repeating unit of time is marked off. Not by accident did history in 1583 choose Galileo as the discoverer of the first simple and practical method for constructing this device. As every student is now taught—perhaps incorrectly in fact, but validly in principle—it was Galileo who, using his pulse as a timer, first calculated that the pendulum swing of a weight maintained a constant, unchanging, ever repeating unit. The distance of the swing might change as the weight came finally to rest, but as long as the length of the suspending cord and the mass of the weight remained the same, the pendulum established for itself a unit of time for each complete swing. The errant flow of time, surrounding and immersing all meaningful human action, could now be broken into units. With a ruler marked off in these units—the dial of a pendulum clock, for example—time could now be treated like space, as a continuum which was ready to be marked off and measured, and entities placed at their appropriate positions along its length. Truly, for the first time in history, man had broken free of time and could now stand outside it, as it were, surveying all time because he had reduced it to a sequence of equivalent units endlessly repeated. A timebound creature had constructed a totally new kind of time for his own use.

This is what the clock meant for men who were determined to subdue nature. It is no wonder that in the first century in which all human energies were turned into this conquest, the clock and its derivative devices became the living symbol for the technology of an age. Even the cosmology of Newton depicted what was essentially a vast cerulean clockworks; the planets swung in their orbits as steadily as, and for the same reasons as, did the lamp that the young Galileo is said to have watched swinging in the cathedral at Pisa. And just as a man bears a certain relationship to the face and hands of a clock, so did the scientist stand in a certain relation to the dimension of time which he now used in his experimental studies. Given a clock, one sees it all of a piece; its entire circuit, from any moment of time through the swing of the dials back to the same point, can be apprehended at one glance. The person who looks at the clock in this way is not himself at any point in the clock's time. As an example, he may know that "it" is now three o'clock, and of course this is one of the numbers marked on the face of the clock itself—but the three o'clock that "it" is, the time at which the person himself is, at the present instant, is not the time of the clock. For the latter is a time which runs along its own course; the clock tells clock time only, a time which one has to handle in a certain way, as by setting the hands of the clock and checking its mechanical accuracy, in order to make it coincide even temporarily with the running-off of one's personal time. A clock cannot be bored with the slow passage of time, nor express surprise that the day has gone so fast, nor recall nostalgically the long, slow days of one's former years. A clock is never at a present moment, nor in fact "at" a moment at all. There is neither past nor future in clock time, only the steady ticking of absolutely equivalent units in a one-directional stream, like an endless sequence of counters laid out on a line. The relation of the person to this line of units is precisely the same as his relation to the units of any other yardstick for measuring. He can break in at any point, place an object on the line, place another object at another spot, and count the number of units between. In this way, either in time or in space—for in principle there is now no difference—he has made the appropriate scientific measurement in a pure world of objects.

But not yet in a purely human world—for in the spontaneous experience of persons, this scheme is only the grossest and most inadequate approximation. MacLeod (1957) poses the issues neatly:

. . . time is an essential dimension of purpose. If time runs in a straight line, then the only things we can consider as the causes of an event are the antecedent and concomitant conditions. The Newtonian system restricts us to these. If, however, we question the absoluteness of time and play with the idea that, in different frames of reference, the relationship between antecedent and consequent may be reversed, we may be left free to think that something that has not yet happened may be an essential condition of something that is about to happen (p. 480).

Even in the relatively uncomplicated instance of the observer who is poised to signal the moment when an artificial star crosses a hairline, the situation cannot be simply described in terms of one event separated by so many counters from another event. It may be more accurate, indeed, to speak of the time of a purely human world as a sequential series of arrows shot out from a living center, each one fitted at its trailing edge with some fixed organization out of the past which, like the feathers fastened at the back end of an arrow, guide its forward flight while being themselves carried inexorably along with it. The relation of the person himself, and therefore of all persons, to the time of the human world is characterized by the word *within*. He is caught within it and made by it, and he himself makes it from the inside. There is no way that he can step out of it, even though in his various pathologies he attempts to approximate such a release —in the stillness of depression, when time slows almost to a halt; in the state of schizophrenia, when he nearly achieves the situation of standing in no present and thus comes close to capturing the illusion of freedom from the bonds as well as the challenge of time and destiny; even, perhaps, in the comfort of familiar and habitual actions, when the casual, will-less running off of known sequences of behavior provides an easy reminder of a mechanical series in which an impersonal happenstance takes the place of the charged and personal deed. It is hardly an accident that behavioristic theories invariably make rote, habitual actions the prototype of all human activity.

Given this line of time as it was ticked off by a clock, the first true experiments on human beings immediately became possible. It is important for us to note, however, that the new science of psychology, if it was to be an experimental discipline, required that a new and more daring proposition be added to those which comprised the methodology of all the natural sciences. By the end of the eighteenth century this methodology had been accomplished—first, in the materialistic conception of the entire physical universe as a huge mechanism ruled throughout by its fixed laws which did not need the intervention of gods, large or small; and second, in the idea, first clearly formulated by Huyghens in 1690, in his "Treatise on Light," that propositions in science need not be justified by being deduced in Euclidean fashion from given axioms but by being verified by tested consequences (Schmidt, 1957). The first of these conceptions guaranteed that man's world as conquered by science was indeed his to master, and the second gave him the freedom to act toward a logically evident "future," rather than merely combine and recombine elements from an established "past."

But beyond these basic propositions, a specifically human science demanded that without exception the events of behavior which we know as meaningful acts be taken out of their setting in motive and feeling, wiped clean of every trace of unique involvement, and strung like any other beads of data along the lines of space and time which are tied across the physical scientist's horizon. Behavior has to be viewed without reference to past, present, or future, for these dimensions have no place in clock time. Fitted into that timeless and spaceless realm in which all of science's events take place, a realm in which the pseudo-prediction of deductive and probabilistic reasoning takes the place of the true forward-reaching thrust we call prediction, behavior now becomes measurable just as though it were an object occupying space. Time is no longer the setting of action but only one more variable, dependent or independent not because of its intrinsic character but solely because of its logical relations to other, usually spatial or numerical, variables.

The structure of *time,* when it is viewed as a historically developed conception in which the past, present, and future are strung out along an irreversible dimension, is of very little help in understanding the case of the person who holds fast with even minimal passion to an idea or a belief. It is a structure that makes sense only in reference to a specific and quite limited kind of mental content—the item which we can hold off at a distance and treat with almost complete neutrality as an object or item belonging to what is past. The idea or belief which is held—in the literal sense of that word—requires for its study quite another structure, to which we have given the name *temporality*. Its model, inadequate but perhaps useful as a first step, would have the form of a number of lines radiating from a continually changing core. One of the lines touches a set of entities which correspond to certain elements found within the structure of *time:* the removed, distant, neutrally conceived packages, as we have called them, all of which have the character of the past event. If these entities are displaced at all along this line, then the known past, the perceived present, and the expected future form the three divisions or categories for their placement. The person himself, in his own lived present, is not somewhere in the middle of these three divisions, but outside all of them. He is just as removed from the expected and predicted future as he is from the completely known past; they are outside of the core of his present, inconceivable moment. A second radiating line of the structure of temporality, in our crude model, touches on the true future—the up-ahead, the not-yet, the hoped-for or feared, the home of challenge and anxiety, of hope and caution and vigilance and faith. As persons who act, we constantly step out along this line, taking the core of our present with us, but with the exception of rare moments—which we sustain only in peril and anguish—we find that we have not strayed far from the everlasting line of pastness that haunts and limits and supports all our action.

Such a model describes approximately the way in which temporality in its various aspects appears to the person. It does not, of course, describe what is *known* about the past, the present, and the future, for this is just what is given by the more familiar structure of the dimension of time. What our model does is help us to depict the way that past things, for example, seem to us; they manifest the character that Binswanger has aptly called the *having-been.* But we can be more concrete than this. There is a most familiar phenomenon with which we deal, an entity which in fact forms the content of much of our thinking. This is the *fact;* and it is the best example we have of pastness in our thinking. The nature of a fact is, as we noted above in regard to an object, that it can be acquired like a thing, possessed like property, and handled like a package. One's attitude toward it—which denotes in simplest form the way it spontaneously appears to one—is precisely the same as one's attitude toward physical things that can be possessed. We speak of accumulating facts, almost as though we could pile them in a heap and sort them into sizes and shapes. We refer to the weight of facts, again suggesting their common phenomenological ground with the tangible. And we are always aware that facts, like discrete objects, preserve their integrity regardless of our psychic actions toward them; we may be upset or happy about a fact, but in stating this condition we thereby clearly distinguish between the feeling that is personal and the fact toward which it may happen to be directed. It is entirely to be expected that the physical sciences, which aim at a dispassionate control of the natural universe of tangible objects and forces, profess to deal exclusively with facts and, indeed, have at times been narrowly defined as nothing but the organized repository of relevant facts.

When we view the fact in this way, we are in a position to affirm its fundamental and essential characteristic: *that its alternative is conceivable*. It is always true of a fact that it fails to exhaust its own realm; there is always another possibility to be conceived and, in most cases, to be stated just as easily as the original fact. If it is a fact that all men are mortal, then it is possible to imagine a race of men blessed, or cursed, with immortality. The moon may, in fact, be made of green cheese—but conceivably, and equally factually, the cheese may be pale blue or not cheese at all but pudding. More to the point for our interests here: A patient in therapy may hold fast to the faith that all women are goddesses, remote and ideal and therefore untouchable; but if he can be shaken loose from his faith long enough to adduce evidence to support this opinion, it will tend to take on nothing more than the status of an established fact in an organized hierarchy. Then a whole series of alternatives may open to his imagining—for example, that all women are worthless, or that they vary as widely as do men, or even that agnosticism is the better part of sexuality because the question which troubles him is unanswerable.

In this respect, that some alternative way of looking at it is always conceivable, the fact again demonstrates its fundamental similarity with the object. For it is the essential characteristic of an object, too, that its other side is always conceivable. One has merely to walk over to it and then walk around it. We always know that this is true of an object. If it seemed to us that this was not so, then it would not appear to us as an object at all but as an image, as a figment of our imagination. The object has its place in our world as a thing which is over-there; the phrase is hyphenated to emphasize a characteristic of which its location in space is only an expression. Because we can always go over to the object, and then move around it without disturbing any of its object character, we know that we apprehend it by being *at* it rather than, say, *in* it. From this, also, we know that we can always find another angle from which to view it; we are certain, in the very grasping of it as an object, that it has at least one more face. Its alternative facet is always conceivable. In the simplest sense, the object is "objective" in this regard: that we can turn away from it. We lose the object when we turn from it, and from this fact alone we are able to know that it is a real thing; for if it were always there whether we faced it or not, we would be sure that it was not an object but, again, a figment of our imagining, not objective but subjective. Thus, the one alternative that is always conceivable in regard to an object is the possibility of its absence. Presence and absence combine to make up the minimum number of facets of the real object. The fact does not have this absolute guarantee of the single other alternative, but like the object it has the same fundamental characteristic: that one or another alternative may always be conceived with regard to it.

Why it should be that the fact, the basic datum for our thinking as scientists, has the same structure as the thing is a question of great interest, and is of overwhelming historical import as well. The convergence may easily be traced at least as far back as the ancient Greeks. It was the Greek creation of a wholly visible world, a world of discrete objects clearly seen, which first enabled thinking man to embark on the endeavor that led finally to his mastery of the physical universe. The world which reaches an apogee in the unspoken metaphysics of contemporary natural science was depicted with equal clarity in the first great epic poem of Greek civilization. Erich Auerbach, in a brilliant evocation of the representation of reality in European literature (1957) describes the "basic impulse of the Homeric style" in terms that might refer as well to many scientists: "to represent phenomena in a fully externalized form, visible and palpable in all their parts, and completely fixed in their spatial and temporal relations" (p. 4). . . . "The Homeric style knows only a foreground, only a uniformly illuminated, uniformly objective present" (p. 5). The world of the Greeks, their reality which gave birth to science, was given by "fully externalized description, . . . uninterrupted connection, free expression, all events in the foreground, displaying unmistakable meanings, few elements of historical development and of psychological perspective" (p. 19).

Initially the person confronts the world in sensory experience, no more. His is a horizon of what John Wild (1958) has termed "world facts," a horizon to which a "world of ordinary language" is fitted; and control over the world as presented is only one of a vast array of possibilities. But, to quote Wild, "the central tradition of Western philosophy has been predominantly objectivist and has been marked throughout its history, ever since Plato, by a strong tendency to restrict and depreciate world facts as relative and distorted versions of reality, and finally to absorb them into a purely objective perspective" (p. 473). The tradition has been followed by history; and the history has been one of a more and more steadily narrowed gaze toward a world of things which are envisioned as a collection of facts. Science is the crystallized version of that knowledge of facts which means power over things. Today we are, presumably, the proud heirs of this victory, but we may also be victims of that way of knowing which is factual because it is patterned after a world of seen things. The fact in our thinking is the counterpart of the thing in our known world, and for this reason, we, as persons who are scientists, find it enormously difficult to think in other terms—though the paradox remains to haunt us, as scientists who are persons, that we will always find it impossible to experience in these same terms.

Two Kinds of Reaction Time

Unfortunately, a misplaced modern sophistication has had the effect, in recent years, of allowing the problem area of reaction time to fall into disrepute. Academically, it has about the same status that the technique of bloodletting does in clinical medicine. But because the problems it raised were once so close to the heart of psychology as a science, it will be in order for us to examine at this point a few of the vicissitudes of the procedure. We noted above that along with the first workable method for establishing absolute reaction time there was born a new and unexpected phenomenon, the negative reaction time. Indeed, it would not be too far from historical truth to say that the positive reaction time is actually a variant of the negative. It ought to be noted, too, that the phenomenon of anticipation, as Mitchel observed it, was not an abstraction, not merely a term for a psychologist's fiction. I say that this ought to be noted in passing because a nearly reflexive action on the part of the modern behavioral scientist is to assign to one kind of phenomenon, such as habit, a reality status which is denied to its temporal converse, *anticipation*—or hope, or wish, or anxiety, or in fact any other term pointing toward the not-yet and the future. On the contrary, anticipation could not have occurred as such until there had been developed a way of measuring absolute reaction time and thus of pinning one end of the phenomenon to the line of objective time. Anticipation is therefore not some merely abstract fiction, but a real, caused event in the real world. Measure the absolute reaction time, set the task to a subject, and you get his "negative" response, his jumping of the gun. The anticipation is just as real, no more and no less, as the green we see when blue and yellow pigments are mixed.

At first glance, there would seem to be no more than a problem of mechanics involved in producing a setting to measure reaction time. All one has to do is measure the precise time at which a stimulus event occurs, then the precise time at which the subject's reaction to it occurs, and on subtracting the one from the other the answer will be found. But the human observer, source of hope as well as of habit, obstacle as often as aid, soon stepped in to complicate this mechanically simple problem. For it was immediately evident that whenever the stimulus event was something the observer could know about, and thus in any way expect, predict, or anticipate, he would, if he were at all motivated—either positively out of a desire to do well and be rewarded, or else negatively out of a desire to avoid punishment—jump the gun and produce a reaction time that was zero or negative. If the observer had no set at all, the problem was solved and the dilemma eliminated at the start—but in such a case would there be a stimulus event? Or would there not remain, rather, only a physical event that triggered off a near-reflex action, much as the neurologist's hammer triggers off the patellar reflex? The hammer is not a stimulus for the knee-jerk but only a precondition; and theoretically the two are by no means the same thing. In short, with no set on the part of the observer, there is no stimulus. With no stimulus there can be no reaction and of course no reaction *time*. On the other hand, if there is any set at all, then there is anticipation, and in such a case the negative reaction time again becomes a possibility. Here is the source of all the woes of the experimental psychologist, for the point is that there is no way at all that the experimenter can ever be sure that he has eliminated the very possibility which will defeat his procedure.

Some experimentalists, showing perhaps more ingenuity than wisdom, have devised elaborate methods in which the stimulus either fails to appear on certain occasions or is interrupted just before the critical moment in its passage. For example, if the observer is being tested on his ability to synchronize his response with the instant at which a steadily moving light crosses a hairline, the experimenter first obtains an average absolute reaction time to a singly presented visual stimulus such as a flash; then the target is occasionally extinguished before it crosses the hairline, the moment of extinguishing being fixed at something less than the observer's known reaction time. If he is anticipating rather than responding to a perceived target, he will be unable to check himself in time and will therefore give a response even to the times when there was no stimulus to respond to. However, this method, like the ingenious trick of occasionally eliminating the target, either changes the problem from the one of pursuing a moving target or else depends on a measurement which is made in a different kind of problem. The stimulus which is approximated by a target that is occasionally interrupted, as well as the stimulus used to determine the subject's absolute reaction time, both differ from a moving target which may give rise to an observer's anticipatory moves. They differ in this significant respect, that they approximate a single, nonrepeated, unexpected, and probably unpredictable stimulus. For the moment the observer can detect any pattern or repetition in successive presentations of the stimulus, he has available to him the very conditions for anticipation which the experimenter has worked so hard to eliminate as a critical factor.

Ideally, the stimulus for determining an absolute reaction time or for eliminating the factor of anticipation or set would be one in which the observer can never detect any clue to help him predict what is coming or when it will appear. But even if this is achieved—and by the nature of the case its achievement can be guaranteed only for the experimenter but never for the observer, for the latter can not even be tipped off by being questioned—it will finally serve only to defeat its own purpose, for there would then be no basis for the experimenter to extrapolate to the observer's processes in a situation in which some degree of anticipation is unavoidable. In short, the experimenter is blocked by the very characteristic of set, or motivation, in the subject which must be minimally present in order to conduct an experiment at all.

Thus hemmed in, experimental psychology began to branch in two directions. On one side, experimenters resorted increasingly to what can only be described as a silent, desperate struggle with their laboratory subjects, their principal weapon an increasingly rigorous and sterile theory and their chief tool a precisely delimited experimental design and procedure. In Bartlett's (1955) apt summary, "When you look at a lot of experiments of the early classical period of experimental psychology, and at many of their direct derivatives down to the present day, you cannot escape the feeling that the experiments mainly provided strings for pulling puppets" (p. 206). By demarcating the situation within sharply drawn theoretical lines, by making increasingly detailed and therefore trivial predictions, and by pinning the subject down to an exactly circumscribed pattern of actions, they boldly attacked one set of problems while, to an increasing degree, faintheartedly bypassing another. The issues dealt with in the laboratory came more and more to be simply a function of the theoretical bias of the day, the hardly ripe fruit of a psychology à la mode which might pass out of style as quickly and as pointlessly as it appeared. Thus, experimental psychology has recently become, to an astounding degree, restricted to those problems which can be expressed in terms of learning theory, or still more recently, stochastic models of the thinking process; yet, at the same time, equally urgent problems—of motivation, attitude, or involvement, of emotional state, of the relation of subject to experimenter—have remained just outside the pale of contemporary experimental respectability. The latter are considered at best the province of experimentally minded social psychologists or of clinicians who are known to use unvalidated, perhaps unvalidatable instruments.

In the other direction, with the tacit admission that there was nothing to be gained by beating the subject at his own game, the earliest experimentalists in the laboratories of Leipzig and Würzburg began to design studies in which the subject could be studied as a free agent. He was, at least at the outset, not enforced but allowed—and he taught his professors a great deal. They learned from him, for example, that his readiness, the direction of his attention, and the particular sense modality which he chose to stress or in which he excelled made all the difference in the speed of his reaction. He showed them that in general he responded quickly to a sharp, clear, sensorially heightened stimulus situation, more slowly to one that was out of focus, uncertain, or perceptually gross; but that both of these extremes were disadvantageous, as in fact the extreme of any situation imposes a stress on the person who is in it; and finally, that he performed best at a less than extreme position in regard to most factors.

The lesson we may learn from the long history of struggle between experimenter and subject in reaction time studies is that there were actually two kinds of time always involved. The experimenter, eagerly following a new and vital tradition in science, was determined to place the situation on the line of time and in this way to subject it to measurement. The subject, on his part, was equally determined to keep the situation within human time, the only time in which he could spontaneously undertake a meaningful act. Indeed, the anonymous human subject has never been given the credit he deserves for his silent, hopeless struggle against methodology, against science, against the awful weight of laboratory authority.

Consider, if you will, the way that time appears to the subject at the moment when the experimenter triumphantly initiates a sequence which, he is sure, he can mark off by the beats of a clock. The latter begins by stating the instructions to his subject. There are some things that will happen, he says—making no mention at all of those that will not; so that we might ask, what is the subject to do with other things that may happen inadvertently? Presumably he is expected somehow to put them out of his attention. In any case, now that he has been told by the experimenter that certain things, and these only, will happen, and that he is then to perform certain actions in reference to the happenings, he has a moment in which to wait. He collects his thoughts, he looks around the experimental setting, perhaps seeing it now in a different light. For it has already been marked off for him in a special way by the experimenter. Certain parts of it have been pointed out to him as relevant, at least in regard to the situation in which he has agreed to participate. He has been told to attend to certain of its aspects and to pass by or put out of his attention some others. Therefore he now sets different values on one or another aspect of the setting. Some are neutral, but most are now clearly not. Whether the latter are challenging or threatening will depend on the subject himself and on his relation to the total situation, but neutral they are not.

In sum, he now finds himself in a special kind of place where he is poised, ready to move, directed in specific ways, oriented in a certain manner in regard to his surroundings, and mobilized to move under only one kind of circumstance. The present moment, as he sees it from his poised and unique position, is not at all a mark on a line. Rather, it is a very special notch which is his alone; and what ever else may be said about this situation, it is clear that the experimenter does not occupy the same notch. Further, the moment which is to occur next is likewise no ordinary moment, not just one more marker out of an endless and indistinguishable sequence on a line. The subject is poised and pointed toward this next moment precisely because it is, for him, now singled out as a moment of a special kind. All the experimental evidence ever gathered goes to show that this is so —for example, even the simple fact that there is always some optimal length of time between setting the stage and precipitating the subject into action in an experiment. If the time is too short, the subject is upset, unprepared, and responds badly; if it is too long, his interest and attention begin to pall and he may be caught off guard.

It is worthy of note that many experimenters who will stake their careers on the evidence they gather in the light of their experimental instructions will ignore or treat as irrelevant the sort of evidence, such as we have just discussed, which happens to occur just barely outside the bounds of an instruction-limited situation. But if we do trust this evidence, we see that the subject has already picked out a certain moment farther ahead along the line of time. It is this one at which he is pointed. He is not just headed in general for what may be up ahead. Rather, he is truly poised, just as a jumper is tuned and prepared when he has to make a leap from one spot to a specified area on the other side of a hollow. Ross and Levy (1958) remark, on the basis of experimental studies of subjects' predictions: "The finding that length of expectancy makes a real difference throughout the course of entire series of predictions indicates that expectancies have a structure of their own and are not mere extrapolations of the past" (p. 122). Similarly, the experimental subject who awaits the start of a situation for which he has been instructed and toward which he entertains expectations, has chosen his point up ahead and is aimed at it—but more significant for our purposes here, he has in a real sense already gotten hold of it in some degree. *It is the outer edge of his present position,* not simply a totally new position which is completely removed from where he is at the present moment. He is already there, one might say; or at least, he has already grasped to some extent what it is to be there. His future is no more a point removed from him than is his past; he can no more keep completely back of the former than he can ever move far enough or fast enough to break completely ahead of the latter. His present moment, in fact, may rightly be considered a kind of stance that he takes so as to hold to both the edge of his future moment and the composite heart of his past.

These are only some of the varied ways in which the time that the subject attempts to institute differs from the time in which the experimenter makes his measurement. In truth, the two times should not even be called by the same name. That they have been is only one more indication that these are matters never discussed. Indeed, they have not really been thought about at all in Western culture, not perhaps since the time of St. Augustine, who felt permitted to deal with such topics because he was comfortably bounded by the fixed and known guarantees of an Aristotelian cosmos. This is how he thought about it: "But time present how do we measure, seeing it hath no space? It is measured while passing, but when it shall have passed, it is not measured; for there will be nothing to be measured. But whence, by what way, and whither passes it while it is a-measureing? whence, but from the future? Which way, but through the present? whither, but into the past? From that therefore, which is not yet, through that, which hath no space, into that, which now is not" (*Confessions*).

However, the ordered whole that constituted the Aristotelian world of Augustine's age is fundamentally different from the kind of world in which the experimentalist of today asks a subject to perform his pre-scribed actions. The space as well as the time of the Aristotelian world was demarcated into zones. It had directions and centers, areas of significance, internally differentiated parts and relations among them. But in the world depicted by modern science, in the post-Renaissance cosmos in which all model events are forced to occur, space as well as time is homogeneous, the former as a neutral array which may be marked off in three dimensions by exactly equal and interchange-able units, and the latter as a line on which equal counters are laid end to end.

The basic distinction [remarks John Cohen (1958)] is between the homo-geneity of physical time in modern science and the inhomogeneity of mythological time. For all the cultures of antiquity as well as in the my-thologies of all peoples, time has a varying quality. It is divided up into holy and secular, lucky and unlucky periods. Hesiod's *Works and Days* ac-tually includes a religious calendar of the months and a list of days which are favourable or unfavourable for certain occupations. Each day is animated by some personal spirit and one's good or evil fortune on a particular day is due to that day. In Homer's *Iliad* the quality of time varies with the seasons and with the weather. It has one value for the victor, and another for the vanquished. Hence it has a quality of fate or destiny experienced by the individual; and so we find Euripedes repre-senting justice as a function of impersonal time (p. 106).

The critical difference between that impersonal time which holds true in science and the humanly articulated time which seemed natural for people of former ages helps to explain the modern experimentalist's seeming blind spot for the subject's view of the situation. The experimenter, if his view is based on contemporary scientific methodology, simply has no way to take account of the kind of time within which the subject, from his own position, carries out a meaningful act.

In the present chapter we have traced out a sequence that spanned two centuries of scientific development. At its beginning, as had been true in the Middle Ages, in the ancient world, and, in fact, in all history up to the beginning of man's rational and deliberate control over nature, the true facts of the world were in some manner ordained. Things were as they were—that is, organized in some kind of order; they were to be studied by men, wondered at, perhaps, and under the right circumstances even to be known, but not to be fully apprehended according to a strictly human scheme. Before the beginning of the modern world, control in this sense was unthinkable. But with the dawn of a secular power, and with man as its agent, the problem of knowledge took on a new cast. If man could remake the world around him, what was the "true" nature of its reality? And whatever this nature was, what of the different pictures of it which were held by men in general and by particular individuals? It was the Renaissance, signal and spark of a great unfolding of men's minds, which for the first time gave us a literature in which the problem of the individual as a uniquely troubled person became a theme worthy of serious treatment. The development in literature from Oedipus to Hamlet tells the story of this vast change in the individual's place in the world.

The answer that psychology seems to need as its first statement—concerning the nature of the real—has, for these two centuries, been given by the world view of the physical sciences: it is that the world "really" is as science describes it. The real thus became the subject matter of a theory in nuclear physics; and the next step, toward the statement that the real is, in essence, merely probable rather than known, was inevitable and therefore easily accepted. On this basis one can, with easy conscience, bypass the problem of the unique perceptual datum which, for all we know, is apprehended by the individual person. The datum for science, as even Maskelyne clearly saw, resides simply in the difference between two perceptions, regardless of the nature of each.

The matter might have rested there, but an issue had been raised which could not easily be quieted. The very same science which gradually made possible a universal and systematic description of the physical world also gave rise to just the instruments to allow, and finally to demand, precise measures of even the individual act. The single, unique item of behavior was at last subject to the same scrutiny in science as were the swing of the stars or the expansion of gases. This last turning of history was perhaps inevitable, that the most dedicated of scientists, challenging what became the final important frontier of technological progress, were hoist by their own petard. As they reached for a way to impress their new subject matter within a scheme adaptable to their instruments of measuring, they blundered all unknowingly into the human dimension. No measurements in space seemed adequate to schematize the unique data presented by the human subject, whereas the possibility of an organization in time provided a challenge as well as a seemingly clear way toward systematically ordered findings. The irony lies in that they were right. They had stumbled into the truly human dimension, which marks the human world and binds together the separable aspects of human action in the dimensions of space. But limited and urged by the demands of a natural science, these dedicated men of the nineteenth century molded the dimension of time into a scheme patterned directly after the manipulable spatial dimensions with which science had so successfully dealt. They created the line of time as the concept within which the temporality of human action was to fit. Thus, the reaction time experiment was the first focus of experimental study in the new science of psychology.

In this light we may now understand John Dewey's (1896) classic paper on the concept of the reflex arc as the one great point of contrast with a flood tide of psychological progress. If Dewey's conclusion is granted, that in even the most direct and obvious of actions the stimulus, so-called, is no point in a sequence on a line of time, but truly represents the *completion* of a constituted organization, then it will follow that the stimulus can occur at all only within time as a human dimension. Dewey's argument, from beginning to end, makes sense only if one allows that the heart of the data in this instance is the person who is organized so as to express himself into his own future. It is this that vivifies his present and makes his past usable; for these are never merely neutral points on a line strung across the endless nothing of science's epistemological vacuum. In the time of the scientist as scientist, there is no future, for here hope has become mere probability, challenge has changed into prediction, and the mystery and dread of the unknown is now no more than a series of gaps in a periodic table whose structure in its entirety is fixed and certain. Nor is there a present in the time of science; this is now merely that artificial and movable fulcrum on which balance two kinds of moments. If time has any meaning at all in the world of science, it has the meaning only of the past, the defining characteristic of which is that in it everything is known, comprehended, grasped, held, encompassed—in one word, all is *had*. It is hardly an accident that, in most languages, the word that expresses possession is the same as that which forms an auxiliary to express the past tense.

If there were only science, we would know nothing of time—and then, of course, there would be no science. The struggle of human beings in a world which presents itself as unknown and resistive gives rise to many ironies, but perhaps none more cutting than this. The scientist, try as mightily as he will, has no choice ever but to conduct his affairs in a human world—though he strains first to invent a realm in which the human dimension of time has disappeared, and then to insist, to his human listeners and his human subjects as well, that the invented realm has a priority in logic as well as in fact. To round out the irony, it is usually the experimental subject, who should have been disposed of by this maneuver, who rediscovers for a science of psychology the dimension that defines a human world and thereby brings back into science the tie that it had almost lost to the only reality that a person can ever know: the full human reality of his own meaningful and responsible actions. With the historic choice advanced by Maskelyne, the experimental subject was created, and with him the wholly new problem of the origin of the human act. In his new position the individual person as subject necessarily became the source of data for the next stage in the development of psychology.

THE CONSTITUTION
OF SCIENCE

The knowledge of a comprehensive entity is an understanding, an indwelling and an appreciation.

—MICHAEL POLANYI

ALTHOUGH SCIENTISTS THEMSELVES HAVE UNTIL RECENTLY RECEIVED but scant attention and poor wages for their efforts, the scientific method itself has always been revered in our society. Today the word *science* is synonymous with *good*—or more precisely, with *true*. There is a widespread belief that the true scientist can do no fundamental wrong, and that it is his method which is the secret of this unique success in a fallible human world. Yet it is never really clear what is meant when the layman refers to science or to the scientific method. In a general way he means something opposed to random, haphazard, impulsive, biased, misinformed, emotional, or frankly human. The slightly unreal figure who emerges to assume this role is utterly rational, cool and unemotional yet passionate, and controlled but dedicated. His white coat is the symbol of his intellectual purity, and the fact that he is male is a guarantee that he will not be swayed by feeling or intuition. Americans are mildly uncomfortable at the idea of a woman scientist. Far removed from the passions that sway ordinary humans in the living room or market place, let alone the bedroom, the scientist is the personification of our collective ideal.

It is risky to quarrel with history or with the spontaneous majority opinion in a democracy. For this reason we would do well to begin by recognizing, as the layman has done implicitly, that the scientific method may not be simply a refined technique, but rather a guiding orientation toward all of nature. It will follow that the man who is equipped to act in terms of the scientific method is a special kind of person, his activities constituting a fundamentally distinctive kind of endeavor. If he is defined exclusively in terms of the physical sciences, they are then raised to a position of unarguable import; and the psychologist who follows their lead can claim for himself much of their prestige, even as he appropriates what he takes to be their metaphysics. Adherents of certain schools of psychological thought or method—the phenomenologists, for example—would then seem compelled either to accept these propositions as basic to what constitutes the scientific endeavor, or else to rule themselves out of the very community to which their professional activities ought to give them access. For this reason we will have to examine somewhat carefully, in this chapter, the notion of science. A convenient starting point, because it accords with the way these investigations are supposed to be undertaken, will be to examine some of the more common definitions of science. The three definitions that we will discuss have to do with quantification, with the scientific method, and with the place of theory.

Definitions of Science

Scientific progress would seem to be inconceivable without some kind of measurement, this term being taken to mean the application of a formal system, such as numbers, to the material under study. By this criterion, metaphysics is not a science, nor is art criticism, nor is psychotherapy—and there appears to be no way in which these endeavors could be so conducted as to be subsumed under a requirement of quantification or measurement. It is of interest to note what the three rejected endeavors have in common. They all spring from the spontaneous experience of persons who are deeply involved in their relationship with the world; they are all attempts to report this spontaneity and involvement to other interested persons; and they attempt to do this without that kind of translation which is implicit when the findings of the scientific enterprise are submitted to some formal scheme of integers. They claim always to make the report in their own terms.

This brings us closer to the nature of quantification or measurement in its relationship to science. Quantification involves the special use of a pre-existing structure to which the data of a science are projected point by point. Only material that can be "mapped" in this way is amenable to quantifying. It would seem, then, that only material already organized in a certain fashion can ever be quantified. Content which does not lend itself to breakdown into units, for example, cannot be quantified—not simply because some counting is required, but because the transposable unit is one of the essential elements in a formal number scheme. This is the idea that lies behind Thorndike's inherently plausible statement that if anything exists, it must exist in some quantity and therefore be measurable. In the course of a thorough critique of the philosophy and orientation of modern empirical science, Sonneman (1954) comments, in regard to this point, that the plausibility of Thorndike's argument is deceptive—for only what can be stated in terms of some unit is measurable; and what would be the unit for measuring, say, an elephant? Would it be elephantness? Following Sonneman, we would add that Thorndike has quite clearly revealed his bias toward a certain conception of reality. He sees it as composed of tangible things that lend themselves faultlessly to unitizing, like rocks that cleave neatly along their lines of inner structure. His reliance on measurement as an ultimate action, then, implies a specific way in which experience is generally organized, and even presupposes that he plans to organize his own experience in this fashion.

In the terms introduced in Chapter two to describe fundamental ways of organizing one's experience, we may now say that measurement always implies the explanatory mode of reflection. But even if it be admitted that the proper place for a quantifying science is the explanatory mode, it may still be questioned whether explanation is ever the whole of science. This question is central to our whole discussion. The fundamental argument for the view that science is a completely explanatory endeavor is, in effect, that at no point in the scientist's activities does he need to resort to anything like faith. Indeed, it is on the issue of faith that there hinges the distinction between the scientist and the theologian, to mention the chief protagonists of the positivists' modern morality play. The true scientist is supposed to be a seeker who moves entirely in the dark; but he is less fortunate than Diogenes, for he does not go forth with a lantern. His ownership of such an item would presuppose the possibility of some light existing independently of the chaos of brute matter, some order or reason prior to his experience of a dark and random world. If one could maintain this view honestly and completely, it would evidence a certain attractiveness: the view that there need be no sense in the world beyond that which is imposed on it *after* one encounters it; that there is no meaning intrinsic to the world of man; and that the encounter itself is sustained in meaning only by what comes out of it, not by what is put into it. The alternative view—that one never moves in the dark except always with the hope, the faith, or the fear that an abyss does not lie before one—is in one sense less attractive, for it forces its proponents to introduce one or more givens; and these, because they lie outside of human experience, must remain undiscoverable. Empiricists in science have always relegated the undiscoverables to the realm of the supernatural. Since their science has been concerned only with the natural world, they have been logically consistent in refusing to introduce what must be defined as unnatural.

The discussion has now reached the point where it becomes evident that the simple question concerning quantification in science becomes, as do all basic questions about scientific endeavor, a question about the nature of man's relation to the world. We began by suggesting that science be properly considered a way of life in the face of nature, rather than merely a set of techniques. Yet it is a quite specific orientation toward nature, being wholly an explanatory activity. Here, then, we may see a first answer to the attractive propositions of empiricism. If we find that we return again and again to the question of man's place in the world, it becomes clear that the question is not merely a propitious way of posing a problem but is itself the necessary basis for our whole discussion. The problem relating to man in his role in the world is itself outside human experience—although experience may contribute light and truth toward some answers—and as a problem it exists prior to any explanation imposed on it. This one problem, indeed, expresses the limits of all possible human problems. If questions about an explanatory science are dependent on some stand on this fundamental problem, there is no point in attempting a solution by means of explanation. Rather, one must choose some starting point which expresses in fact one's relation to the world, and from this point one may then proceed to construct some organization to impose on *subsequent* experience. It is in this way, and to this extent, that we say that science is not wholly a matter of explanation but that it always presupposes a trust and a commitment which are expressed through the mode of understanding.

Science has sometimes been loosely defined as a body of knowledge, or more specifically a method of arriving at its body of knowledge. The latter has come to be known as the *scientific method;* and in these terms there is often stated a second major definition of science. As one example, the scientific method is demonstrated by clearly stating a proposition in advance and then putting it to test, either by obtaining additional evidence bearing on it or—what amounts to the same thing—by conducting an experiment relevant to it.

The essential feature of this view of science may be summed up in terms of its public nature. All its demonstrations take place out in the open—for even when they are carried out in the actual privacy of a laboratory, the rules are established in advance by the community of scientists; the results must be available in full along with a complete account of the relevant procedural details; and the report must be clear enough so that any other scientist may repeat the experiment. In place of the public character of the scientific event, we might better talk about its *communal* character; it is public in the restricted and root meaning of this term: that it belongs to other people. In this way, so the argument runs, the scientist is enabled to avoid that bogey of all good empiricists, those overt or covert biases and prejudices which might enter into and color his results. It is always recognized that the completely unbiased scientist is a dead one, but it is maintained with pride that the scientific method enables one to bypass prejudices by forcing the scientist to play a specifically delimited role. Once he has performed the creative act of stating a problem and deciding on a way of attacking it, he is constrained by a specific procedure over which he exercises no real control. In his affairs with nature, he plays the role of Prince Consort. His duty is to take part in conception but thereafter to have no personal voice in the activities of his productions.

The flaw in this carefully organized picture is relatively easy to spot. Science has here been defined in terms of a nearly mechanical procedure which runs its course *after* the creative work of the scientist has been finished. There is no scientific method which teaches a scientist how to create a new construct like the meson, no procedure for spotting and pinning down the core of a problem area; there is not even a technique that guarantees that one will be ingenious in designing apparatus to test out an idea. In short, the scientific method could not have attained its present eminence if it were in fact no more than a set of cautions to insure the repeatability of experimental results. Actually, repeatability is often difficult if not impossible to attain, for reasons of historical accident or even personal ability, yet this has not served to detract from the scientific respectability of many discoveries in astronomy or clinical medicine. So we shall have to take another look at the scientific experiment to see if there is a feature still hidden in the method that will define it for us.

Not all questions which might be put to nature are scientific questions. Not all expectations are testable; nor are all ways of testing an expectation logically equivalent. To take a common and trivial example, suppose A says to B, "Have you stopped beating your wife?" There is one sense in which this question provides a test and one sense in which it does not. In order for A to ask this question— that is, if he is sincerely motivated to obtain the information which might be forthcoming by way of an answer—he must assume first of all that B has been doing this reprehensible act. It is for this reason that the question is often considered the perfect example of a loaded question. By this expression one usually means that A does not give B the chance to state what might well be the truth, which was that he had in fact never started beating his wife. Thus there is a sense in which the question does not provide a test; it presupposes a certain restricted class of answers—all of its members being variations on the themes of admission, apology, or denial of the one given fact of wife-beating—and allows no possibility of an answer outside this class. On the other hand, the sense in which this question does provide a test is given when one accepts as a fact that B has indeed been beating his wife. In this case the question allows for two classes of answers. The first of these is a form of the affirmative, the second a form of the negative reply; and the question is then a test, not of whether B does beat his wife, but of whether or not he will admit to the known and accepted fact that he does.

These two senses of a question—that it allows no answer outside of a restricted class, and that it sets the stage for a choice between two opposing answers to an accepted fact—apply to any question that one might frame. Since the asking of a question presupposes a ground of agreement between questioner and questioned, the question limits its answers to that class defined by the agreement; in this sense, and in this sense alone, to ask a question is not to engage in a test of anything but merely to review a presupposed set of answers. But if the question can be answered either affirmatively or negatively, asking the question allows more than one possibility; and in this sense the question is a real test, perhaps even a test of the questioner's expectation in one direction or the other. No question, therefore, is either completely loaded or completely unloaded, although in each case we have a right to ask whether the way in which it is loaded is relevant to the issue that is stated as being under test.

It is clear that the questions which are put to nature in science must be questions of the second kind. That is, they must allow for more than one class of answer, and every class must be relevant to the problem being examined. The creative aspect of devising experiments, in fact, would seem to lie precisely here, in the scientist's ability to frame questions which bracket the relevant issue between the two classes of allowable answers. The scientific method, then, would in this sense be defined as a means of assuring that more than one class of answer is allowed and that every class has a democratically equal chance of being represented in the results.

The experimental method, and its associated techniques and procedures, comprises a way of posing questions. However, we may now see that it is in addition a set of devices for implementing the asking of just one kind of question—the kind in which the datum that is sought is sandwiched, as it were, between a relevant *yes* and an apposite *no*. But this, too, involves the scientist in a special kind of relationship with the world. Unless he is content with manipulation of trivia out of a clerk's repository, his method demands of him a continuing evaluative maneuver. It is not an exercise in logic but a fine balancing of the pertinent against the practical, of knowing where the limits of relevance lie. The experimental method, we suggest here, must always be acted on against a ground of the suppositions out of which science is constituted.

There is a third criterion which is commonly offered as defining the scientific endeavor. The basic proposition relative to this criterion is that thinking, even at its most rigorous and organized, rarely takes place exclusively in terms of a fixed body of statements. A scientific doctrine is supposed to be unique in this respect, that it is compounded of special kinds of propositions which are linked together in a special way.

Theoretical structures which conform to this criterion of science usually take their cue from the more established disciplines among the natural sciences. Physics, particularly atomic physics, commonly serves as the ideal and is offered as the most perfect example of the hypothetico-deductive method. From a limited set of generalizations concerning the nature of the physical universe, there is generated by purely logical devices an extensive network of testable propositions which are so interrelated that the clear contradiction of any one, no matter how small, by the observable facts of nature would be sufficient to shake the system down to its axiomatic roots. Indeed, perhaps the great virtue of such a gauntlet thrown down to nature is the awesome responsibility it imposes on even the smallest proponent of the least important of its derived propositions.

However, since psychological science presently lacks the kind of theoretical structure out of which there might flower some all-embracing system that will reach to every possible datum—as the body of theory of physics does for the natural world, from atomic nucleus to the very limits of the universe—there have recently been offered a number of stopgap substitutes. These are neither systems nor parts of systems, but something quite special in the history of scientific theorizing. Their authors usually call them models, and we shall observe this convention here. But it must be remembered that these offerings are not models in the sense in which the term is applied, for example, to some children's toys—they are not replicas of larger, pre-existing structures. Nor are they models in the sense in which the word is used for people who pose for artists; they are not existing structures to be copied in order to make some derived product. A useful term for these analogues might be *mock-up,* meaning a device which is put together in order to give its creator some first concrete idea about a final structure which is as yet unformed.

The mock-up, or model, serves the useful preliminary purpose of organizing sparse or loosely cohering sets of propositions into the appearance of a whole—but even at its most elaborate it is never more than an illustration for a story. Theory-builders and model-makers alike tend to forget, in their enthusiasm for the structures they create, that a theory is not a discovery of laws that already exist in nature. It is, rather, an organized attempt to superimpose some order on the presented flux of events; and therefore it follows that the scientist must adopt some stand in relation to the world before theory-making is even possible. He cannot stride boldly into a universe of facts unless he starts out with a trust that intelligible facts are both possible and probable; he cannot impose order unless he senses in advance what the idea of order might mean and unless he is prejudiced in advance in favor of order as opposed to disorder, chaos, or emptiness; he cannot make a discovery unless he is prepared to recognize the discovery when he has made it; and finally, he cannot select, prefer, or rank unless he is equipped with a set of values and the tools by which he implements them.

Model-making and theory construction have tended to be barren in the large, or economy, size, or else trivial in their smaller versions, precisely because their authors emphasize formal schemata at the expense of concrete data. Burke (1954) has expressed very well the two kinds of emphases: "Experimental scientists must have for data a permanent respect that transcends their passing interest in the stories they make up about their data" (p. 589). The relation of his observation to the recent history of theory building in psychology needs little further comment. But it may be useful at this point to emphasize that the recent loss of interest in observation in psychology, and the consequent proliferation of story-making *about* past, present, and future data, may be more than a trend. Perhaps it represents a fundamental position regarding what constitutes the scientific enterprise. If it is assumed that the experience of the scientist has no genuine place in the scheme of science; that all trained observation is essentially of the same kind and value; that we require ingenious techniques and methods rather than gifted observers in order to gather data; that the whole truth to be obtained inheres in whatever the stimulus object happens to be at the moment, whether it is the white rat or the Rorschach subject, the target dot or the hallucinating patient—if these are the assumptions, then indeed there is a logic in emphasizing inferences concerning data at the expense of the process of gathering data. Such inferences, when presented in elaborate and often quantified form, become theoretical structures.

But if our emphasis in psychological science shifts toward the primary data and the process of making observations, then it will be recognized that in the creative act of organizing his experience the scientist creates as much as he organizes. There would then be an increasing tendency to study the observer himself, his activities in the experimental situation, and his ongoing relations with his subjects. Out of this there might come a renewed interest in the processes of social perception as basic to the understanding of science and scientists.

In discussing the three criteria by which science is usually defined, we have come back each time to the same point. If science is, as we began by stating, a special kind of endeavor, then it should follow that the activity of the scientist involves him uniquely in his relationships with the world. The layman's recognition of this fact, that there is something about science which sets it apart from workaday activities of all sorts, should be our clue in this direction. Let us now consider, by contrast, some generalizations about what we have referred to as workaday activities.

In the course of acting on whatever motivates him as a goal-directed organism, the person will always move selectively in reference to various observable aspects of his environment. That is to say, he does not answer to every possible stimulus but changes direction, holds a course, accepts certain kinds of direction and influence—in short, he uses his energy in part to pick and choose rather than to absorb indiscriminately or in wholesale fashion whatever he meets. As a result of acting in this way, he seems to the observer to achieve goals. He reaches points where he pauses or stops, points which may be defined either by us or by him or by all of us in concert. We must assume, also, that in the normal course of events this selectivity with its consequent satisfaction by way of goal-achievement is biologically correct; and we have a right to assume as well that as the person proceeds in this way—again in the normal course of events—his goals seem proper to him and his efforts at choosing and striving seem to be the right thing to do. Presumably, if he felt that the goal was completely wrong or that his use of energy was taking him away from a wanted goal, he would do something to correct the situation. Viewed from a little distance, then, so that we may see his activity as a whole, he usually appears to act in accordance with a basic principle, that what he does seems to him to be right. The one guide he cannot adopt is the deliberate set to demonstrate to himself and to others that he is wrong.

The social psychologists in our discipline are fond of pointing out very much the same basic aspect in human cognitive and attitudinal structures. They tell us that much of our activity is, beneath its trappings of reason and rationalization, essentially a consistent effort to demonstrate that we are right and to maintain a situation in which we will be proven right as often and as thoroughly as possible. Indeed, even when the person has seemingly abdicated from his normal stance of acting as though he is right, the same motive continues to determine his resulting humility. This, too, will seem to him to be the proper and the right course to pursue. In the normal course of events—that is, unless he is confused or bent on self-destructive ends for some highly deviant purpose of his own—he devotes his energies to pursuing what seem to him at the moment positively valent goals. If his momentary goal, in the light of all the relevant circumstances, is to be humble rather than rigid, this he will be; but he will be one rather than the other for no different reason. He is always committed to his own endeavors, no matter how righteously or humbly, how rigidly or flexibly, he maintains his position.

If these statements are acceptable as generalizations about most human activities, then it becomes apparent that the deliberate disavowal of such a determining base will represent a unique and fundamentally different form of human endeavor. Only an endeavor so basically different from those of the workaday world could have become a pillar of a whole civilization and could have so profoundly altered the consciousness of mankind. Our definition of science, which we offer now as a summary description of just this alternative direction of one's guiding motive, is: *science is a way of proving that you are wrong; it is the deliberate experience of error.*

A brief consideration of the relationship of primitive man toward the natural world—a relationship bound by magical rituals and ruled by the unknowable acts of mysterious forces—reveals immediately the tremendous stride forward which was taken by the first men who were able to act in terms of an experience of error. Neither quantification nor experimental procedures nor theory-construction rank in historical significance with the step taken when men were first capable of deliberately acting with a view to proving themselves wrong. They had somehow, we cannot conceive how, to give up their guiding experience of the world and, by this step, to lose touch with the data of the world of sensory experience. In the end they came back to a totally new manner of apprehension of data; the world appeared to them in a different mode, as probable rather than certain, and as suspected rather than known. They cast their skepticism out into the world and it came back to them as the first scientific data. All of the operations which today usefully define science have flowed organically out of this changed mode of apprehension, out of this fundamentally changed relationship with the world. It is no wonder that two thousand years of civilization have profited from this achievement, for good as well as for ill; small wonder that in his naïvely sensible moments the layman deeply appreciates this fact.

The wonder of this achievement is that it ever occurred at all. Consider what it must mean to take this first step, which involves stepping back from one's position in the world, agreeing that what ought to matter does not matter and that neither knowledge nor truth is more than probable. There are, perhaps, rare occasions in adult life when one's fundamentals are shattered in this way; but it is difficult to conceive of an adult deliberately bringing this about in order to achieve an end that is only vaguely sensed. It may be chiefly in adolescence that this event occurs with any frequency at all—for example, in the traumatic crisis during which the adolescent loses a set of religious faiths which had sustained him during much of his childhood, or in the romantic tragedy when, bereft of his first love, he cries out that he will never love again. Children may even have such an experience at every loss which seems small to the adult. But whether in childhood, adolescence, or adulthood, it must be a striking event. When it occurs at all, it must be so devastating that the question one asks immediately is: what does the person have left for himself at such a moment?

There seems but one answer. When the certainty, the immediacy, and the value of one's experience are called into question by the power of events that overwhelm one, it is possible to continue without turning away completely from the world only if one is sustained by a trust in the long-run rightness of one's purposes. Allport has described the nature of the crisis:

If we looked into the matter, we might question whether any mortal can ever free himself from a feeling of fundamental rightness in his own conduct. Peripheral evils and errors he can put into perspective and report accurately; but the pivots upon which the whole life turns are sacred. To expose them to ridicule or to deny their fundamental rightness would be to devastate the very foundations of his life. Therefore, he must consider his own course as justified, and his own ego in the last analysis as inviolable. Suicide would be the only alternative (1942, p. 131).

One must continue to believe that it will come out all right in the end, that what cannot be seen because it is up ahead is still to be relied on.

Every person starts with a faith, as we may call it, in the immediate rightness of the presented data of the world. But in deliberately seeking the experience of error, the person steps back from this faith; he agrees to give up certainty and to doubt what seems naturally to be right. How has the embryo scientist gained by this transaction? He has lost that by-product of faith which we call certainty—but it would appear that by the same step he has gained a new position in respect to that other by-product of faith which we call truth. The truth can be apprehended by anyone who will undertake to see into reality; but not everyone will therefore conceive of the truth or be able to reflect upon it. This is reserved for the doubter, the skeptic, the embryo scientist, whose new vantage point is such that the additional possibility of nontruth or partial truth now appears to him. Truth is no longer the outer limit of his faith but now consists of a possibility and its coupled alternative possibility. For the first time he can himself learn, and he can teach others, that the apprehension of truth is possible for anyone.

We must understand, in regard to the very earliest experiences of science, that things still made sense, that they meant something, that it was important to know or not to know. There was no thought of the meaningless except as a kind of blasphemous chaos which was no part of knowledge. This science was just naïve and passionate enough to insist that things were real. All of this has now changed, of course, and in our own day, when the self-proclaimed arbiters of science will touch only a pure, mechanical, once-removed kind of data, the reality of things is hidden from the very disciplines which ought to grasp them fully. The things of science no longer present a face and an inner essence, but only a flawless and depthless shine. The scientist does not trust nor distrust; he only tests.

Because the experience of error, as it is sought in science, starts from a position of faith and can always return, it is distinguishably different from the experience of uncertainty, let alone confusion. It remains a mode of reflection, an experience which is entertained for what it will gain the person. "The pursuit of science is motivated throughout by a passion to understand," says Polanyi (1959, p. 84). Because of this, and because it is guided intrinsically by whatever lies ahead of it, the error which may be experienced enables the person to set some part of his world aright. In this way he arrives at an increased understanding of the world and of his place in it. The many techniques by which we recognize science, the methods that are its common guise, the tricks of its trade with the natural universe—these will arise at just this point. Quantification, experimentation, and orderly theorizing serve the basic requirement of benefiting from the scientist's initial challenge to faith. These techniques and methods are not inevitable in science, not its start, but are the profit to be gained from a skirmish with fate. Taking the first step by deliberately losing touch with the guarantees of one's data of experience—this is what makes scientific methods and techniques possible, not the reverse.

A Clinical Science of Man

If we agree that the goal of science is not explanation but, as in all other basic modes of human action, an understanding of the world and of one's relationship to it, the way is then open to adumbrating a clinical science, a science of man. Our agreement may first of all enable us to avoid the trap into which so many scientists and critics of science have fallen. If a true science that uses explanation to arrive at understanding is possible, we will not have to insist that understanding be degraded to the level of mysticism. We will not have to call all modes of reflective endeavor that do not stimulate machines *merely intuitive,* and we will not have to refer to all nonquantifiable data as vague or esoteric. We will not be restricted to a design and technique which are more properly applicable to the experiment in organic chemistry. Most important, we will not be forced into handling the kind of data most germane to the clinical field, such as is found in the psychotherapy session or the test protocol, by imposing on it from without some scheme better fitted for experimentation.

It may well be a disheartening and thought-provoking experience for the aspiring scientist in psychology to look over the kinds of experiments that have been done in the clinical field. Even in the case of clinicians who are amenable to a scientific approach that respects the concrete data of their professional experience—and one cannot summarily dismiss or degrade these data without risking the loss of the very phenomena one starts out to understand—there is almost no experimentation which arises organically out of the very event being examined. In an extensive series of experiments by members of the nondirective school (Rogers and Dymond, 1954), for example, which is surely the outstanding example thus far of a careful and intensive attempt, made with respect and loving care, to mold these complex data into some sensible unity, the form of the experiment is always one taken over from what is classical in science. The example of the experiment in organic chemistry was suggested above and is relevant here as well.

The essential element of the chemist's experiment is that in carrying it out he maintains a specific vantage point in respect to the material with which he works; he is completely independent of it, not only in regard to the possible influence of his own bias toward one or another result, but far more important, in regard to the possibility of his personal connection with the *history* of the objects under study. This may seem an odd term to introduce at this juncture. Let us pursue the point to see if it is not more appropriate than appears at first sight. If the material being studied is inanimate, as will be true in the experiments of organic chemistry, it is to be expected that the experimenter deal with them as though they had no history. He acts as though their presence at this time and in this place were in no way related to what they are or how they are defined. But this is self-evident, you will say; this is just the nature of the inanimate object. They are where they are, at one particular time, by virtue of forces that operate independently of the definable "nature" of the objects themselves.

The self-evident, because it is often the living instance of the concrete, has much to teach us. From the self-evident fact that rocks and tables and chemical compounds exist as such independently of the place and time at which they are, we may realize what usually escapes our notice—that objects have no history. They may be moved from place to place, or they may be in one place at one time and in another place at another time, but their changes in location are demonstrably a function of those circumstances to which we give the collective name *environment*. Their movements and appearances are never a function of whatever defines the objects themselves, such as the fact that a table has from one to a dozen legs or that a liter of sulphuric acid contains so many molecules of hydrogen.

In the psychological literature, this point has been made explicitly by Lewin (1931). He showed that in the science of the Greeks, as represented in the writings of Aristotle, the history of a thing was not distinguished from the history of a person. In regard to both, it was assumed that the place that each of them, person or thing, occupied through the course of time was a function of whatever was intrinsic to them: in the case of the person, his will or his destiny, and in the case of a falling rock, its heaviness. These intrinsic and determining characteristics, the Greeks thought, existed within the entity itself; heaviness was inherent in the rock just as will was inherent in the person. Lewin demonstrated that Galileo first gave to science the distinction between objects of interest with histories such as persons, and ahistorical objects of study; the latter, like the rock falling through space, move through time and space, not because of any characteristic inherent in them, but as the demonstrable result of forces external to them and acting upon them. According to Aristotle, the rock falls because of its heaviness, and therefore its falling is a moment in its history that is determined by its "personal" characteristics; whereas for Galileo, the fall of the rock is an event in that field of forces which defines the position of the rock at any instant of time. For the Aristotelian scientist, therefore, the movements of rocks and of persons fall within the same realm of "historical" study, whereas, since the time of Galileo, science has concerned itself exclusively with those phenomena which, like rocks, have no histories.

Like his fellows in the natural sciences, the chemist has profited through the years from the distinction made by Galileo. The term *profited* is quite applicable, for it is clear that when one restricts one's scientific endeavors to inanimate entities, one would do well to keep this distinction in mind and to study the forces at work in the field of which the thing is a part rather than to look for a quality that is presumed to inhere in the thing. It is only when one turns to animate objects—that is, objects that demonstrate that they can independently maintain a direction of activity through time—that the distinction, and the limitations imposed by attending to only one half of it, become rather binding on the activities of the scientist. Perhaps it is stretching a point to refer to the tobacco virus, let us say, as animate, and then to suggest that the microbiologist seriously consider his own history in reference to this animate object under his scrutiny. But the suggestion becomes a good deal more pointed when the scientist works at the phylogenetic level of the white rat and proposes in all seriousness that these objects of study entertain hypotheses and solve problems through the use of cognitive maps. For here we have propositions that can be made with equal cogency about the experimenter himself. And since the experimenter demonstrably has a history—that is, he has come to this place, at this time, at least in part because of what he is rather than because he is completely the unknowing victim of pressures that may have been at work on him—there arises the possibility, *which can never be ruled out by the experiment itself,* that the animals also have histories and that their histories and that of the experimenter are in some way intertwined.

Perhaps we are still stretching a point when we suggest that because the white rat is not treated completely as an inanimate thing, and because the experimenter and the rat both have histories which have crossed at the moment of the experiment, the experimenter cannot maintain a completely independent vantage point in regard to his results. In the case of laboratory studies involving rats as subjects, this caution may not always be of central importance. True, there have been some recent rumblings in rat psychology to the effect that the animal's familiarity with a certain handler may operate as a variable differentially affecting certain experimental results. But it is probable that our strictures are relevant in regard to experiments when they are guided by theories that assign a place of primary importance to a "subjective" type of data. To the extent that rats are dealt with as though they rather closely resemble human beings in this important respect, then, the experimenter will have to keep in mind the consequences of the vantage point he is assuming.

For the vantage point of the experimenter who accepts the proposition that both he and the subject are historically experiencing organisms is profoundly different from the vantage point of the experimenter whose prototype is the organic chemist. The latter is, as we have agreed, truly independent of the activities of the objects he is studying. To repeat, his independence is not a result of his rationality or his lack of bias. It arises from the fact that he has a history and his object of study does not; having a history implies that the object "contains" inherent characteristics that determine its actions, whereas not having a history means that the object is determined by the total play of determinable forces in operation at any moment. Therefore, in the meeting of a historical object with an ahistorical one, as occurs when the chemist confronts the material he is studying, the experimenter's position is the same as that of any other environmental force impinging on the object being studied; it is equally determinable and controllable, and it may be included or ruled out of the results by appropriate techniques. In this sense, then, the experimenter, insofar as he is a person with a history and not an automaton or a complete creature of habit, is independent of the object he studies.

Two points must be considered, however, in this connection. The first is that supporting evidence for the line of argument being pursued here may be found in the great difficulty we have in finding a single term to apply both to the historical person and the ahistorical thing. I have used such terms as *entity* and *object of study,* but these are makeshift attempts to gloss over the problem; the very absence of a term which is applicable to both indicates the great difference between them. The second point has to do with the necessary relation between independence and the histories of the participants. The independence of the experimenter in chemistry from the object he studies is only partly a function of the object's ahistorical character; equally, it is a function of the fact that he himself does have a history. For if he, too, were ahistorical and "encountered" the chemical compound, he would not long remain independent of it. One or the other of two ahistorical things, when they "meet" and affect each other, must give way or be destroyed as such; this is the meaning of the physical event which includes the simultaneous presence of more than one object. Independence, then, may occur if both the entities have histories or if only one has a history, but not if neither does.

But in the encounter between two entities when each brings a history to the situation, this kind of independence can be attained only if at least one of the participants adopts a set in which he deals with the Other as a thing rather than a person—that is, if he denies that the Other is determined in his actions by anything outside of the determinable pressures of the experimental situation. He may, of course, deliberately make this denial, in which case the situation is set up for the usual experiments one sees in psychology. In these encounters the experimenter decides in advance what, for his purposes, constitutes relevant information; he so arranges the experimental situation that just this information and, if possible, no other is obtained; he restricts the subject to these limits by means of the instructions to him; and he proposes to rule out as either irrelevant or contaminating all data that do not correspond to the restrictions which he enforces. Bruner has argued very plausibly that no other course is logically defensible, particularly in experiments on perception: "We as experimenters must decide in advance what constitutes relevant information and not allow the subjects to decide this for us; otherwise we would be in a complete circle" (1951, p. 131). Whether or not other alternatives are indeed logically admissible, the fact remains that in adopting this procedure the experimenter imitates the vantage point held by the chemist. He maintains as complete an independence as possible from his subject—again, not because he has manfully searched out and insightfully ruled out all of his own prejudices, but because in dealing by preference with an ahistorical object he has eliminated the possibility that two histories will meet and affect each other.

To appreciate the difference between this procedure and one in which both of the participants in an encounter freely admit and display the fact that each has a history, consider that prototype of the human encounter which we call the *psychotherapy session*. It is the essence of the process in therapy that primarily the client, but also the therapist to a great extent, come face to face in all their humanness—remembering, judging, feeling, hoping, and fearing. The client who avoids this requirement, or degrades it by techniques of distance—"intellectualizing," forgetting, evading, or denying—will make but little progress; his history will stop at the point where, to use one kind of terminology, his resistance begins. And equally, the therapist who never stops diagnosing and independently judging, who degrades the client by failing to allow his freedom to grow in the directions for which he is suited, will be judged a poor therapist—although he may, if he is sufficiently skilled, implement his ahistorical approach by authoritarian techniques, choose only those clients who will welcome what he has to offer, and perhaps present a surprising record of successful accomplishment. Involvement on the part of each of the participants must therefore necessarily follow upon the juncture of two histories, as indeed it does in the productive psychotherapy session. It is easy to see why involvement of this sort threatens the very foundations of most scientific procedures. This is not simply because during a therapy hour, or in a similar situation, the clinician is unable to steer clear of his gross prejudices and biases; for most clinicians, testers and therapists alike, will testify that techniques for this end may be learned and do not present insurmountable difficulties. The reason that the involvement in a human encounter poses a problem for conventional scientific procedures is, rather, that it is incompatible with maintaining the experimenter's independence of his object. As an experimenter, his vantage point is outside of whatever history his subject may have; but as a therapist, he agrees to link histories with his subject for the period of their meeting. In contemporary psychological science he finds few techniques available for operating in such a situation. Organic chemistry has no lessons to teach the psychotherapist.

This is the sense in which most experiments in the clinical field have imposed an organization on their subject matter from without rather than allowing the scheme to arise organically out of the concrete data—and this has occurred whether the experiments have stemmed from the sympathetic orientation of those already working in clinical areas or from the prejudice of those who are grimly determined to lay the clinical ghost once and for all with the shining sword of factor analysis, objective tests, or whatever happens to be the season's methodological fad. As Freud sensed, the psychotherapy session ought to be the model for a scientific experiment in clinical psychology. Instead, a limited kind of laboratory strategy, with the experiment in chemistry as its model, has bludgeoned and probed and laid waste a fertile and inexhaustible field of data. The cry has always been that unless one uses whatever methods and techniques are fashionable at the moment, and unless one's orientation is completely compatible with the kind of methodological independence achieved by the chemist, one is not contributing to science at all. But the argument in this chapter, tied to the argument of the rest of this book, has been that science must be of greater import in human affairs than is a specific and changeable set of procedures. If it is indeed as significant as we hope it is, its referent should be some fundamental relationship that a person sustains with the world. The definition we have offered above, that in being a scientist the person deliberately seeks the experience of error, seems to conform to this criterion of significance; and with its use a clinical science can be taken seriously. Our science, then, need not be restricted in its operations to a prototype taken over from the natural sciences. It ought to be completely compatible with a clinical method, and a clinical science of man should be within our reach.

CHAPTER FIVE

A PARADOX
OF DIFFERENCES

HAMM:	Sit on him!
CLOV:	I can't sit.
HAMM:	True. And I can't stand.
CLOV:	So it is.
HAMM:	Every man his speciality.

—SAMUEL BECKETT, *Endgame*

IN ONE OF THE RARE DISCUSSIONS IN PRINT OF THE PROBLEM WE will examine in the present chapter, Allport (1953) points out that all current psychological theories, from psychoanalysis to reinforcement theory, join in rejecting the contemporary, conscious report by the individual. Without exception they choose to depend on data which are "uncovered"—uncovered in the present in the unconscious dynamisms of the patient, or else traced back toward the past, either by means of a genetic reconstruction as in psychoanalysis or by means of a search for the rewards and punishments of primary drives.

146

This prevailing atmosphere of theory has engendered a kind of contempt for the "psychic surface" of life. . . . It is now easy to understand why the special methods invented by Jung (forty years ago), Rorschach (thirty years ago) and Murray (twenty years ago) were seized upon with enthusiasm by psycho-diagnosticians. At no point do these methods ask the subject what his interests are, what he wants to do, or what he is trying to do. Nor do the methods ask directly concerning the subject's relation to his parents or to authority figures. They infer this relationship entirely by assumed identifications (p. 108).

The evidence which Allport then reviews from extensive experimental studies of semistarvation during World War II (Brozek *et al.*, 1951) demonstrates that such indirect methods may well miss "the most urgent, the most absorbing motive in life." A battery of projective tests failed almost completely to produce material concerned with the subjects' constant, agonizing need for food; yet this need was so overwhelming that it utterly dominated conscious, waking hours. It is evidence of this sort, as well as the clinical literature of half a century of "irrationalism" and "geneticism," that leads Allport to ask with some spirit, "Has the subject no right to be believed?"

The view to which Allport refers is no minor opinion but rather the first proposition of contemporary clinical theory: that there are two kinds of data—the immediately present or observable, and the postulated, hidden, or covert—and that the latter is more "real" than the former. A corollary of this fundamental proposition is that in order to arrive at an explanation and understanding of a man's true nature, one must somehow uncover the real data, and to do this one must have some way of bypassing the less real and the immediately observable. If the proposition sounds crude, do not blame its proponents; for in open and clear-cut form there is no way to make it sound more impressive. Perhaps this is why it is so rarely spelled out in the clinical literature as an explicit statement which might be judged and examined. Kept partly under wraps, so to speak, it functions admirably as a kind of motor for thinking rather than as a fixed conclusion, as a general framework on which to hang observations rather than as a theorem to be stated and tested.

A Man's True Nature

There is a well-known statement by Francis Bacon—it is quoted, most appropriately, by Beck (1945)—which provides an excellent starting point for our discussion: "A man's nature is best perceived in privateness, for there is no affectation; in passion, for that putteth a man out of his precepts; and in a new case or experiment, for there custom leaveth him." Now, the topic which Bacon introduces here, "a man's nature," is rarely discussed in contemporary psychology. But even at the risk of rushing into unfamiliar territory, we may begin by defining, with Bacon, man's essential nature: the nature which is to be elucidated by means of the clinical test; the nature, or personality, which, by virtue of its special characteristics, may be tested most successfully with these specific instruments; the nature, that is, which poses the clinical problem for us, which sets the limits, defines our techniques, and contains the answers we seek.

Bacon seems to argue, at least by implication, that when we observe a man in the course of his customary public activities, without putting him in a special situation and without subjecting him to stress, we can, though perhaps we seldom do, distinguish three characteristics in how he acts. There is, first, a certain degree of "affectation." He plays a role, so to speak; he tries to be or to act in a special way, and more often than not this somehow runs counter to another part or element of his total nature. Whether the "public role" is flatly in opposition to this other part of the man's nature is not clearly stated by Bacon but merely suggested. Second, the man who is the object of our casual observation is, in his ordinary and public life, a man of reason. He acts in terms of his precepts, that is, in terms of a set of maxims or rules for his moral conduct in which he has been instructed by his betters. The term *precept* clearly implies, not the rote behavior of the slave or of the disciplined ignoramus, but the schooled conduct of the reasoning man in whom certain principles have been inculcated. Thirdly, the innocent subject of our study often behaves in terms of habit. He does things by "custom," because that is the way they are usually done, by himself and by others; and the presumption is that in these instances he rarely pauses to think about the significance or even the details of what he is doing.

These are the ways, says Bacon, that characterize a man in his usual routine: he is a creature of habit, he acts in terms of developed principles, and he plays out some role in his public life. Are these elements, then, the sum of human personality? Decidedly not, says Bacon. They are, most remarkably, precisely the factors which stand in the way of our perceiving a man's true nature. If we wish to get at what constitutes the essence of the man, we must discover and utilize special techniques. We must begin by observing him in private, or at least without his knowing that he is being judged, for only in such a situation does he reveal himself most truly. He drops his "affectation," he ceases to play a role, and thus he no longer acts by reference to the presence or importance or possible responses of another person. And since we have adopted the tactic of observing him without revealing our own presence—for how else could we perceive him in "privateness"?—we must also forgo the privilege of a normal relation that we might have with him. We can no longer approach him as a friend; and equally, we have given up the possibility of acting as a visible stranger.

How might this be accomplished? How are we to learn this much about another person while he remains in his own "privateness"? Bacon almost seems to suggest that the ideal instrument would be one in which we are able to be significantly in the subject's presence while being psychologically absent; or better yet, one in which the subject would act as though we were not in fact observing his every move. At first sight this seems to be an impossible demand to make of an observer. To the great credit of modern clinical psychology, however, success in just this direction has been achieved. A way has been found to do private testing in public. The proposition which refers to this achievement, in fact, quite rightly occupies a cornerstone in the existing, if implicit, doctrine of clinical testing. But before we turn to a discussion of this key proposition, let us note Bacon's two other suggestions for obtaining a picture of a man's true nature. In order to strip away that mask which is formed by the operation of his precepts and the effect of habit, we must first get him aroused and then place him in a situation which is completely new and strange to him. Since he will be in the grip of his emotions, and since it is well known that affective elements serve to guide a man's perceptions and thinking in autistic directions and away from the strict demands of reality, he will no longer be able to act in terms of his established precepts. And equally clearly, habit will do him no good at all if he is in strange territory; he had, in fact, better learn very soon that habit is often a detriment rather than a help. The Englishmen celebrated by Noel Coward, who refuse to give up their London habit of a stroll after lunch, are operationally indistinguishable from mad dogs.

Notice that it is not stated what a man's true nature *is,* but only what it is not. It is not what is usually seen, it is not what he has been taught, and it is not what he simply does—in short, it is not at all that which is there to be judged. One can easily see that at this point a theory of some impressiveness is required in order to answer two obvious questions: First, what are we to say about the immediately presented data if they are not the essence of man's nature? Second, "where" do the real data reside? For we seem to be in the curious position of denying the validity of what customarily confronts us; and in order to do so with any semblance of coherence, we must advance some theory to explain away what is there as well as to postulate some other, presumably hidden data as more true or more valid. It has been the task of recent psychodynamic theory in clinical psychology to state the theoretical relationships between these two levels of data, the observed and the postulated, and to suggest some reasonable explanation of the nature and systematic characteristics of that which is covert.

A number of alternatives immediately suggest themselves as to the logical relations among the two kinds, or levels, of interpretation of test data. The first of the alternatives is that both interpretations say the same thing, that they are not two interpretations but one. The second alternative supposes that the two versions are different and that the psychodynamic one, as we usually term it, is closer to the real truth of the matter; and the third alternative is the converse, to the effect that it is the interpretation stemming from the immediately presented facts which comes closer to the truth.

It will be evident at this point that one of the interpretations is made up of statements that belong in a theoretical system, and that the other encompasses the observable phenomena that form the field

of social perception. The two interpretations are thus more than explanations. They stand for ways of handling whatever is available for
the clinician's use; and because they represent two kinds of attitudes,
they produce different sorts of data and lead to dissimilar goals. Statements made within either of the two interpretations, therefore, are
by no means variants of some single, all-embracing proposition. Substitution is out of place, and translation a waste of effort.

These assertions may sound extreme. If so, it will be worthwhile to
consider two propositions, familiar to everyone, which exemplify the
divergent interpretations we are examining. To maximize the probability of recognizing the propositions, we will add to them a third;
the set will then read:

> A. He is a man;
> B. Men are good;
> C. He is good.

Our interest at this point is not in the entire syllogism but in the second
and third of its propositions. We choose them for discussion because
they are good examples of two kinds of statements: the one called
B is a statement belonging in a theoretical system; the last one is
a statement out of social perception. The proposition "Men are good"
is meant to refer to all persons without exception. Thus, although there
is no way at all that it can be substantiated—unless we grant the possibility of evaluating all the men in the world—it states a determinable
fact which can be validated within the limits that science sets for
accepting such propositions. The proposition, "He is good," however,
is a statement of a different kind; Husserl would call it a *judgment*.
If it is true, the truth which it expresses is found in one person's perception of another and is therefore self-evident. To say, "He is good,"
is very nearly the same as to say, "I believe that he is a good man."
Only if the statement "He is good" is not self-evident can it attain
the status which the statement "Men are good" has initially—the
status of an objectively verifiable proposition in science. Only then
would it make sense to refer to a test of its accuracy, for this suggestion presupposes that there exists some independent criterion
against which the statement may be compared. The self-evident, phenomenal proposition, "He is good," satisfies itself, so to speak, and in

so doing it rules out the possibility of a criterion which is on principle independent of it.

There are still other fundamental differences between these two propositions. A little reflection will reveal that, in spite of the way we usually think about it, the statement, "Men are good," is not a generalization of many instances of statements such as "He is good." One reason for this is simply that the latter statement is not an instance at all. The term *instance* implies a series of equivalent representatives of a class to which they all belong. To use the term, then, is to assert that the statement is not unique and self-satisfying, but only one other evaluation which is interchangeable with its fellows. But this is the question we are examining at this point; a question cannot be examined by presupposing its answer. It would be more appropriate to say that the logical relation between our two statements, if there is any relation at all, must be effected by some person's inductive processes. He must learn, in one case, that a person is good, then learn the same thing about another person, realize it about a third, and in this way arrive at the point where he makes the inductive generalization that people in general are good. However, it is precisely this kind of process which is not reducible to deduction, no matter how rigorous. The deductive mechanism of the syllogism, therefore, appeals to us because it rests on our appreciation of the inductively grasped relation between its last two propositions.

A Pluriverse of Data

The topic we are pursuing in this chapter is not the place for an extended discussion of the questions raised by the logic and the psychology of the syllogism. We may only note at this point that the structure of logical relations first worked out by Aristotle can be understood as the first major attempt to reconcile the two kinds of propositions we are examining. Because of its nearly universal appeal and utility it has finally been turned back on its source and, in an excess of inverted psychologism, held up as the mode and prototype of the thinking process itself. But even our brief review of the issues involved indicates that the two kinds of statements, one determinate and the other perceptual, belong to two different realms. A bridge between them cannot be made by fiat or out of a hasty application of syllogistic reasoning to the situation which alone makes the syllogism possible. We will, therefore, have to turn to the second of the alternatives that we posed above, to the effect that our two sets of interpretive propositions, and the data they produce, are not the same and that it is the one out of a theoretical system which is primary.

Spelled out in terms we might find in conventional clinical theory, this alternative is to the effect that the concrete clinical data are one thing and the inferences to be drawn from them quite another; that the former in fact mask the latter; and that the entire examining procedure is essentially a method for obtaining the latter while ostensibly aiming at the former. The subject's invention is, in this view, a kind of facade, but the very nature of this facade is that the stronger it is held the more it gives way. The less it reveals in actuality—that is, in relation to the subject's deliberate communication of facts about himself insofar as he knows of these facts—the more it reveals in another order of reality. The strange and wonderful psychic process here described is known, in this manifestation at least, as *projection;* and the extra order of reality which is thus displayed, as the subject's invention recedes further from the sphere of conscious communication, is of course the *unconscious.*

It is important to emphasize the mutually inhibiting interplay which is supposed to take place in this process. Its essence lies in the fact that as one of the elements rises, the other sinks; as the subject tells more about himself by way of a forthright and reasonably factual report (just as he might account to a census taker or in the confessional booth), he thereby tells less in the way of invention; as a consequence, he furnishes less material that may be assigned to the realm of the unconscious. Conversely, as he tells more and more from which important psychodynamic truths can be ascertained about him, he offers less and less from which a factual report about him can be reconstructed. The facade, in other words, reveals only when it conceals.

The term *facade* and other terms used to describe the nature of its functioning in the clinical situation have been taken from an article by Margolis (1945). In this paper Margolis discusses the phenomenon ·of the facade, which, he says, is invariably presented at least initially by students who are being counselled for low grades. The facade, as he describes it, is that exterior which is presented initially to the counsellor—but it need not for this reason be considered a mask or a stratagem that works by contrast. Says Margolis:

Accepted in a spirit of enterprise as the first step in the exploratory process, it becomes an invaluable reference point to which other facts, feelings and relationships can be oriented. This holds true for evasive statements as well, since the need for evasion is part of the student's total picture and is connected by threads of logic to the rest of his problem. The facade is thus seen to play a positive role. It is a function of the interior and, when properly apprehended, reveals as much as it conceals (p. 139).

This is the difference to be emphasized: that in the one view the facade reveals only to the extent that it conceals, and in the other that it reveals as much as it conceals. In the one view the reference point is a predetermined truth to which the subject's invention is forced to conform, even though in the course of doing so the invention may be degraded. In the other view the facade, or the immediately presented clinical data, is taken as the orienting point for the examiner's construction of the subject's functioning. When the first view is held by a clinician, the subject is not allowed the freedom to state in his own terms whether his invention is indeed a facade, for since it is defined only negatively, as an intriguing but expendable mask, it can bear only one kind of relation to what is supposed to lie behind it. It is not "accepted" at all, nor does it become a "reference point," nor is it seen as a "function of the interior." Its usefulness is temporary only, to gain for the subject himself an entrance to a formal ritual which prescribes that at the proper moment the mask is pulled aside to reveal what it really hides. In the second view, however, the subject preserves the freedom to declare the logic of his presentation.

Margolis presents the example of the student who has in fact a very good excuse for his low grades: he has been sick.

The student himself in such instances is invariably fascinated by the simple logic of his position, and finds himself cheerfully blocked, as far as any impulse to explore the situation further is concerned. [This, however, is clearly not the presentation of a facade.] It is not an exterior which can be penetrated. It is solid through and through, immutable and final. . . . This underlines by contrast the operational significance of facade. The latter carries with it the idea of movement. Only that explanation is a facade which is amenable of alteration within the counselling process. A facade must be capable of ceding its position (p. 140).

Only when the issues are posed in these terms is it possible for the clinician to take a position on the vexing question of what to do with contradictory data which are factually accurate and objectively true. All sorts of logical gyrations are resorted to by testers and test theoreticians to deal with this kind of response, for it always puts them in the uncomfortable position of distrusting what may well be, by their own criteria, both true and plausible. Suppose we undertake to examine the way in which a subject's hostility is reflected in his Rorschach protocol, and for this purpose hypnotize him, tell him that he hates a certain person, and then have that person administer him the Rorschach. Will the test results be different from a test given either before or after the one under hypnosis? At least one group of experimenters (Counts and Mensh, 1950), faced with a choice between accepting the immediate data as true or holding to one of their clinical principles, chose to hold to the principle and to an orthodox interpretation of the test. Since no differences were apparent in the subjects' protocols between Rorschach indicators of hostility before and during hypnosis, they concluded that the Rorschach really measured basic, and therefore stable, elements in the personality, elements not likely to be changed by the mere influence of a hypnotic session. In a word, they tossed out those data which gave the factual truth that their subjects did not give "hostile" Rorschach responses to the examiner. Rather than accept this as true and then proceed to understand it in the way in which Margolis understands an equally true fact about his clients—that their excuse of having been sick is correct—these experimenters chose to ignore the true statement and to view all possible responses as variants of a mask hiding their own version of the truth. As a consequence, they were then able to look on the absence of hostile responses as a logical indicator, not of the lack of hostility, but of the inadequacy of the responses themselves as measures of the "real" or basic elements of the personality.

It is easy to point the methodologist's finger and mutter accusingly about reasoning *post hoc,* but the matter goes deeper than that. We are all reasoners after the fact, as indeed I am at this point. It is not that these experimenters arrived at their conclusions only after gathering their data rather than before or during it, but, more significantly, that they end with no way to distinguish between what is facade and what is not, between the response based upon a fact that is independent of the testing situation and one that exists as such totally within that situation, between the immutable and the alterable. They are as bemused by the logic of their own position as the student with a good excuse is by his; or else they are as trapped and helpless in their own situation as the paranoid is in his. Whenever the concretely and immediately presented data are dealt with as though they are at best a substitute for something else, something more real or more valuable, no useful judgment can ever be made about them. They are in one sense all that the tester ever has, yet he acts as though he hopes to make of them something better than they are, to see in them a hidden and perhaps opposing reality, certainly a reality of a higher order. In the event that they do in fact correspond to a verifiable event outside the testing situation, the tester is forced to discard them completely; or if they seem to reveal something to him, he must immediately suspect the disclosure and turn to that theoretical construction of his own which stems essentially from this suspicion. If, as Gough (1948) has suggested, the subject, in his own frame of reference, often wants to use the test therapeutically (perhaps as a means of talking about himself without shame), the tester has no way of gracefully accepting and skillfully using the opportunity. The examiner can never allow him to act in this way; in the completely open and unstructured situation of the projective test, the subject is therefore quite drastically limited in his range of attitudes and aims.

The third alternative we are considering states again that there are two kinds of data to be considered in every instance of interpreting a person's behavior; but its position is that primary emphasis is to be placed on the immediate, concretely presented data—that is, the content of the observer's social perception. To take a position in support of this latter alternative requires that we examine, as we have not done thus far, what is involved in the process of observing and interpreting. As we shall always find ourselves doing when confronted with a significant issue in psychology, we here begin to round a circle and come back on ourselves as source and end of the problem, as origin and aim of the solution.

The question posed by the object of our observation may be stated simply enough: How may we understand the phenomenon of the other person? Were we to make explicit the view that directs contemporary clinical thinking, it would be to the effect that persons are ultimately knowable as an organized collection of facts. For the purposes of a psychological science, according to this view, man as an object of observation is essentially a source of useable data. Frequently enough, of course, the view is also inspired by a faith in man's essential goodness and by a concern for the more positive aspects of his functioning—but equally, there is often a crucial element missing, one which is emphasized in the approach that starts from the concept of the intentionality of meaningful acts. I mean by this phrase that the act, whenever it becomes an object of observation, is always toward an object. From the observer's position, the act embraces its object from start to finish; and from the performer's vantage point, the object is to some degree in hand by virtue of the very fact that the act is begun at all. There is no splitting apart the two, act and object, for they define each other. That which they comprise was stated a century and a half ago by Hegel as "simply and solely a unity of what is given and what is constructed—a unity whose aspects do not fall apart, as in the idea of psychological law, into a world given *per se* and an individuality existing for itself. Or if these aspects are thus considered each by itself, there is no necessity to be found between them, and no law of their relation to one another" (1931, pp. 335–336).

The act is not a response but a performance. Therefore it makes sense to conceive of kinds of roles which make the performance manifest. However, we will lose sight of the phenomenon as soon as we conceive it in terms of a set of facts which define a response. This is why using a term like *disguised* to refer to a subject's performance in a clinical setting is at best a haphazard rendering of his multilayered act. In Murray's (1943) rationale for the Thematic Apperception Test, for example, it may appear that a transcendent meaning is suggested for the subject's story: ". . . before he knows it, he has said things about an invented character that apply to himself" (p. 1). But skilled though he may otherwise be in the face-to-face encounter, Murray here expresses a view of the person as no more than a mechanism for one kind of response, in this case the response of revealing or not revealing certain private data. The alternative possibility, that the person is *both* the one who says things about an invented character and the one who says these things before he knows it—a possibility that thrusts before us the mystery and riddle of human reflectiveness—can hardly be accounted for by a scheme which so limits our understanding of the meaningful act.

We are coming around to stating that there is a sense in which clinicians of a psychodynamic persuasion are certainly correct. Although the person whom they depict by way of the theoretical construct is flat and two-dimensional at best, they have at least kept alive in psychology the idea that, just as direct observation will always tell us, the person carries in him more than he presents directly to others. Indeed, if we can talk intelligibly about a facade and what it conceals, then it would seem that there is indeed both an outer and an inner aspect to the person. If the outer is what we have called up to this point the *immediately presented data,* then the inner ought to refer to something else. It will not be a construct like those we have just discussed, nor is it immediately present; but on the other hand it is just as real as what is directly seen. I do not think we can deny the common perceptual experience of seeing a person, observing what is immediately presented by him, and at the same time noting that it seems to diverge from something else expressed by him. We have all known poor liars and amateur actors. A more subtle instance, which perhaps points more directly at the heart of the matter, is our perception of the immediate data in the person's behavior and, concurrent with it, our clear feeling that he could be other than the way he appears to us at the moment. One way to describe this is to say that we see the other person as a system of possibilities. If we see a roomful of aspiring children go through an elementary sequence of positions in ballet, and one of them strikes us as potentially a great dancer, we are engaged in the clear distinction between what is and what might be; we are matching possibilities against actualities. The magical charm of the infant, and one source of our simple and often foolish pleasure in perceptually stimulating it, may arise largely from the fact that the infant appears to us as all possibility. As his proud parents will tell us with every fond look at him, he can be anything, for the future belongs completely to him. When we observe the infant, we see, in one sense, his gross thrashings, his changes of facial expression, and his various anatomical characteristics, all of which comprise the immediate data; but within and even beyond these we see the set of possibilities that truly identify him as an infant for us. At the other extreme, perhaps, might be our perception of the chronic schizophrenic who appears to us as devoid of possibility; his expressiveness is stereotyped, his facies washed-out and relatively undifferentiated, his emotional status inconsistent with the significance of the situation. We are free to gather the concrete and immediate data because that is just about all there is.

In his *Vision of the Last Judgment,* Blake expressed it thus:

I assert for My Self that I do not behold the outward Creation & that to me it is hindrance and not Action. . . . "What," it will be Question'd, "When the sun rises, do you not see a round disk of fire somewhat like a Guinea?" O no, no, I see an Innumerable company of the Heavenly host crying, "Holy, Holy, Holy is the Lord God Almighty." I question not my Corporeal or Vegetative Eye any more than I would Question a Window concerning a Sight. I look thro' it & not with it.

Blake's "Corporeal Window," our common perception of the infant, the sight of the schizophrenic, and the act of the subject telling a TAT story are all examples of that apparent divergence between immediately presented data and a something other. The latter may be a central characteristic, an enduring disposition, or a range of possibilities, and in seeing it into the other person, as it were, we may be greatly mistaken or even the victim of our own wishes. But the phenomenon which is there, regardless of explanations that may be offered about it, is the inescapability of our perception of a meaningful act as many-layered. The person is both what he is and what he might be. He is in the present, but it is a present having meaning only in terms of a past that was once meaningful for him and which has therefore impressed itself on him; and his present is expressed toward a future which marks him as a creature involved in the continual process of becoming something other than he is. If our social perception is veridical, it cannot eliminate its reference to this dual aspect of the person—that he is both the past and the future as they meet in the present, that he is both in the world as an existent and beyond the world as a creature of anxiety, guilt, and despair. Only to the psychologist turned experimenter does the human person ever appear in some more limited ways, perhaps as a matter of necessary rigor but certainly at the expense of full understanding.

The Person Appears in Psychology

Nothing seems so natural to us, in our normal social world, as other persons; no phenomenon appears so little in need of explanation. But here again, as we might have expected, the natural contains a mystery, and what is self-evident will turn out to be filled with puzzles and surprises. Of these, none will astonish us more than the uniqueness that the person demonstrates by virtue of his very similarity to other persons. Here, if anywhere, the transcendent and multilayered person poses his special problem of individual differences, a paradox that the science of psychology had to try to explain at the very beginning.

It is not easy to trace how the person as an object of interest first entered the science that was aimed at understanding him. That the circumstances should have been so confused is, perhaps, sufficient indication that there may be nothing simple in the conception of the person as a subject for psychology. It is quite likely that the overwhelming influence of biology, stemming from the impact made by Darwin's work on all the sciences, was largely responsible for the new emphasis on the person; for biology had always taken the whole organism as its unit for study. Galton, for one, immediately undertook to apply to his anthropology, or science of man, the benefits gained in biology from a consideration of differences among species. But as a target of psychology's interest, the person is a phenomenon of a different sort. First of all, there is the fact, so commonplace that we do not usually reflect on its significance, that differences among persons are by no means self-evident. If as a group they are distant or strange, they will all seem to look alike; in the familiar example,

Chinese all look alike to Americans, and the reverse is said to be true also. But even if the persons observed are close or familiar, seeing the differences among them is apparently something that has to be learned. Children are able to draw many of the details of their environment before their drawings begin to depict differences between one person and another. The "types" which they spontaneously draw suggest that it is the class which is seen first and differentiation within the class only much later. Indeed, it may be that children's greater interest in animals than in humans as literary subjects in their pre-school years is a result of this fact that differences among kinds of animals supply the variability which they are not as yet able to observe in persons.

Even today, in the high state of our current sophistication, it is painfully evident that we have no theory that will account for the person in psychology. The science has come to deal with parts, with processes, with principles, with constructs and with aspects, but almost never with the plain and simple subject of people. Throughout its recent history, psychology has been at various times the scientific discipline concerned with consciousness, or the mind, or faculties, or the soul, or experience, or finally behavior, but rarely with persons. Of course, it may be argued that this is because the topic is so obvious that it requires no emphasis. Psychology is without any doubt the science of persons or people, and it could hardly be otherwise; the problem is how to spell this out in rigorous and systematic fashion. But the issue may not be stilled this easily. Its history, from pre-Socratic Greece through the magnificent theoretical structure of the medieval scholastics to modern Thomistic psychology and the philosophy of existence, repeatedly emphasizes the fact that there are profound problems to be met and faced when one begins to ask about the person in the most common form of the question, "What is man?" The issue which cannot be evaded is posed as soon as we ask why the person should be the subject matter for a special province in science. Is the person some unique entity that does not fit into one of the divisions of biology? And it becomes even more complex when we note that the person, and his typical activities, is the province also for all of the disciplines that make up the social sciences—social psychology, sociology, anthropology, even political science and economics. This, then, is not a biological organism, though it is also that. It is an entity of a special order, as children and animals are quick to recognize. The person has a special manner, a certain mode of being, a way of life unique in all the array of living creatures, a position occupied by nothing else in nature. The final issue, which complicates almost ruinously the already complicated aspects of these problems, is that it is the person himself, and no one else in all nature, who is called upon both to ask and to answer these very questions. There is little to wonder at, little cause for feeling superior, in the troubles of those who made the first attempts to put the person into psychology.

What is it like to look at or cognize or think about another person? What are persons like as objects of our knowing? We do not know, of course; herein lies both our psychology and our lack of a psychology. Knowing another person is both the beginning and the end of the psychologist's task. But we can be clear about this much: that just as a psychology of nonsocial perception has to do with people's experience of the world of nonsocial entities, so a psychology of social perception has to do with our experience of persons. The scientist is no exception. He, too, when he considers the whole person as data for his activities, begins with a process of social perception. As a scientist he has just the same choice that all of us have as persons, between that experience of the way things are which in an earlier chapter we called *understanding,* and that construction of the world which we discussed as *explanation.* And to some extent at least, this is a distinction that can be traced out in the subsequent events of the early psychology of individual differences.

The general notion that persons differed was never more than a layman's observation, at least as far as psychology was concerned, until the last half of the nineteenth century. It is missing, for example, in such relatively sophisticated developments as faculty psychology or the associationism of James Mill in the first half of that century. Thus, in Germany a psychology developed which had no need to look at the individual subject. At most it was concerned with differences between groups. Cattell's interest in individual differences found little favorable reception in this atmosphere, and the tests that he worked out were delayed in their publication for a number of years until he was settled in America, in an atmosphere friendly to the conception of the worth—including the scientific worth—of the individual person. During the period from 1885 to 1900, a large number of younger persons, in their interests halfway between the burgeoning biological science sparked by Darwin's theories and a psychological science which was beginning to spread beyond the confines of moral philosophy or sensory experimentalism, worked on the problem of devising specific tests to measure differences in functions between persons. Jastrow, Münsterberg, Cattell, Boas, and Witmer in this country, and Galton, Kraepelin, and Ebbinghaus abroad, were among the many who worked eagerly on these problems. But although much of their work was consciously meant to be a break from the traditions of the laboratory as established by Wundt, they did not manage to get hold of the whole person as a target for their interests. They pioneered in developing detailed, objective measures; they submitted the simpler sensorimotor functions to elaborate and ingenious analyses. But somehow all they managed to do was to cut the person down to the size of their measuring devices. One might have supposed that the testing of thousands of fascinated visitors at the Columbian Exposition in Chicago in 1893 was proof that here at last the person had entered psychology; yet in all this dedicated effort the emphasis was on function rather than person, or on differences between persons rather than on persons who differed.

These alternatives are not trivial, and the choice between them was no accident. On the contrary, it may now be seen as almost inevitable when one considers the outlook of its chief architect, Cattell. Organizer and entrepreneur of the early stages of American psychology, Cattell was the man who, more than anyone else, became responsible for the direction it has pursued since then. In typically American style, he combined an intense interest in individuals with the conviction that he could treat them as members of working groups; and the two strains which he represented and fused, the stress on the single person combined with the love of the democratically massed group, bear fruit even today in a discipline that combines a worship of the statistics of groups with a faith in the dynamics of democratic group relations, a dependence on quantitative laws with the widespread practice of face-to-face psychotherapy. What was established under Cattell's influence, therefore, was a psychology of individual differences—but it never led to a clinical psychology. In fact, the psychology of the clinic, although it arose at the same time, in the same atmosphere, and apparently in response to the same problems as did the psychology of individual differences, actually represented a quite different current in the history of the science. The extent of the difference may be seen if we compare the approach, the outlook, and the work of Cattell with that of Alfred Binet, who may well deserve the title of the first full-fledged clinical psychologist. Lightner Witmer, who founded the Clinic at the University of Pennsylvania in March, 1896, probably was the first to use the term *clinical psychology,* but to Binet belongs the credit for exemplifying, and in many ways demonstrating and developing, an approach which begins and ends with the whole person.

The psychology of individual differences, under Cattell's enthusiastic guidance, was rapidly developing into a Wundtian experimentalism. To this Binet contrasted an emphasis on higher and more complex functions and then, as his interest shifted to educational problems, a further insistence on what Goodenough (1949) has aptly termed a "sampling" method. By this she means an approach which consisted of testing intelligence by using tasks requiring intelligence; the range of possible total manifestations of the phenomenon was sampled, and from the sample results the tester extrapolated to the subject's possible activity in general in regard to the phenomenon. Consider, by way of contrast, an approach in which "speed of association" is tested, as Cattell did in one of his numerous batteries. What could the results of such a test tell us about the subject, even supposing that the tester's interests were—as was Cattell's—in the subject as an individual person? Clearly, nothing could be learned by this method about the whole person unless—and here is the crucial methodological issue to distinguish Cattell's psychology of individual differences from Binet's individual psychology—there was also available some means for relating this single finding to the subject's total behavior. Speed of association has no value as a concept unless it is fitted into some explanatory scheme; and in the absence of such a scheme (which goes by the general name of a *theory* and which in relation to a test is called a *rationale*), the tester is left with an empty or trivial datum.

The issue we are considering here is fundamental to the problem of testing, and for this reason it has not disappeared but in fact is still very much in our midst. At this point, however, we may digress to examine more closely the logical problem besetting the first psychologists whose unit of study was the person. In Cattell's hands the attempt to introduce the person into psychology was made not by confronting the whole person as an observable entity, but by the same method as Dalton had used. Comparisons were made between persons, and in this way the entities being compared could conveniently be ignored. Given a first step away from the concretely presented phenomenon—the measurement of differences between persons rather than some crude and immediate apprehension of the person himself—it was logically necessary to stress the measurement of isolated functions which, in themselves, were meaningless or trivial. Only two paths were then open to the tester. He could attempt to string his findings together and relate them as an organized structure to a theory, which in turn referred back to the whole person and to his action in the world; or he could develop some means for finding how far the results obtained on one function might be compared to results obtained on others. The latter path, which required no attempt at theory but only a mechanical, or preferably a mathematical, procedure, led quite naturally to the various correlational methods. They were developed at this time to satisfy a very real need. The need was the direct outcome of Galton's work on individual differences, and it is therefore no coincidence that the methods were developed by his pupil, follower, and later biographer, Karl Pearson. The logic of the method of correlation is this: the presence together of two bits of data, or their concurrent varying, suffices to demonstrate some relation subsisting between them. Associationism in the realm of theory, expressed in terms of the copresence of ideas in the mental apparatus, is here perfectly mirrored in the realm of statistical practice. Vastly more sophisticated versions of this logic may be seen today in the thinking which underlies the use of factor analytic methods; but the fact that quite recently Guttman (1958), for example, has had to ask for more psychological theory and less "algebraic manipulation" would seem to demonstrate that there are still unbroken, even if unrecognized, historical links from contemporary behavioral science back to the turn of the century.

It was another breed of person, however, whom Binet struggled to bring into psychology. His problem had its origins outside of psychology; specifically, in the humanitarian work of Edward Seguin, to whom we may trace the idea that mental defectives are educable. The schools established on the basis of the model institution that he set up, and the vast spread of popular education in the nineteenth century as well, had made pressing the need to distinguish reliably those school children who required special attention and training. Binet and Simon, therefore, were faced from the very start with an issue of social import. Because what they would do was bound to matter outside their laboratory, they were constrained from the beginning to consider consequences. Theirs was, from start to finish, an applied psychology. Today this term is hardly in good repute, and in fact, since the second decade of this century, it has quite often been used in a mildly derogatory sense; for it refers to a field in which the source of questions and the immediate uses for their answers have their locus in everyday, practical affairs. For a psychology which was bent on following the path of its more respectable older sisters, in swift retreat from the concrete facts of the world, this was a kind of endeavor for which science had little use. But Binet and Simon had no such qualms. In order to test school children they began by intensively studying children themselves, guided by the general notion that they had to find samples of a fundamental capacity or they would not have a usable test at all. This capacity they defined as the ability to "judge well, to comprehend well, to reason well." The result of their work, and testimony as well to their approach, was that by 1908 they had essentially achieved a grasp of the whole problem and that no one has added appreciably to their thinking in the fifty or more years since. They clearly distinguished intelligence from learning, knowledge from aptitude, and global impressions of intelligence from a total score obtained by the addition of discrete "signs." They saw that one had to assess the subject's present state and not confound clinical judgment with either prognosis or the estimate of etiological variables. They separated the concept, and therefore the testing, of intelligence from that of "instability" and from various other personality characteristics and conditions. They noted that the clinical tester must see the subject himself, as distinct from his family or his situation; that one must gain the subject's confidence or else discontinue the testing; that the bare results of the test score gained their "true value" only when coupled with observations of the subject's behavior during an examination; and that the subject must not be aided or impeded either by overt or covert suggestion. They recognized that one becomes a clinical tester by practice with tests rather than simply by learning a method. They made some excellent guesses about such modern problems as the development of intellectual ability and intrasubject variability. They stated the concept of mental age and all but defined the intelligence quotient. They classified tests by age, a method which served testers very well for the next thirty-five years. They pointed out that the purpose of intelligence testing was not to categorize the child, not to fit him to an educational system, but rather the reverse— and in the course of making this statement they came very close to defining what is now known as *reading readiness*. They tried very hard to construct a "culture-free" test. And finally, they made the concept of intelligence a statistically usable construct, thereby establishing the foundation of modern work in test construction.

It may be claimed that many of these were no more than insightful technical contributions. Yet in all of this they were inspired by a unique interest. They never thought of measuring speed of association for its own sake, but they did ask, for example, how one might measure such attributes as "richness of inspiration" or "accuracy of judgment." Binet himself conducted a number of surprisingly sophisticated studies of teachers' judgments and educational methods. This is why is it disheartening to note that their views found no really friendly reception in America. But paradoxically, the general lack of interest in their approach occurred at almost the same time as a marked upsurge in the use of the very instruments for which they were given credit. Various reasons have been offered for this seeming historical oddity. Peterson (1925), for one, attributes it to the influence of a pair of experimental studies which were published about this time, one done by Stella E. Sharp under Titchener and one by Clark Wissler; both tended to cast doubt on the efficacy of the new tests of intelligence. But one ought to look, rather, to a climate of opinion which failed, on the one hand, to nourish the rich clinical fruits of Binet's inspiration and, on the other hand, gave support to ardent, if shallow, proponents of the principle of mass testing. Cattell had no difficulty in finding support for his role as entrepreneur of American psychology. Similarly, the times were ripe for the "hard sell" practiced by Henry H. Goddard, whom Wallin (1955) has knowingly described as "a personable, kindly fellow and good social mixer, a productive worker with a flair for popular presentations of scientific data and also for the practical . . . the trail blazer for the Binet-Simon Scale in America and the chief protagonist for its use even by 'novices' and 'the untrained or the wrongly trained person' " (p. 39). It is difficult to believe that a scientific community would recoil from using the Binet-Simon tests on the grounds of two sets of experimental findings but welcome their use when they were glowingly touted as "accurate to one or two points" and perfectly valid and useful in the hands of "untrained teachers" (Goddard, 1913). But the fact that it occurred suggests that scientists, like laymen and Supreme Court justices, have some tendency to go along with what the times demand. They will welcome the findings that fit into the thinking of the day, and they may even act as the social psychologists say we all do, selectively perceiving only that evidence which maintains harmony within their existing views.

It was in such a climate that intelligence tests flourished during the next two decades, but they flourished in a very special way. The field of intelligence testing was so completely empirical, so lacking in a theory of any sort, that by 1921 Boring could suggest in all seriousness that intelligence be defined simply in terms of what intelligence tests test. Psychologists ought perhaps to consider soberly the fact that the function of intelligence testing is the one with which they are most closely associated in the public consciousness, the practice which they have controlled as completely as the medical profession controls the practice of surgery—yet their contribution to understanding their practice or its results has been next to nothing. It seems undeniable that the person, who had finally entered psychology with the work of Binet, was almost immediately squeezed out. No person appears in today's theory of test construction; nor is he to be found in the discussions that filled the journals some twenty years ago on single- and multiple-factor definitions of intelligence. For a period during the 1930s, we recall, there occurred one of those rare flurries which occasionally disturb the placid surface of scientific progress: studies at the Iowa Child Welfare Station (Skodak, 1939) appeared to show that there were changes in intelligence test scores accompanying marked improvement in social and educational opportunities; but the discussion, we may note, usually referred to whether the IQ could be changed and only rarely to the child himself and the changes in his world when his opportunities enlarged and his horizons broadened.

In the history of the beginnings of intelligence testing we can discern a paradox: that the same development which effectively blocked the person out of clinical psychology also put a major emphasis on individuals and differences between them. The second would seem to be inconsistent with the first; yet if we consider the record that we have traced thus far in our biography of clinical testing, a turn of events that seems paradoxical will, I believe, be revealed as historically necessary. Recall that by the close of the nineteenth century a tradition was firmly established in the intellectual life of Europe and consequently of America as well. It was based upon that great movement toward secularization and rationalization which defines the modern age. In the propositions of science may be found the chief expression of this movement—that in an arbitrary cosmos, man is just one more particle among the rest, different by virtue of his organization but otherwise a sheer factual entity in a universe of knowable facts. To the scientific student of man—and what psychologist is brave or foolish enough to disavow this claim?—there is no human purpose except what a man discovers in his own behavior after he has acted; and there is no human world aside from the collection of data gathered on the basis of past and recorded behavior.

Cattell, as the first full-fledged scientific student of man, did his work within these propositions of modern science. What he studied, therefore, was a set of complex relations among certain factual entities. What he did not study were the differences among people. For a difference makes sense only in the context of a possible similarity; without one, the other disappears. The study of differences between persons presupposes that although they are seen as unlike, they are known to be in some manner joined. This, in turn, implies a human world within which their identifiable acts exist. If there were no such world, if Cattell and those who followed him were in fact correct, differences would not be discernible at all. Each person would appear—if there were a sentient being to whom the appearance could even occur—as just one other discrete integer, and a population of persons would seem to be like the molecules of a gas, separable only by means of an additional conceptualizing effort. And this is indeed what has happened in the psychology following Cattell, despite the occasional flash of protest from such figures as Binet or the early Dewey. This may also be the explanation, in brief, for our paradox. In the same way, and for basically the same reasons, a self-styled psychology of individual differences killed off the individual as effectively as the citizens of the Enlightenment had killed off God. The rest of the history of psychology, especially in its clinical aspects, is in essence the story of the vicissitudes of what was left.

THE PSYCHOLOGY
OF AMBIGUITY

Psycho-analysis . . . tells us what we really think when we think we
think a thing. Without psychoanalysis we should never know that
when we think a thing the thing we think is not the thing we think
we think but only the thing that makes us think we think the thing
we think we think.

—EWEN HEALEY

The "New Look" in Experiments

FROM THE INTRODUCTION OF THE BINET-SIMON SCALE TO THE FULL
flowering of clinical psychology in its "golden decade"—as George
Kelly has called the years immediately following World War II—there
is a half-century of growth which remains almost undocumented
(Watson, 1953, 1960; Wallin, 1955). With the highly publicized
screening of millions of recruits by means of the group tests of World
War I, it became apparent to even the most dedicated academician
that the clinician, like the Negro slave in America during the 1840s,
was here, and although he might well become the basis for conflict at

a later date, inevitably he was here to stay. By sheer pressure of numbers on an APA in which the amount of the annual dues—one dollar a year—was as low as entrance requirements were high, the national organization became, within the space of a few years, profoundly altered. From a "very modest organization," the APA soon became a "big business" (Fernberger, 1932), and in so doing, its attempts to police its own ranks and to supervise the activities of clinical psychologists faded to second place in the face of the more pressing demand to create an acceptable "image" of organized psychology in a boom culture. For a most remarkable and largely unexpected turn of events had made the science of psychology an important force in American life. Though contributions of perhaps equal value had been made by many psychologists before this time, Watson's politically adept and perfectly timed teachings found a nationwide audience which was unprecedented in the history of psychology. Every literate parent, and many whose literacy extended only to reading as they ran, knew and had an opinion on Watson's daring thesis of the limitless improvability of the plastic human organism. And at very much the same time the similarly daring ideas of Freud were being introduced into American social life, finding perhaps too ready a ground among a generation which delighted in breaking every taboo it could find and name.

A wholly new clinical profession seemed about to be born during the 1920s, marked by two significant events—the founding of the interdisciplinary American Ortho-psychiatric Association in 1924 and the establishing of the Harvard Psychological Clinic by Morton Prince in 1927. The picture of American psychology from the middle of the 1920s almost to the outbreak of World War II is thus one of two professions in peaceful coexistence—the one rather vaguely formulated, respectable, and academically quiet in outlook and tone, and the other noisier and more active in its dealings with the public and other established professions; the one proposing mildly to advance psychology as a science, emphasizing the acquisition of the Ph.D. degree and centering in the universities, and the other more worldly, perhaps even opportunistic, accepting the Master's degree as an appropriate level of formal training, and located in clinics, hospitals, and occasionally in schools.

During the decade of the 1930s the larger organization changed but little. Applied psychology, however, underwent a number of significant and far-reaching developments. To pass them by with no more than a mention—there was, first, the change in classical psychoanalytic theory that, during this period, developed a new and more systematically stated concern with ego functions; now the clinician no longer had to be satisfied with a complex, vague, yet enticing set of poetically phrased legends about mythical figures in a morality play of cosmic scope. Second, the Rorschach test was introduced to American workers, and was followed a few years later by the Thematic Apperception Test. Both turned out to be difficult instruments to use and were of such a nature that their applicability in research presented horrendous obstacles: of doubtful reliability and unknown validity, they were also time consuming to give and interpret. We may note that here, if anywhere, the fundamental opposition between applied psychology and its conservative older brother is exemplified, for although these tests are useless by every scientific canon they are the most widely used and the most vehemently defended of all clinical instruments. By the beginning of World War II, then, clinical psychology, which was at this time the most active and impressive of the applied areas, was solidly established as an institutionalized profession of its own; it had specialized instruments, its own training methods, some basis in research, a host of eager practitioners, textbooks by the dozen, two flourishing journals, a national organization, and a widely accepted theoretical orientation. It was, of course, a psychoanalytic orientation, words that seem to mean *leaning against* but not quite *falling for*.

In his role as member of an increasingly organized and identifiable group, the clinician now began to reach out for specifiable techniques. One such direction was toward that most prestigious of scientific achievements, the laboratory experiment. However, the clinician's special interests led him to seek at least a different kind of data from that which had occupied psychologists since the days of Wundt. His was a new kind of orientation, and it took some fumbling before he found a place for himself in the laboratory.

During the ten years before World War II, the most sophisticated and elaborate of the gropings toward a clinical experimentalism were taking place under Henry Murray's direction at the Harvard Psychological Clinic. Here, an elaborate study of fifty-one normal college men was undertaken, with many workers whose names are now familiar contributing to it—among them Rosenzweig, Sanford, White, Frank, Beck, and Shakow (Murray, 1938). Here for the first time the procedure was used of "building in" needs, as Gardner Murphy has aptly called it, producing and controlling wishes and motives so as to make possible laboratory predictions as to their effect. With the demonstration that significant motivating forces of the person could thus be manipulated experimentally, the way was open for the next generation of clinicians to bring their theory into the laboratory. Implicit in any clinically based theory, particularly one which depends on psychoanalytic hypotheses, is the conception that the person is engaged in a continuous remaking of a world in terms of some version of his unsatisfied needs. The most impressive statement of this idea, supported by an array of historical material, proposing a new terminology, and tied to most of the forward-looking developments then current in the physical sciences, had been the monograph on projective techniques by Frank (1948). Thus, a complete foundation had been laid, block by block, from a psychoanalytic theory to Murray's procedure and Frank's rationale. There was now needed only a set of actual experiments to provide clear evidence that the needs—so basic to functioning, so amenable to manipulation—did indeed find their way manifestly into overt action. The proposition chosen for test was the obvious one, that the wish is father to the perceptual deed.

Two experiments began the program. In the first of these Proshansky and Murphy (1942), starting with the "thesis that perception develops by virtue of its capacity to mediate adjustments, to serve needs" (p. 295), studied what they termed a "restricted autism," or drive-determined perception. Their results suggested that reward and punishment may be effective in changing such perceptual processes as are involved in estimating lines and weights. In a second, more elaborate, and apparently more definitive study, Schafer and Murphy (1943) presented a Rubin-type figure, similar to the profile-and-vase design of figure-ground experiments, rewarded perception of either one side or the other under conditions of tachistoscopic exposure, and, on presenting another exposure at the same speed, obtained most frequently perception of that profile which had previously been re-warded. Unfortunately, the issues here have turned out to be meth-odologically complex and not easily tested in a definitive manner. Rock and Fleck (1950) have replicated the Schafer-Murphy study with negative results; and more recently Jackson (1954), upon re-peating both studies, seems to have demonstrated that the results one obtains will depend on the precise method used.

Others, too, had been working the same field during the war years, particularly Bruner and Sanford. One study a few years later (Bruner and Goodman, 1947) appeared to demonstrate that a need for money, as differentially experienced by rich and poor children, will affect perception of coins so as to lead to significant differences in estimates of their size. In these pioneering experiments, and in dozens later which pursued the same path, the evidence indicating that actions of a laboratory subject were a function of permanent or temporary needs and desires seemed to pile up. The underlying thesis, that peo-ple do what they do because they are motivated to do it, of course needed no laboratory proof; a psychology that denied this would be inconceivable. But experiments of the sort described here managed to take a major step toward opening a domain of experimentalism which had always been closed to clinicians. No psychologist would have disagreed with such a proposition as: Food looks more appetiz-ing when we are hungry than when we are satiated. However, agree-ment on the common-sense, everyday level of discourse was by no means the same as an experimental demonstration under conditions as rigorous as those which usually provide evidence in regard to a scientific theory. What was needed, at least according to the canons that directed experimental psychology, was an observable and quan-tifiable anchor point at the stimulating end and an equally measurable anchor point at the behavioral end of a directed sequence of events. Only in this way could the psychologist put to test the notion "looks more appetizing." It had to be shown that subjects were measurably different in terms of some stimulating variable, and following this that their behavior was altered in objective fashion. The two methods used for this—either to pick groups known to differ according to acceptable sociological criteria, as in the Bruner-Goodman study, or to build in differing needs by a pretraining system involving reward and punishment, as in the two Murphy studies—enabled the experiments to satisfy customary requirements as to rigor. Clinical psychology now had its experimentalism—and therefore, one presumed, the accolade of science.

But the experimental results were by no means as straightforward as they seemed, and their complexities merit further examination. The novel element in the studies just described consisted in the particular stimulus situation to which the subjects were asked to respond. Indeed, the apparent proof in each experiment rested in large part on this fact: the stimulating situation was contrived in a special way. What the subjects were asked to look at, and then to do something about, was not the usual object for perception. This latter is, for good reasons of experimental method, usually clear and unambiguous; for the experimenter will say, with some justification, that if the object for perception is not clear, how will he himself be certain that the subject has perceived it in the required manner? In contrast to this, in the clinical experiments that we have examined thus far the perceptual object was deliberately arranged so that it could be construed in more than one way. In the Proshansky-Murphy study, the percepts were viewed under conditions of near-threshold illumination. Schafer and Murphy ingeniously utilized an ambiguous figure which might be seen easily in one of two ways, and then used a tachistoscope for very rapid presentation. In the Bruner-Goodman study, it is true, one part of the data was obtained when subjects were able to view the standard stimulus in clear light and at their own speed, but a replication of the experiment by Carter and Schooler (1949) indicated that positive results on this part at least, were probably an artifact of the subject population. The latter were able to duplicate the original findings only in regard to one situation, involving the remembered size of coins, in which it may be presumed that the stimulating percept was neither clear nor unequivocal as to size. Studies later than these early ones have standardized the procedure through the use of a tachistoscope, the stimuli being presented at speeds which assure that as viewed they will always be equivocal rather than clearly and unambiguously one thing or another.

So striking a change in the very elements of experimental procedure was not arrived at by chance. Rather, it must represent in effect a theory of perception, a kind of dynamic psychology in miniature. The issue, and some of its logical consequences, have been well put by Bruner and Goodman (1947) in discussing the matter of "equivocality, or ambiguity in the perceptual field . . . The greater the equivocality, the greater the chance for behavioral factors in perception to operate, all other things being equal . . . insofar as equivocality reduces the organizing capacity of autochthonous perceptual determinants" (p. 36). This is to say that a balance is struck between the forces of the environmental field and others—called extrastimulus, or autochthonous, or personal—which stem from the subject himself. Raise one and you lower the relative effect of the other. Make the environment unclear, so that its effect is scattered, so to speak, and you increase the chance that inner needs, which have been waiting an opportunity for expression, will burst into the perceptual open and determine what the subject sees or hears. For a discipline concerned chiefly with the nature and expression of private constellations of such needs, this must indeed be an ideal method. Recall that the theory on which clinical practice rested had to do with a person's felt and unfelt needs, and that in fact the most important propositions in the theory, the most far reaching in their consequences, referred either to nonconscious processes or to the relation between these and overtly observable aspects of functioning. Therefore it became highly useful to have a situation in which the subject could be brought to respond in terms of needs of which he was unaware. To do this, of course, the target for perception had to be something less than clear and definite; the subject's conscious life could then be bypassed and the workings of his inner dynamics exposed.

But progress is never easy, not in science any more than in other worldly endeavors. As soon as one set of problems—in this case methodological—was solved by changing the nature of the stimulating situation from clear to ambiguous, a new set arose, this time basically theoretical. The problem was this: If the conclusions to be drawn from experimental studies rested on the fact that subjects responded to what they did not clearly perceive, how was one to explain their apparent effectiveness in perceiving? The first answer was given by Bruner and Postman (1947), who postulated at least two kinds of reaction to emotionally disturbing stimulus material, the defensive and the vigilant. On the basis of the experimental evidence they argued that the reaction of defense was associated with higher thresholds for traumatic material, and the reaction of vigilance with a lowered threshold. In this way there was explained the finding that when anxiety-arousing percepts were presented at tachistoscopic exposures too rapid for unequivocal perception, some subjects showed marked delays and others significant increases in reaction time. Exploring the issues further, Bruner and Postman later went on to suggest (1949) a "hierarchy" of thresholds. The subject, they proposed, could respond on one level without the stimulus reaching a "higher" threshold; the latter was to be defined in such terms as *reportable experience.*

The issue that these developments suggest is, of course, unconscious perception, or, as Miller (1939) had termed it, "discrmination without awareness"; later it came to be called "subception" (Lazarus and McCleary, 1951). Our interest here is not in surveying the area, a task which has already been capably done by Adams (1957) and Eriksen (1960), but in tracing out and identifying some historical currents. Murray, whose pioneering influence is unmistakable wherever one turns in the field of clinical experimentalism, offered, in an early study (1933), the first laboratory evidence on these problems. He showed that children who had been put through a frightening experience changed their estimates of the maliciousness of faces seen in photographs; the increase in unpleasant characteristics spontaneously and naïvely perceived in the faces suggested that the changed psychological situation of the perceivers was a significant determinant of their subsequent perceptual behavior. Some twenty years later, when a similar result was achieved in miniature in the laboratory, experimentalists of what was now called the New Look in perceptual theory attempted to explain this key concept in clinical psychodynamics. Its relevance to the behavior universally observed in clinical patients was, of course, immediately clear. Everything pointed in the same direction, the theory as well as the experimental results, to provide evidence for unconscious perception, with all the thorny problems that this held for theories of perception and cognition. In some respects the question is still up in the air; but although theory seems to lag behind results, thereby hinting at one of the dangers in a completely empirical approach, one conclusion appears to emerge—that explanations and explanatory schemes aside, the special kinds of perception observed in these experiments could not have occurred unless they were in response to a special kind of stimulus material.

Consider, in this connection, the study by Miller (1939) in which, as part of a series of experiments, he presented one of five different geometric designs through a one-way mirror. The lighting was so controlled that the design was, as far as the subjects were concerned, below the visual limen; yet some subjects did better than chance in "guessing" which design was presented. Now, the kind of stimulus material to which subjects in this study tried to respond may be described as factual. This is to say that its characteristics as an experimental datum could be adequately specified. Regardless of the standards or methods by which the subjects attempted to determine whether a specific design was present, it can be asserted—by Miller and consequently by anyone else who reads his report or replicates his study—that a specific design was in fact really present to be observed; and such relevant characteristics of the design as shape, size, or class of figure may also be unequivocally affirmed. Because a certain design was, in this sense, certainly there and describable as such, the only issue on which subjects were asked to judge was one the answer to which could be stated as a fact, that the design was or was not actually present.

In direct contrast, the double-profile design utilized in the study of Schafer and Murphy (1943) was by its very nature ambiguous in the extreme, and even a correct response—that is, a response that followed predictably from the treatment accorded a particular subject—could not be said to refer to a factual datum. Rather, the kind of stimulus material used by Schafer and Murphy was chosen by them *precisely because no relevant factual statement could be made about it by way of a description of its characteristics;* because, to put it another way, one would be hard put to state what might really constitute a "correct" response. In regard to the Miller design, one might state, and then objectively verify, that a design which was not visible according to the subject's report was in fact really present; but it would make no sense to say, in regard to one profile or the other in the Schafer-Murphy study, that it was "really" there to be perceived. And if the stimulus pattern is not verifiably present as an objective datum, what is one to say about the apparent response to it? What kind of perception is it which answers to what is not there?

By this last phrase I do not mean merely that the subject fails to report his awareness of the stimulus, nor that he reports one thing about the stimulus and something else, on being questioned, about his awareness of the stimulus. These possibilities are easily taken care of in the various kinds of studies on learning without awareness. I mean rather that in the New Look experiment, as exemplified in the study by Schafer and Murphy, there seems to be no way that a definition of the term *objective* can be stretched to encompass the necessary characteristics of the stimulus. By the usual canons, the subject is acting in terms of what can neither be defined nor reported into existence.

Here is a phenomenon which is totally unique in psychology, and indeed in science in general. It merits a more extended examination—which we will attempt in the next section—but not only on grounds of methodological interest. Of equal significance is the fact that this phenomenon—the special kind of stimulus and the consequent unique order of perceptual data—constitutes the basis of clinical psychology's experimentalism. Further, it has led to the only theory that may be said to belong to the clinical orientation. It is all the more surprising, therefore, that the theory should not be openly proclaimed but largely hidden or ignored, as though it were an underground movement, and that the pioneers in the New Look—Bruner, Postman, and Murray are examples—should without exception have turned more recently to other areas of interest. The term *New Look,* with all its implications of a breakthrough in methodology and theory, has found its way into the literature, and since then has been embalmed in textbooks; but it no longer refers to an actively cultivated experimental field.

Notes on the Ambiguous Stimulus

In the preceding section we began discussion of the concept of ambiguity, that more or less accidental innovation that is central to such theories as clinical psychology possesses. We noted that the stimulus material in the typical New Look experiment is not observable, not reportable, and not definable operationally, by either experimenter or subject. Everyone is silent in its presence—if, indeed, it is present in any objective sense; or if, indeed, such terms as objective and subjective may properly be applied to it.

What is it that characterizes this very special kind of situation? What do we mean by a stimulus that is ambiguous? Unfortunately, at this crucial juncture, as is so often true in the clinical theory we are engaged in examining, the theory fails us. No formal definition is ever offered. More than this, the conception is such that it is extremely difficult to discover and state a precise set of criteria for ambiguity. It often seems that the concept itself partakes to a certain extent of the very qualities which it seeks to represent—for it is self-evident yet elusive, and obvious at the same time that it cannot quite be pinned down.

This may well be one reason why the concept of ambiguous stimulus is so widely used yet so poorly defined. It is simply because everyone understands immediately what is supposed to be meant by it, especially when the concept is used as a basis for a test situation. All that one has to do is offer the subject a stimulus which might reasonably appear to him in a number of different ways—depending on how he feels at the moment or on his past experiences or even his personality characteristics—and, on the basis of his responses and the way he offers them, draw conclusions about his "inner" state. The ambiguous stimulus may now be defined in preliminary fashion by way of this operational criterion: it asks a question for which there is more than one good or correct answer. The incomplete sentence, "Two plus two make . . ." or a photograph of da Vinci's Mona Lisa with the question, "What might this be?"—these are not ambiguous questions, for in our society only one good answer can conceivably be expected to each one. They are unambiguous in the extreme; whereas the ambiguous test stimulus allows each subject a range of possible responses and thereby makes possible a range of different but equally acceptable answers from different subjects.

It follows from this characteristic of the ambiguous stimulus that the various answers offered by a population of test subjects can be interpreted as products of the individual peculiarities of the subjects themselves. Any test using an ambiguous stimulus, then, becomes without further ado a way of testing new subjects. This was in effect the logic used by Murray in constructing his Thematic Apperception Test. He knew that different subjects usually told different stories about the same set of pictures and he was willing to accept all stories as equally "good." Therefore, he gathered a group of pictures and a group of known, or previously studied, subjects; and he chose the pictures for his test on the basis of how much information they provided him about the subjects. The characteristic of ambiguity, then, is inevitably tied to its use in a testing device; the ambiguous stimulus is defined in terms of its ability, so to speak, to test subjects. Ambiguity is one facet of a more general characteristic of the whole testing situation that we may call *detectability,* which is the ability to obtain the true or real data hidden behind what is immediately present. And this is perhaps the reason that the concept of ambiguous stimulus made its appearance at about the same time that clinical tests began to be widely used, and why it does not appear anywhere else in psychological theory. Ambiguity need not be defined, for if one accepts the common-sense notions implicit in a logic such as Murray's, the ambiguous stimulus is defined in a self-evident manner.

One of the classic statements of this view of ambiguous test material is to be found in the two volumes by Rapaport (1946), a work which should stand as the definitive formulation of a psychoanalytic approach to clinical testing. Rapaport refers to the ambiguous as "unstructured," defines it in general as offering the subject "wellnigh infinite possibilities for structuring and organizing," and then discusses the relation of this particular kind of material to clinical tests (Vol. 2, p. 5). Stimuli of this sort are of value in clinical instruments because their use opens the way for responses which are "unstilted." In responding to them, the subject will not "find support" in approaches that are superficial, formal, or conventional. As an example, in the Word Association Test the subject may respond in any way at all, whereas in giving answers to a conventional vocabulary test he is not only constrained in specific ways but it is the specific business of the test to determine the extent to which he abides by the constraints.

What is clearly implied though never openly expressed in this plausible argument is that a person's true bent is better revealed in the unconventional than in the conventional, that the real truth about people lies somewhere below the socially acceptable surface, and thus that the purpose of elaborate testing procedures is to get at this subsurface vein of personal reality. There is more than one good reason, as we shall see in this chapter, for referring to contemporary clinical dogma as an "underground theory." It deserves to be called underground for the obvious reason that it has never been openly and fully spelled out; one gets the impression that clinicians who act in terms of the theory would be made uncomfortable at seeing its full implications. A second, and possibly more interesting, reason for using the term, however, is that the theory states a dependence on the hidden, the not-present, the subsurface; wherever a choice is possible, theorists of this bent imply that what is not immediately available in the person, what is implied and suggested or perhaps even denied and resisted, constitutes the abiding truth about him. In the preceding chapter we discussed some of the consequences of this conception of a pluriverse of data; and here we will examine further this "underground" bias in reference to the particular kind of stimulus material which is used in clinical testing.

Rapaport's unexpressed conviction, we have just noted, is in the Hobbesian tradition, to the effect that man is a citizen in spite of himself. The adult is so "fenced-in with formal information, conventions and traditions, as to rarely display his individuality undisguised" (Vol. 2, p. 5). Individuality, then, is just that which is masked by the formal, the conventional, and the traditional, and psychology's task comes to be to uncover the nature that is hidden behind what the person knows and does and says. In another analysis, too, Rapaport builds his theory on his bias toward the underground. Discussing the continuum which runs from structured to unstructured perceptions (Vol. 2, p. 90), he notes that when our perception is directed toward the completely structured we immediately recognize what something is. In unstructured cases, by contrast, we are forced to call into play other perceptual processes; these include memory, concept formation—to organize, compare, and sift among memories and to establish new links—and finally concentration guided by anticipation. As the perceptual object becomes less structured, the perceptual process itself changes to involve new subprocesses. Thus, as the subject can no longer rely on the familiar, the easy, and the conventional response, he will be forced to display to us some other, less common processes, in this way providing "the examiner with a rich treasure of insight into hidden aspects."

Here again there is either expressed or strongly implied a theory and a philosophic position supporting it. Notice how little trust is ever put in the ordinary and the familiar, how little positive weight is ever assigned to the conventional surface of life. And notice too that the "structured" end of the continuum of perception, when it is dealt with at all, is assumed to be essentially a process of recognition of given objects—analogous, in its function, to the primitive olfactory sense. In this view, the task of everyday perception, when allowed to be of any significance whatsoever, is to orient the person in a world of hard facts and concrete objects; and any other aspect of the person's world, whether it be of challenge or interest, diversity or uncertainty, is assigned to the realm of the hidden, the unexpressed, the denied and resisted. It is evident, then, that the concept of ambiguity is of some significance in contemporary theory, but that it can hardly be understood without considering its logical converse, the unambiguous.

To state that there is a possible stimulus which is not clearly and exactly any one thing—which is the way the ambiguous stimulus is usually described—is also to say that there exist other possible stimuli which are quite clearly and definitely something specific and exact. A stimulus can conceivably be ambiguous only if the concept of unambiguity also has some meaning. Fortunately, one does not have to look far to see what is meant in the simplest sense by a stimulus which is unambiguous, for this is what surrounds us all the time. Chairs and tables, problems and situations are usually and in the ordinary course of events unambiguous. They seem to be whatever they are, and conversely they usually are whatever they seem to be. Further, they seem to be just that and not anything else, at least not at the same time. Finally, most persons would agree on these propositions.

So runs the earnest and sensible argument of most psychologists. Their reference is always, as it must be, to a world of unambiguous stimuli. Nor are they in this fundamental respect any different than the

rest of us as we go about our activities in an equally serious manner—
for what is true of the scientist as I have just described him is true
of people in general. The description above is not only a theoretical
and philosophical position but, as all such positions must be, an
underlying attitude, a set which determines one's perceptual activity.
The scientist is an experiencing human being and his science is
embedded in his ongoing experience; therefore, any general statement
about the basis of his science must also be applicable to the ongoing
experience, perceptual or otherwise, of himself and of his nonscientific
fellows. What I have described, then, is the vantage point from which
the human perceiver undertakes his perceptual engagement with his
world. When he is in his normal state, which is most of the time, and
when his activity is directed toward his accustomed environment, he
bases his perception upon the naïve and sensible empiricism just
described. Things are what they seem to be, and whatever it is that
they are, the "is-ness" and the "what-ness" reside out in the observed
world.

There is one compelling way in which this proposition can be
demonstrated to our own satisfaction; the method is simply to examine
the nature of our perception. When we look back into our own
perceptual activities, reflecting for a moment on the way things seem
to us *as we perceive them,* we will notice that usually the act of
perception is fully summed up and rounded out at the time of its
occurrence. However we see things, we always see them as they seem
to be at the moment—not as they will be or might be or have been, not
as an alternative or a variant or a less than explicit possibility. All of
these latter ways of perceiving are possible under certain circumstances, but reflection will surely tell us that they are all special
cases. They are different from the usual way of perceiving, which is
simply to see what is there to be seen, to see it in whatever way it
appears to us, and to accept the perception as such. The essential
factor here is the difference between perception *as it occurs,* to which
the preceding statement applies, and some sort of extraperceptual
reflective or introspective act, such as the variants I have listed. We
must be careful to keep in mind this distinction between the act of
perception in its occurrence, on the one hand, and the introspective
or reflective act, which is directed toward the perceiver or his own

perceptual act, on the other. Any of us can quite easily undertake this separate act, but it takes little self-examination to reveal that it is distinguishable from the perceptual act itself. All of the questions about the original perceptual act, or all of its variants, therefore, arise exclusively in the course of the separate act of reflection or introspection. The perceiver may entertain an attitude toward his own act; he may contradict it or be puzzled by it or deny it; he may entertain it as merely one of a number of equivalent possibilities; or he may even direct himself toward a stimulus describable as unclear—but each of these acts is separate and quite different from the perceptual act itself. Perhaps one of these extraperceptual, reflective acts might even occur simultaneously with the perceptual act itself; but perception itself will never tell us whether this might occur and will not indicate when it does occur. Perception is a unitary process; any of us can discover this much about ourselves, no matter how many slices are made of our perceptual act by a sophisticated theory.

Consideration of the nature of our own perception tells us something else about the usual perceptual act and its results. This is that in the normal course of events perception is of a world which is in some sort of order. As long as our spontaneous perception is of what seems to be there, it is perception of the world so arranged as to be sensible to us. By the very act of perception there is constituted an order in whatever is there for us to perceive. With the exception of abnormal conditions such as confusion, fatigue, hypnagogic revery, hypnosis, and the like, the order presented in perception simply precludes ambiguity in the stimulus. If the stimulus is perceived at all, it is perceived spontaneously and unreflectively as *something*—or else it is perceived with equal definiteness as *not*-something, which for the purposes of our discussion is the same thing. At the time of the occurrence of the perceptual act, the stimulus is not ever ambiguously something; this is a contradiction in normal experience. If ambiguity ever occurs, it, too, has the characteristic of every other field toward which attention is directed: if ambiguous, it is *definitely* ambiguous, and the perception as it occurs is of the definiteness rather than of the possible ambiguity.

In one of the very few papers discussing the concept of ambiguity, Luchins (1950) presents a cogent argument to the same effect:

Consider Boring's "beauty-hag" picture. If the subject sees the young woman, it may be for him a very strong structure, difficult to alter. Once he does perceive the hag, she may become so dominant that he encounters difficulty in restoring his former view of the picture. Each of the two organizations is strong and compelling. Thus ambiguity is not equivalent to a low degree of structural clarity. As a matter of fact, it does not at all refer to the strength of structurization, but rather, to a range of possible structurizations" (p. 28).

An example taken from a Rorschach protocol will perhaps best illustrate the conception of the priority of order in perception. The subject, Thomas, after a certain amount of vacillating between making light of the clinical situation and manifesting great concern over its significance, offered the following response, with almost no delay, to Card I:

Might be a butterfly. [After waiting for him to continue, E urges: *And anything else that you see*. Patient leans back and clasps his knee.] That's about all that I could see. Could be a—flying fish or some—Could be a kite. [Patient pushes card back.] [E: *Anything else?*] That's it. [70"]

Asked during the inquiry about the determinants for the "butterfly" response, the patient says:

Well, the way its—its wings out like this. [He makes some vague motions with his hands.] Pretty jagged for a kite. These little dots out here, of course, it could be a—you have a kite, and a flying fish, and what else was it? [Pause] Butterfly.

The examiner asks him about his reference to the dots, and Thomas says:

These out here—it could be a map of some kind, with an island, that part of it don't take a flying fish or butterfly or kite either. I suppose this might be a kite or butterfly—wouldn't have these little dots. Could be an aerial map. Wouldn't have dots out there for a flying fish. It would depend on what you're trying to imagine. It could be a person with shadows cast, but the dots wouldn't be there. I guess that's all I can make out if it. [E: *Show me the parts of the butterfly*.] Well, this—the wings. I mean, actually when you go into it, it isn't like a butterfly, it's like a person with a shadow, then folded over. The duplicate is over here. If you want to be explicit, it wouldn't be either a kite, fish, or flying fish.

It would be something made and an exact duplicate—except for this one thing. [Patient points to the little dots. E: *The person?*] This could be a person with her hand up, casting a shadow. It's actually almost as if it were made here and folded over.

The degree of this patient's slipperiness raises some fundamental questions concerning precision and order in the Rorschach response. When a subject accedes to taking the Rorschach test he agrees at least implicitly that the test has certain limits and the test situation certain defining characteristics. The examiner spells out most of these in the test instructions and the remainder as required during the course of administering the test proper. There is, for one, the characteristic that the inkblots are to be responded to rather than either ignored or bypassed in favor of some other percept; they are to be considered figure rather than ground in the subject's perceptual field. Within this very general kind of limitation, the subject agrees with the examiner that the blots might very well "be" something—although of course he adds to this that by the nature of the test it will be up to him alone to declare what it is they might be; thus, for example, the anxiety displayed by some inadequate subjects which leads to their insistence that the examiner reassure them as to the blots really being something. Finally, the examiner and subject agree that however he arrives at his response and whatever he produces in the test situation is to be sensibly communicated so that the one can understand the other.

The way in which the subject accepts these limits indicates to the examiner how reality is constituted into an order for him. It is the patterning of this order which appears to other persons as his individuality. If he does not accept the task as a task in the first place; if he does not agree that the cards are figure rather than ground; if he denies that the blots might be something or will not agree to frame his responses as a comunication to the examiner—in short, if he does not take the blots as real and to be responded to as such, there is nothing that can be said about the order of reality for him. It may be that even in such an extreme case there is a reality constituted for him with its own kind and degree of order, but this can no longer be discovered by means of the test. As a specialized instrument, the Rorschach requires that the subject act so as to guarantee to us that his is a perceptual act which is directed toward an order of things.

The patient Thomas fails, apparently, to achieve even the minimal precision needed for an examiner to assign his responses to some formal scoring category. But even this way of responding, pathologically slippery and fluid though it may be, manifests order. He is not perceiving nothing; he is directed to a task; it is in some way constituted for him as a perceptual object; and he is communicating in his own fashion to the examiner. The inkblot may be an ambiguous stimulus, but it is definitely ambiguous.

Where, then, does the ambiguity of the blot have its effect, and what are we to make of the patient's idiosyncratic mode of responding to the ambiguous blot? The answer must be that these aspects of his response occur within the context of the order that he manifests. Given a world which is in some perceptual order, Thomas displays a singular lack of a certain pattern or organization—and it is this to which we refer when we talk about his fluidity or absence of precision. Having said this much about him, we can now go on to consider the uniquely individual way in which he utilizes order in the service of imprecision. He is clearly not like the person who achieves an organization or even the lack of it by means of his own active efforts—that is, the person whom we would see as compulsive. Rather, he is among that group of persons who arrive at whatever mode of organization befits them by accepting it from whatever source is available—that is, the hysteroid personality. We may note that only a few and quite limited kinds of precision are ever available to him, and that he uses them in turn, just as though this were really all that were possible for any person. The first of these is given by the little dots, and their organization is actually a perceptual given; they stand out perceptually as black dots against a white ground. The second kind of organization he achieves is also based on a perceptual gift, through no effort of his own: it is geometrical. The cards are in fact nearly symmetrical, and although he discovers little else about them he soon finds this out. Much of the rest of his Rorschach protocol, in fact, consists of his comments about the symmetry of the cards.

Through the use of the dots and a recognition of symmetry Thomas manages to attain a kind of precision, but it is nothing created by him. It is always something that he stumbles across—and often, in fact, cannot immediately utilize, as in his complaint that the dots spoil his vaguely sensed images of the kite and of the person—or something he has given to him, as it were, by the very formal character of the cards. It is interesting that his acceptance is not completely flaccid. Because he cannot or will not easily fit things in when he comes across them, he has a whole set of techniques for grasping at straws, for shading things a little or twisting them around. In this way he often arrives at a facsimile of a construction, one which even seems to resemble the painfully evolved construction done by the compulsive person. In diagnostic terms, he would be viewed as a hysteric personality with superficial compulsive defenses.

When perception is considered in this way—that is, as the ordering of presented appearances by means of a unitary process—it is evident that the unambiguous is in fact the perceptual correlate of unreflectiveness. Unambiguity is the essential characteristic of a stimulus, whether it is a table or a child, a situation or an event, whenever I apprehend that stimulus in an unreflective way. If it seems to me to be simply and definitely whatever it is, and to contain this "whatever" rather than to have derived it in part from myself or my own efforts; if I deal with it spontaneously, without hesitation, and with some degree of certainty; if I appear to an observer to be responding in this familiar and straightforward manner; or if I customarily apprehend things in this way and do not usually pause, contemplate, pose alternatives, make choices, or have regrets—in any of these instances my perception would tend to be unreflective and therefore the stimulus could properly be described as unambiguous for me. And it would follow from this that my perception of what is, since it is unitary, rules out any other position that I might take in respect to the stimulus. I could not both see it unreflectively and at the same time maintain the possibility of seeing it in any other way. As long as I persisted in perceiving it in this way, which we have referred to as perception of the unambiguous stimulus, then ambiguity would be ruled out either as a characteristic of the stimulus or as a possibility that I might entertain about the stimulus.

In short, the division between reflective and unreflective modes of apprehension also serves to dichotomize two different orders of stimuli. Unreflective apprehension, in the immediate and straightforward way I have described it thus far and without examining the conception more elaborately, always refers to the unambiguous stimulus; to the unreflective eye, stimuli are just what they are, without question, doubt, or possible remorse. But reflective apprehension is quite different; and the ambiguous stimulus, as one specific kind of object in the perceptual field presented in reflectiveness, is something more than merely a vague and indistinct version of its unambiguous cousin. The proper analogy here, plausible though it may appear at first sight, is definitely not the microscope which one may move in and out of focus. In reflectiveness we step away from the immediate and spontaneous response to an unambiguous stimulus and assume some position in which it may appear to us in more than one light. The ambiguous stimulus is only one of the many ways in which the world may appear in the course of reflective apprehension. By contrast, in the course of unreflective apprehension, the stimulus appears to us simply and therefore often clearly, in one light only, nakedly as what it is, and bare of possibilities, however remote, which might serve to charge it with significance or valence. The distinction has been developed in rich detail by Merleau-Ponty (1960), in his "philosophy of ambiguity": we constantly give meaning to things, but with each act it is from a new perspective and in a new light; in this way, although man builds a many-faceted world, full knowledge of it, as though it were a fixed and preordained thing, is never given.

We noted above that in the concept which is current, though usually unexpressed, in clinical theory, the quality of ambiguity is not the denotable presence of something but rather the inherent absence of any relevant stimulus characteristic. The ambiguous stimulus is therefore not clear but vague; it suggests nothing though it may imply everything; it contains no promise of goal or fulfillment; it lacks any demand character; and it does not present itself in respect to any directive for action. It is, in short, the very absence of the "thingness" or the "whatness" that ought to characterize the identifiable stimulus. It is this "thingness," on the other hand, which binds the unambiguous stimulus together, so to speak; binds it into a perceptible unity, encompasses it or pervades it, and holds it for us so that we can grasp it in the present and maintain it in the past. The ambiguous stimulus is not this at all. It is, in short, no stimulus. We can only imagine that, in the unspoken metaphysics of modern clinical theory, it is meant to be contrasted with objects and entities that are the more familiar representatives of the real world. Only if we understand the ambiguous stimulus in this way can we explain why the concept is so elusive, why it is so indefinable yet so persistent in clinical theory, why in spite of its apparent logical emptiness it furnishes one important pillar for the theory, and why it seems to be central to any explanation of perception yet bears so little consistent relation with the known data or experience of perception.

A psychological theory based, as is that of the contemporary empiricist's, on the kind of limited world which is described by the physical sciences, will deal with nothing but the unambiguous. It will insist, from beginning to end, that perception is always of discrete and tangible objects with spaces between them, and it will manage to reduce every psychic phenomenon to some kind of physically manipulable thing. But the world that the clinician is dedicated to understanding is in many ways not like this at all, for first of all it is not "world" but "worlds" that attract his interest—the private, often deviant worlds of unique individuals. Here, then, is the basis for the concept of ambiguous stimulus, that it provides a novel category which will suffice to contain the phenomena that seem central to clinical problems.

The Artist and the Nonartist

Undeniably, there is a half-truth to be found in the set of propositions concerning the ambiguous stimulus. There is, first, the underlying notion that the concept of the unambiguous, as this is expressed in the activities of experimentalists, will not suffice to explain some of the most significant and perhaps fundamental instances of perception. There is more everywhere than meets the fact-seeking eye, and therefore people do more, or they are capable of doing more, than is found in their customary and unreflective apprehension of the familiar objects around them. If this were not so, there would be no clinical problems to be dealt with by means of clinical testing, no instances of anxiety, guilt, or disturbance pointing to perceptual ways that differ from the familiar and the ordinary. The concept of ambiguous stimulus is one attempt to encompass these phenomena which are in important respects out of the ordinary, and to the extent that the concepts refers to problems requiring other ways of under-standing, it contains a measurable portion of truth. Second, and more specifically, a half-truth is contained in the emphasis on some sort of individually creative process on the part of the test subject. The test instructions accomplish this by inviting the subject to be creative, in the examiner's insistence that the subject make of the material any-thing he pleases, and in the further guarantee—which no one else but the artist ever has about his own perceptual products—that whatever results from the endeavor will be correct or true. Indeed, an analysis of the ambiguous stimulus teaches us a crucial distinction between the work of art and the practical accomplishment: that there can be no judgment of accuracy, of rightness or wrongness, about an artistic creation. It may be good or bad, well or poorly done, inspiring, interesting, revolting, or dull, but the idea of its correctness is as irrelevant to its aesthetic value as the idea of its height above sea level. In this respect at least, the subject's performance on a clinical test is exactly like that of the artist's performance before an easel, in the latter case as a result of his special view of things and in the former because of the instructions and set that initiate the testing situation.

But the differences between the two are equally important, especially in view of the tendency on the part of some critics to belabor a clinical approach as resting on art rather than science. Again, we may turn to some evidence, in this case a test protocol of the sort that seems to lie on the border between artistic creation and projective expression. The following response to Card IV of the Rorschach was given by Donald, a 23-year-old, hospitalized, male subject who was being retested after a course of psychotherapy:

[Smile] [10″] Well, I remember this creature. I sure had something made up on him.

He's got huge feet—and he's standing facing anteriorly—facing, or rather—and bending over backward so his head is at a level lower than his feet. His pants are ragged, his shoes are worn. He has the head of a monster—sort of a caterpillar-like head or dragon-like head. The very definite conversion [sic] point where the—the buttocks leave off and you can see the head being bent over behind them. [Pause] On the axis of the body you can also see his anus and the underside of his scrotum. His arms are very small—short, shriveled. [Pause]

There's some interesting effects of shade and light here, that forms a picture, within themselves—just the light and dark shades. Just the light and dark shades—the face of a man. Probably a God, or the features of a God—a long Hebrew nose, hollowed cheeks, a mask-like face, and the long hair of the ancient Hebrews. His eyes are absent—well, I don't know, not absent, because they aren't there. They're much more powerful than they would be otherwise. [Pause]

The forehead's wrinkled, and hard—Ahah! I know what it is—it's Jesus Christ, and he's got a wreath of thorns about his head, poor fellow. Narrow, martyrish shoulders, very weak character, asking for sympathy— a beggar. The coat he's got on, something like burlap—and the arms are extended in supplication. [Patient here raises his own arms, fingers outstretched.] A beggar, strictly a beggar, whatever it is. [Pause]

Isn't that a wonderful combination—Jesus Christ, and the ass of a caterpillar? [7'30"]

Fascinated, and understandably so, by the elaborate and revealing richness of this patient's productions, we might easily tend to equate it with what the artist does. This is, unfortunately, particularly true because of the current influence of psychoanalytically oriented practitioners of the critic's demanding craft. In their understandable eagerness to make their own degree of understanding seem universal in scope, they indulge in the broadside application of psychological concepts which are either elementary or overly special. Art has not suffered from their efforts, but aesthetics as a discipline has; and the remarks that we make about the Rorschach response just quoted may therefore help a little in righting the balance.

By some criteria Donald has "created" an organized, finely articulated, and exquisitely sensed percept out of what is for some other subjects only a grossly perceived blob and for most persons simply a more or less accurate representation of a two-legged figure. He has given two responses, the first the full figure of a "caterpillar-like" creature as seen from the rear, and the second the face of a Christlike person with arms outstretched. Both percepts are well developed and reasonably accurate as to form; both utilize all the elements of the blot, in particular the nuances of shading and texture; and both are elaborated with a great deal of associative content. It is undeniable that they are also revealing of many aspects of his personality and that pathological indicators abound in the formal as well as associative aspects of the responses—but this should not concern us here. Art, as such, ought to be judged independently of the known or estimated disturbance of the artist himself. Our interest is in whether or not this production differs essentially from what the artist accomplishes in his own chosen medium.

However, even if we may properly disclaim any interest in the interpretable aspects of Donald's responses, we cannot help noticing that they are most prominent. Indeed, when we examine what he says we are struck by the fact that the seemingly artistic qualities of his performance are given by just those characteristics which inform us as to the nature and extent of his emotional difficulties. The almost obsessive concentration on the anatomical detail and precise positioning of the anal area of the first figure; the elaborated artificiality of the face seen as the second percept, especially its emphasis on light and shadow, on its distance and unreality, and on the power generated in what is almost a death mask; and the concluding associations which have nearly the form of a deductive argument based on a highly charged syllogism of great personal relevance—these are both evidence for his "creative" accomplishment and material for extended clinical evaluation. Now, this is not the way it is in a true work of art. We could never tell an artist's work habits from the finished painting; nor could we deduce a writer's traits of character from the kinds of personalities he creates for his novel. Rather, the reverse is true. Only to the extent that he is a poor artist are we ever able to make a diagnosis of him as a person from the work that he produces. Insofar as he produces art, he disappears into it. Herein is the difference between the short story and the TAT protocol; as we are able to grasp the latter, we lose touch with the former.

It is particularly in the way that Donald approaches his "creative" task that he reveals how little of the artist there is in him. His approach is one of searching out, feeling his way, and finally by a process of associative accretion coming to a major concept or image. He begins the second response in this way, with the remark, "There's some interesting effects of shade and light here," and he concludes it with a discovery which is signaled by his exclamation: "Ahah! I know what it is." We need only contrast this with the miracle of confidence that the artist somehow possesses. He may often search for a word; or he may scrape away and redo a detail in a painting; or try a dozen different pieces of clay on an armature; even make a series of preliminary sketches for a larger work. But these are not attempts to discover what he is trying to do. He knows this already, in some way that is peculiar to an artist; and these are really trial efforts to guide him as to how he might best do it.

Finally, there is one other way in which Donald shows us that he is not an artist at work. This is in his relation to the viewer of his finished production. The artist has a strange bond with his public. He is not a teacher, nor is he engaged in writing a private diary. Whatever the nature of his performance as an artist, from the calculated eccentricities of Dali to the tortured singularities of Joyce, the aim is not to keep something secret from the viewer or reader but to draw him into contemplation of a greater mystery, not to explain to him but to enthrall him and move him. Donald, on the other hand, is quite adept at explaining what it is he has "created," and he will extend the explanation to even greater lengths as soon as he is requested. His relation to the examiner is analogous to his relation to his own work, for he demonstrates in all of his comments that he distinguishes clearly between the real and the imagined. In this respect the artist is again unique, for he would be lost if he ever began to make such a distinction. It is his mission to fuse the real and the imagined, and therefore when he is at work he *is* his work. He has no position from which to make comments about it—as witness the fact that artists are often the poorest critics of their own most deeply felt work. An inquiry, which forms the heart of a clinical test because it helps us to find out the way in which the subject is reflectively related to his own performance, would be blasphemous if applied to the artist.

For all its value, then, the concept of the ambiguous stimulus would seem to be lacking on two counts. First, it would be psychologically inaccurate to apply it to any aspect of the artist's world; it must stand or fall on its own merits as a recognizable part of clinical psychology's underground theory. We have already examined some evidence in this regard as it appears in a test protocol, and to this we may add some propositions concerning the artist himself. In brief, he finds his place, not in an ordinary perceptual world, but at the very boundaries of human experience. The artist transcends and therefore transmutes; he does not arrange disorder or disorderliness into order. The term that most centrally applies to the perceptual field of the artist at work is not ambiguity, but *possibility*. He sees things in their nearly infinite nexus of possibilities, as though a light had suddenly been turned on behind them. The moment of creation has as its truest symbol the blinding flash of inspiration or insight, not the poorly formed or unstructured, the unfamiliar, or the badly seen blob.

Second, and perhaps more significant for our purposes, the concept of the ambiguous stimulus is lacking because it is at best an unknowing version of just the simplistic metaphysics which victimizes the empiricist. While seeming to set up a novel theoretical category which will contain many of the phenomena unique to the clinical disciplines, in effect it represents not much more than an illicit subscribing to the very concept of *un*ambiguity which underlies the doctrine of nonclinical experimentalists. In the conception of the ambiguous, or intentionally neutral, screen upon which the test subject somehow projects his needs, we may see replicated in less than explicit fashion that pseudo-task which the neutral experimenter always presents to his anonymous subjects. His subjects are nameless integers who are manipulated in various complex relations within an impersonally neutral world—and all that the contemporary clinician has added to this is the notion of autochthonous determinants serving to decide the outcome by tipping the balance of forces toward the subject.

For all its value, a clinical science of persons would seem to need more than this. Only if we have some grasp of the world which is given to all of us in our normal, waking activities will we have the basis for understanding the special world that we create in moments of artistic endeavor, insight, decision, and travail. A psychology of ambiguity, in short, finally needs a foundation in a psychology of the norm; and if we should achieve this goal, both the ambiguous and its correlate will fade away.

PART III

SITUATION
AND ENCOUNTER

THE
INTENTIONAL
SUBJECT

Yet now and then, at the sight of my name on a visiting card, or of my face photographed in a group among other faces, or when I see a letter addressed in my hand, or catch the sound of my own voice, I grow shy in the presence of a mysterious Person who is myself, is known by my name, and who apparently does exist. Can it be possible that I am as real as anyone, and that all of us—the cashier and banker at the Bank, the King on his throne—all feel ourselves ghosts and goblins in this authentic world?

—LOGAN PEARSALL SMITH, *All Trivia*

IN THE FIRST VOLUME OF HIS BIOGRAPHY OF FREUD, JONES (1953) describes the historic moment when the clinical concept of resistance was born. Listening to a patient try to express some of her thoughts, Freud noticed that she seemed to be struggling to bring some things to clear expression. It was as if she were a battleground for opposing forces, one set of forces pushing the thought toward expression, the other acting to set up obstacles. Her hesitation, stammering, difficulty, and final inability seemed to him supporting evidence for this way of depicting the event (p. 285). It was out of this observation, and probably many similar ones as well, that Freud developed a set of concepts concerning the psychic apparatus as the ground for the play of opposing forces. The tendency of one part of the apparatus to set up blocks to the operation of some other part seemed to him to warrant the term *resistance*. "An early conclusion about the cause of unconscious resistance was that it must be produced by the same forces which had, in the first place, created the repression" (Thompson, 1950, p. 96).

Of the many changes that took place in the Freudian system during the ensuing years of systematization, one of the most significant was the steadily increasing emphasis on the relationship between patient and therapist as a central aspect of the clinical situation. From Freud's original formulation, which had been couched entirely in terms that referred to psychic phenomena internal to the patient, the focus of theoretical interest gradually shifted toward formulations and concepts that referred to the perception of each other by the two participants. Transference, and later countertransference, came to be seen as the key pair of elements in the therapeutic situation, and the working through of the so-called *transference neurosis* became the goal of the treatment. And as this general shift of interest took place, it carried with it at least some concepts that had been at home in the original formulations, necessarily changing their meaning through the years. This is what happened to the concept of resistance, among others. At first it had been conceived as a way of describing the opposition of one set of forces to another, both sets being within the patient's psychic apparatus. But some years later, resistance came to mean, not a struggle taking place within the patient's psychological economy, but a tug of war between patient and analyst.

The Model of Power

The difference between the two meanings points up not only the change in conceptual emphasis from a system of intrapsychic stresses, checks, and balances to a system of interpersonal tugs and strains, but more significantly, a change in the status of the patient, himself, in the clinical situation. In Freud's earliest formulation the patient moved within a certain range of possible roles: she was at one extreme an interesting, if puzzling, object to be observed sympathetically and judged in tentative and humble fashion; and at the other extreme she was a free agent who played out a struggle of her own while the analyst could only watch, wait, and encourage—perhaps pressing her forehead to aid her "concentration." But within the range bounded by these extremes she maintained a certain dignity, for her role was never prejudged solely in relation to the therapist; she always had a better than even chance to establish for his benefit what role she was going to take in their meeting. By the end of a period of systematic development and reformulation, however, the patient's status in the analytic situation had changed to a significant degree. She now moved within a much more limited range. Both ends of this new range were, and are, bounded by a specific relationship between patient and therapist. This is a relationship that postulates the two acting in opposition to each other. More accurately put, the patient and the therapist are assumed to be set in mutual opposition, not as peers arrayed in a combat decisive for both of them, but as one protagonist holding firm against a second who is irrationally and, in the long run, hopelessly attacking an edifice of truth, stability, and wisdom. The status of the patient, as it is revealed in the half-truth of the joking question, "Why are you resisting me?" is the status of someone who at best tilts futilely at windmills and at worst nibbles at the corner of a great structure. To maintain that the patient, in expressing certain ideas and failing to express others, is playing a role of resistance against the therapist is to say that the patient's role is always limited to one or another variant of irrational opposition to the greater truth, stability, and wisdom of the therapist. The patient is no longer either a fascinating object or a worthy opponent, no longer an agent who is free to work out his destiny in the helpful presence of the analyst, but now a creature cast in a role of resistance to the easy forward progress of insight and change.

This is a far-reaching development; it is, in fact, one that has not yet been fully documented in the critical literature of the clinical professions. It has given rise to some most paradoxical phenomena— for example, that if the patient, on the basis of limited evidence, insists on perceiving the therapist as though the latter were a member of a class about which he has had prior knowledge or feelings, the phenomenon is called *transference;* whereas if the situation is reversed, and the therapist, on the basis of not much more evidence, views his patient as a member of a class about which he has some prior knowledge, the phenomenon is called *diagnosis.* One other phenomenon which has resulted from this clinical development is known as *interpretation.* In order to examine it at closer range, with a view to understanding it in terms of the struggle for status between therapist and patient, we may consider at some length a familiar example from clinical practice.

In the course of a session with a new patient, a novice in therapy— a first-year resident, perhaps, or a beginning trainee in psychology— obtains certain information about the patient's social and sexual relationships over a period of years. The patient reports, with seemingly little ability to arrive at an interpretive generalization about the facts, that he has had few heterosexual contacts in his life and that, in fact, he is not very much interested in girls, although he will go along with the boys to a party if urged by some of his more forceful and outgoing friends. He usually manages to find this kind of male companionship, although he himself is rather retiring and clinging in his relationships to them. He has seldom lived alone, preferring rather to share a small apartment with one or another of his male friends, and for some reason he has always seemed to carry the burden of work required to keep the apartment presentable. He has bought the food, prepared the meals, managed a sort of budget, and seen to it that the place was reasonably neat. Although none of the arrangements for living in this fashion have lasted very long, most of them breaking up in violent quarrels when he accused his roommate of being more interested in having a good time on dates than in keeping the apartment running properly, he has usually managed in short order to embark on a similar arrangement with someone else.

Now let us suppose that the novice in therapy brings this material, gathered in an early session, to his supervisor for their regularly scheduled control session. A review of anamnestic data of this kind easily enough leads the supervisor to entertain certain ideas about the sexual adjustment of the patient in question. Were the supervisor, himself, trained in the theoretical tradition which today dominates the clinical field, he would have little hesitancy in postulating that in the course of these abortive affairs with various roommates the patient was acting out what are commonly called latent or repressed tendencies of a passive homosexual nature. It would seem clear to the supervisor that the patient's womanly relationships to his more active and masculine consorts, as well as his extremes of frustration and anger when they "deserted" him for heterosexual objects, provided clear evidence in favor of this generalization. We would guess that the supervisor will now attempt in the best semidirective fashion to lead his pupil toward grasping this idea and expressing it in his own way. But suppose the novice does not manage to do this. As the supervisory session continues, the teacher's best efforts to have the pupil see the patient in this way come to naught; the student simply fails to organize the relevant data along these lines, although after a while his supervisor is providing him with some rather broad hints to this effect.

I am not using this example to make a point about how to teach someone to be a therapist, but to describe a common situation in which a generalization or mode of understanding is clear to one of the participants in a therapeutic-like situation but apparently not as clear to the other. When these two participants occupy the roles of teacher and student, as they do in the case I am using, there is one gambit still open to the supervisor at this point. He can make an interpretation about the student himself. Stated in its most innocuous form, the interpretation might go like this: "The point that I've been making is about the sexual relationships that your patient maintained, not with women but with men. It seems that you have some difficulty in considering this possibility."

Whether or not this statement, or one like it, ought to be made at this point, or indeed at any particular place in the course of supervision, making it constitutes what is usually called an *interpretation*. The supervisor's point in making the interpretation is a complex one. It includes the proposition that certain things are true about the patient, in addition to the proposition that certain other things are true about the student therapist; the first proposition is evidence of a sort for the latter, though the interpretation itself is more than simply a logical deduction. It is primarily and essentially a way of describing the novice rather than his patient, and of course it is offered for exactly this reason. As a result, it changes the whole focus of interest in the three-way situation among patient, therapist, and supervisor.

An interpretation when it is made in a therapeutic situation is meant to advance the therapy; in a situation in which one is taught to be a therapist, it serves a similar purpose in advancing the teaching. We have now to consider how the interpretation, as one person's way of describing another person, differs from the usual interpersonal description. One answer to this is to ask the purpose of the description, that is, what it accomplishes in the interchange. Some statements are informational; they add to the common store of knowledge or facts. Others express a mood. The interpretation does neither of these. Consideration of it reveals that what it accomplishes is to delineate certain specific aspects of the relationship between the two participants. It refers, not to them, but to the relation between them. It is usually taken for granted that the interpretation rests on some sort of knowable fact or states some sort of provable proposition. But the logic of the situation—for example, the one I have just described—is such that this way of looking at the interpretation cannot be maintained. For the interpretation is clearly offered as a different kind of statement from one of fact. It is not, for example, a statement like the ones I am making in this paragraph. It differs from propositions which constitute the premises or the conclusions of an experimental study. It does not even have the same status as a claim in an argument. Rather, associated with it are certain presumptions about rights, powers, privileges, and status. One presumption, for example, is that the statement is probably true and that the student's denial of it constitutes his resistance to revealing its truth. For this reason the interpretation cannot be considered a proposition susceptible to proof or even amenable to dispassionate examination. This is, in fact, the logical status of most such statements, all of which occupy key positions in the systematic presentation of the teacher's position. His interpretations, though they claim to be related to the facts of the situation and to arise in some demonstrable and logical manner from the data, are more properly understood as summaries of the relative status of teacher and pupil.

Interpretations refer to power, not to information; to status rather than to fact.

We can see this clearly if we consider the result that must follow the teacher's interpretation in the example we are discussing. Suppose the teacher makes the interpretation given above and suppose this interpretation "hits home." This is quite likely since we have all been taught that there are major problems which are suffered in some measure by all of us, and whether this is so or not, we all do certainly suffer from the conviction or the fear that we *do* have these problems. The teacher strongly implies that the student, himself, has a problem concerning repressed homosexual drives, a problem sufficiently demanding to make it difficult for him to handle his patient's similar problem directly and without scotomata.

Hit in this way, the novice may react in many different ways; but whatever he does—laugh it off, become angry, accept the blow—something will have changed in his relationship with his supervisor. A significant part of him will have been captured, so to speak, by the supervisor; it will remain the teacher's property, as a kind of datum which will intrude between them whenever they meet. Each time they see each other, no matter where or when it is, the meeting will, for the novice, be colored by his thought: "He knows this about me which I had to keep hidden even from myself." And it will do no good for the novice to appeal to the possible *factual* status of his teacher's interpretive proposition—that is, whether it is right or wrong, valid or invalid—for to do so would imply that the interpretation was offered as an informative statement in a therapeutically and interpersonally neutral context. To maintain this would imply, in effect, breaking off just that therapeutic relationship between them which, we assume, the novice is interested in continuing for the purpose of his own training and advancement. It is small wonder that the problem of resolving this dilemma and finding a way out of the uncomfortable and distressing situation must become, finally, a matter of major concern to the student (or patient) and then, at last, to the teacher (or therapist). The process of breaking out becomes, of course, one of working through what is called the transference neurosis in the ending phase of dynamically oriented treatment or teaching.

But short of this resolution, which is in the end the only alternative to a complete rupture in his relationship with the teacher, the student must bear the cross of this changed status in regard to his supervisor. At the time it is offered as well as for the rest of their relationship —and unless it is superseded by another, "deeper" interpretation, which usually implies an even broader scope as regards a change in status and power—the interpretation is a way of stating the interpreter's power. It underscores the silent struggle between them and points to a realignment of forces. Initially, the student's acceptance of his position as semipatient in a semitherapeutic relationship is equivalent to his agreement to give up his position as peer and accept the possibility of interpretations that could be denied only on pain of being accused of resistance. In so doing, and in being relegated to a certain status in subsequent meetings, he also agrees, although perhaps quite silently, to the further possibility that their positions of relative power can and will change as a consequence of the "depth" of the teacher's interpretations. Finally, he accedes to the promise, glowing vaguely at the far distant end of the period of training, that if he advances properly, he may in due course achieve that status of equality in which the teacher would no more be able to make interpretations of his behavior than of the behavior of other professional colleagues who are his peers.

In the course of acceding to all of this, the student—or the patient in a similar situation—in a full sense accepts the meaning of interpretation that has been suggested above. Other meanings are quite possible, for the phenomena of resistance and interpretation may be profitably viewed from many aspects; but as key elements in a clinical theory, we suggest that they need to be defined as weapons in an interplay of forces, as tools for achieving interpersonal status in the clinical situation. Their use in this way will help us to spell out some basic propositions concerning status, role, and power.

First of all, it should be clear that power, in its reference to the tension between the subjective and the objective in human existence, need not be synonymous with violence nor even with force. Beerling (1955) has aptly defined power as simply "the possibility to carry out decisions by which reality becomes changed" (p. 215), and he notes that it is restricted to the realm of human relations, since only man can make decisions and carry them out, and that it is always effectuated through resistance. Although our language has such expressions as "brute power" and "drunk with power," both of which point to that kind of aggresiveness which may in fact sometimes accompany the expression of power, we should keep in mind that this is not just one kind of expression of feeling but rather a basic theme in all human relations. In his subtle analysis of love, power, and justice, Tillich (1954) writes:

In any encounter of man with man, power is active, the power of the personal radiation, expressed in language and gestures, in the glance of the eye and the sound of the voice, in face and figure and movement, expressed in what one is personally and what one represents socially. Every encounter, whether friendly or hostile, whether benevolent or indifferent, is in some way, unconsciously or consciously, a struggle of power with power. In this struggle decisions are made continuously about the relative power of being, actualized in all those who are involved in the struggle (p. 87).

These words do not describe a fight but a struggle; for as long as we maintain for each person some right to self-determination, we introduce the possibility, perhaps even the certainty, that the cogent decision will always be made by one person against, as well as with, the other. When it is understood in this way, the element of power in the clinical situation may be discussed openly as a necessary aspect of every meeting. It is perhaps because a narrow view of the concept of power has pre-empted discussions that one so seldom finds a straight-forward evaluation of psychotherapy from this standpoint. A serious paper by a political scientist (Hacker, 1956) and a witty essay by a psychologist (Haley, 1958) are rare and welcome exceptions.

We have said that there is a set of conceptions concerning status and role which comprise an unexpressed current theory of clinical relationships. In our day, the question that follows immediately on even the suggestion of a theory is: what is the model which describes the structure postulated by the theory? For the model serves to bring out into the arena of public discussion those matters which, like a person's intimate biological functions, are taken for granted but rarely mentioned. A consensually adapted vocabulary for dealing with them has never been developed. They lie, therefore, just over the ever-present horizon of sociality, emphatic in their influence if not in their mode of expression.

We may note here that it is by no means unusual for a matter to be apparently beyond the ken of a person even as he seems to act in reference to it. It would seem to be a basic characteristic of human cognition that a person takes a stand so as to grasp that order which is his perceptual field, and that in taking his stand he marks out boundaries, so to speak, which define the absolute limits of his dealings. The nature of the limit, we may note, is that it bounds but is not contained within; it is just at the outer limit of, but is never a part of. Because the bounded area is thus contained and defined, as it were, by the nature of the limit, it is always possible for the person to act in directed and organized fashion toward just that which is clearly beyond his ken. In this way, we may understand how a model may be implicit but still directive; and we may see that on occasion it may be made explicit, and that this, when it happens, may be an answer to a question that has not even been asked.

How, then, shall we proceed to examine the model which, we have supposed, implicitly guides much of today's clinical thinking? Questions that are not asked refer to the outer limits of a way of thinking. The kind of model that properly describes a clinical situation, especially if it is marked by different roles that are distinguished in terms of status and power, cannot be discussed within a framework of acceptance of the situation itself. Discussion of the model requires that we step beyond the conception as it is offered by proponents of this clinical situation. We might proceed in the simplest way by denying the usefulness or the reasonableness of such an interpersonal arrangement as depicted in the usual clinical situation—but our purpose at this juncture is not to criticize but to examine. How may we reach beyond the limits of the conventionally accepted clinical situation without embarking on an extensive criticism of it? The most obvious way open to us is to consider it in relation to the historical development of some of its guiding ideas. In this way we will be able to grasp the model with some degree of completeness, and perhaps can examine it in its totality.

As scientists, we are part of the continuing stream of scientific development and progress. This is as true today as it was in the time of

Galileo or Freud. Thus, in the broadest terms it is possible to place Freud's whole system within the boundaries of a set of ideas which dominated European scientific thought during the latter half of the nineteenth century. His portrait of the human personality was, in its structural aspects, essentially a boiler system with a complicated arrangement of valves and pipes to account for the misadventures (or "vicissitudes") of the energy of the sexual instinct. It mirrored quite neatly that grand invention, the steam locomotive, which was the proudest technological achievement of the age as well as the foundation of its industrial growth. Freud's great insights into the subtleties and interconnections of the presumed parts of the human psyche equalled in grandeur and consonance Josiah Gibbs' conceptions in the field of thermodynamics. Both men were supreme—one almost says necessary—products and leaders of an age, just like Newton, who, in his thinking, summed up and perfectly expressed the guiding conceptions of an earlier century by portraying the universe as a grand clock which repeated on a celestial scale the great and basic technological achievement of his own age, the navigator's chronometer. In our time, the steam engine has been replaced by the electronic brain, and associationism by cybernetics and information theory, but it is a revealing fact that the model implicit to present-day clinical theory has not kept pace with this significant change. The model is, in fact, one to which Freud subscribed—but in this one respect he produced nothing in the way of an innovation. Rather, he based his implicit conception of the clinical situation on a model handed down to him by a former age of science. His model, as is ours, was Newton's.

The Newtonian model to which I refer here is best expressed by its greatest exemplar, the structure of the solar system. In the scheme of Newton's mechanics the solar system was conceived as made up of a number of nearly spherical bodies which were separated by empty space. The bodies moved in mathematically regular patterns according to certain rules prescribed in the Newtonian scheme. The bodies were, however, not independent of each other but rather exerted pushes and pulls on each other across the vast distances of intervening space. The nature of the force thus exerted was hardly guessed at, but according to the model it was perfectly analogous to the action of a

magnet, from which forces of attraction and repulsion were also conceived to issue and to affect bodies at a distance from it.

This sounds familiar to us, for most of us were brought up on some
such conception of the structure and activity of the solar system.
It is perhaps because of this familiarity that we find no difficulty in
accepting as a matter of common sense a model of the clinical situation
which contains very much the same constituent parts. The psychodynamic model of the clinical situation, therefore, has our own
common sense to appeal to as support; it sounds correct because it
appears to us, at least at first glance, as inherently plausible. In this
conception the planets of the solar system are replaced by the participants in the clinical interaction, and they turn out to retain to a
surprising degree the characteristics of the spheroid bodies for which
they substitute. They are restricted to a certain range of acts, the
pattern of their activity arising as a function of certain intrinsic
characteristics that we sum up as individual role and status. But the
clinical participants are no more independent of each other than are
the observably separate bodies of a solar system. Forces issue from
each and affect the other, forces which go by the names of *emotions* and
defenses. One set of forces, for example, has to do with a kind of
action and reaction which takes place at the expense of one of the
participants—although a conception such as "at the expense of,"
with its connotation of value, dignity, and personal experience, strikes
a strange note in this model. This set of forces relates to what is
termed an aggressive action by one person against the other. It may
produce in reaction a retaliatory movement of aggression, in which
case the force issuing from the reactor is called *hostility;* or else there
may arise a situation known as *frustration,* in which the push of one
person against the other is somehow blocked. An elaborate, specious,
and ingenious theoretical scheme has been developed to account for
many of the less pleasing aspects of interpersonal contacts which, in
the terms of this model, are seen as requiring explanation. The actions
and reactions of the parts of this miniature solar system, as they move
in their patterns around each other but within the space of movement
prescribed by the limits of the situation, are strikingly similar to the
observed orbits of the larger planetary bodies after which they are
modeled. Although no general mathematical statement of the smaller

situation has as yet been offered which is comparable with Newton's Laws of Motion, the broad scheme of psychodynamics (since that term is usually used to refer to a psychoanalytically influenced personality system) is usually offered as at least a stopgap, pending a more precise calculus of interpersonal push and pull.

We should bear in mind that this model, like any other conception, can be sensibly maintained only when we take a certain position in respect to its contents. Consider first the position, or vantage point, that was required before the Newtonian model of the solar system made sense to thinkers in Newton's own time. There was required a historic step forward in which the scientific mind was freed from pre-Copernican notions about the relationships of the heavenly bodies. As long as scientists held to the belief that the earth was the center of the solar system, it was hardly possible to conceive of a set of bodies, of which the earth was merely one representative member, obeying a complex of mathematical principles. The Newtonian scheme was applicable only to a solar system as it might be viewed by an observer who stood outside it, perhaps on some distant star; the scheme could never be imagined, much less utilized in science, by an observer whose position was on a planet which had been postulated as the unique center and origin of the rest of the solar system. Man had to step away from himself and assume some independent and external position—a vantage point is the term we are using—in order to make sense of the Newtonian model. And this is precisely the vantage point which, I propose, is also required in order to maintain the Newtonian model's applicability to the clinical situation. The participants or interactors in the situation must be viewed from the position of an observer who is external to and independent of both of them. He must be a completely nonparticipant observer; and by this we mean, not simply that the particular observer who talks about any specific situation must stay out of it while describing it, but in general that the clinical participants must be described just as though the observer were not a person at all. The hypothetical witness must be the ideal of scientific theory: the generalized observer who has shown up so many times before in our discussion. Only to this observer—and never to a human observer who retains a shred of the possibility of mutual interaction with the participants—can the interactors ever be discrete bodies which simply move in relation to each other, pass through patterns of movement, and exert forces on and toward each other. As I have emphasized before, this is not a practical but a methodological issue. The very use of the model at all calls for the generalized observer; the methodological requirement of the New-tonian clinical situation requires that someone occupy a vantage point perfectly analogous to the out-in-space position of the hypothetical observer of a Newtonian solar system.

This generalized, nonhuman observer cannot ever attain to data that concern human beings in a social *situation;* at most he can arrive at data that concern objects in a homogeneous, isotropic *space.* But for none of us, as long as we are human observers, do other human beings actually exist and move in a space of this sort. They do not appear to us as equivalent and interchangeable objects in a space that seems the same no matter where one stands. For the space from me to you is outward; whereas the space from you to him is out-there. You and he are over against each other in space, yet both of you are opposite to me. A look, a throw, or a move from me to you is in no way the same as a look, a throw, a move from you to me; it is not the same either to you or to me, so long as each of us apprehends the event as persons in a meeting with other persons; yet it would be the same if we were entities in space as viewed by the generalized Newtonian observer. The distinction between these two kinds of data, Newtonian and truly social, is a transitive and reversible distinction: it works both ways. The generalized observer cannot ever observe a truly human event, cannot ever apprehend the social phenomenon in the clinical situation; and the human observer, or the scientist whose data reside in human events, will not grasp the clinical situation as the planetary circling of bodies in Euclidean relationship to each other in a neutral space.

We may ask, as perhaps participants in a clinical interaction often do, whether there is an alternative to be found to this model and to the uses of power which sustain it. As it turns out, we must search in an unlikely place to find an expression of a sentiment in which power is absent. One sociologist who essayed a tentative trial (Foote, 1953) discovered that he could find hardly a colleague who would treat his subject with the seriousness that it merited—for his topic was love. Suttie (1948) treads in similarly dangerous territory in describing the situation when mother and baby meet:

. . . there are . . . moments of reunion or at-one-ment in which interaction is in no way competitive. In these moments there is no question of a "balance of trade" of benefits conferred or obligations incurred. It is not even "more blessed to give than to receive," for every gift is in fact a gain; every transaction liquidates itself immediately; the baby is solvent and there is literally no occasion for anxiety. Power at this moment is as meaningless as credits and debits. There is no criticism, so that "goodness" and "badness" are nonexistent. This is the age (or the "moment") of innocence (p. 50).

Here indeed is a situation in which each of the participants is suspended, as it were, beyond striving, beyond status, beyond goals and competition for goals, and beyond the use of power. It is a naked and open encounter. As we can see, the essence of a love situation must be full acceptance, in the same way that the mother accepts the baby— all of him, every moment and detail and aspect of him, every act and smell, fully and unquestioningly accepted with no thought of ruling out any part or of setting up distinctions; in the same way, the growing baby accepts and embraces the world, seeking out everything in his grasp, rejecting none of it, fully and unquestioningly accepting it just because it is there. As the infant begins his life bathed in the love of all others who matter to his development, so, by the very transitive nature of all genuine human phenomena, he begins his life loving the world which loves him. As we grow, we cannot maintain this; and in our reflective moments, whenever we consider our past, our transient present, and our unknown but knowable future, we are aware (perhaps nostalgically) that such a state of bliss would finally smother all our strivings. We must learn to live beyond the comforting sphere of love; we must find and then transcend our own limits; and we must face up to finality and fixedness in ourselves, from the thingness of our settled characteristics to the certainty of our mortality. Our aim, in the end, must be, not to recapture a primordial state of full and loving acceptance, but to share with each other person the risk involved in our participant and unfulfilled striving toward love. Side by side with this striving are a constant set of companions to mock our efforts, the immutable fact of status, the inevitability of prejudice, and the possibility of assumption of power. The choices in place of love are two, hate and power. We thread a narrow and dangerous path in the clinical situation; anxiety is the ever-present hint and beginning of alternative paths to hate and prejudice and power.

We can see these alternatives most clearly in the matter of the risk attendant upon change and in the judgments that one member passes upon the other. A judgment necessarily involves a statement of status and an expression of power. In the judgment the person immobilizes the other and fixes him in some terms that have meaning beyond the moment. The person says, "You are immature," and in this statement he wraps up the other person in a cloth which may now be handed from one to another; the object of the judgment is then somehow less than the mode in which he is judged; he is a part of this mode, indeed a specific example of it rather than beyond it as he must be if he is to retain his full individuality. To the judger prior to his act of judging, the other person does not appear as a challenge nor as a partner in sharing the risks involved in changing together. Rather, he seems, as Rogers (1951) puts it, like a puzzle; and in dealing with a puzzle one may be defeated or baffled, but never involved in the risk and uncertainty of changing oneself. The expression of power is always apparent in a situation in which only one of the two participants runs the risk of change. In our science we have constructed and then accepted a kind of clinical situation in which the encounter is dominated by considerations of status and power; in which change can take place in only one of the two who meet, and then only by permission of the other; in which judging is reserved as a function of the one who wields the power; in which the discovery of truth flows in one direction only; in which similar expressions by the other person are defined as resistance to clinical progress or as transference or as irrational manifestations of unresolved issues out of the past. In this "hierarchical structure," as Cole (1953) accurately describes the testing situation, the chief weapon is interpretation, the chief aim that kind of formalized prejudice we call diagnosis, the chief avenue the use of power rather than love. As the limited experimental evidence also goes to show, the characteristics of interchanges founded on elements of power are unmistakable. Concluding an elaborate study of cohesiveness in two-person groups brought together under different conditions, Back (1951) concludes: "If cohesiveness was based on group prestige, members tried to risk as little as possible to endanger their status. They acted cautiously, concentrated on their own actions, and adjusted to their partners as the social environment. One partner would easily assume a dominant role, and the submissive member was influenced more, without their actually trying to establish this relationship" (p. 23).

A relationship which is expressed only along the dimension of power, whether conceived by one or both of the participants or by a determining outside observer, will maintain a situation which is best described by a Newtonian model. It will serve to rule out the data of social perception on the part of the observer, for he will see the target participants as equivalent or comparable objects rather than as humans and brothers to himself; just as, conversely, the true meeting between two persons is unique in that no observer can ever be an independent third party to it. It will also serve to rule out the commitment to love on the part of either or both of the participants, for they will be engaged in limiting each other rather than providing opportunities for each other, and each will see a risk to himself as a threat to his status rather than as a necessary challenge to his participation or a chance to learn about and declare his own limits. As unselfishness is the arena for the practice of love, so competitiveness is the natural expression of the commitment to power.

All of this may seem a far cry from matters of immediate concern to the clinician who tests, diagnoses, makes interpretations, or practices psychotherapy. It will seem particularly far-fetched in the face of the clear fact that the two persons in the clinical situation, though both may loosely be called participants, assuredly differ in regard to their purposes, their standing, their problems, their psychological processes, and, most importantly, their reasons and needs for being there at the same time. Indeed, it may even appear that in arguing against such differences I have been surreptitiously advocating a kind of interpersonal relativism—which is counterpart to that occupational disease of the contemporary behavioral scientist, an-ethics-which-is-no-ethics. It will be objected that the mere fact of a difference need not always lead to the commitment to power, as witness the inherent distinctions among participants in a democratic process as well as between partners in the act of love itself. To this objection may be added, also, the point that perception of differences is prerequisite to preferences, values, and probably for any action at all. A situation without differences, like a world without variability, is grey and congealed.

There has been no intention in these pages to deny such basic considerations. The discussion of the effects of power in the clinical relationship has been meant, rather, as a counter-balance to a current conspiracy of silence and sweet smiles, and as an antidote to the claims of the status-ridden wing of the clinical profession. Now that this case has been made, however, we may conclude by considering the matter of power and love under the aspect of a clinical philosophy rather than as a theme in clinical practice. Our reference in the present chapter to the bipolar relation between power and love has to be understood in its own way: it is not a continuum which provides an independent definition of man. For we insist that a philosophy befitting man and his condition has to arise within and remain inside that condition, and therefore cannot rest on a supposed dichotomy which surpasses man. All that we will be able to do from the vantage point of a philosophy and science of man is to discover some duo-tensional simultaneity in human action; when we think that we have reduced man to his "ultimates," we will find instead that we have only found some face and counter-face, which together pulse beneath a major sphere of possibilities.

If, then, power and love are conceived as two limits of the theme of action-with-others, we may say that each one "picks up" part of the other: power picks up and feels at home with the necessary inequality that resides in the loving and sharing encounter; and love picks up and uses the "care" that power requires in order not to destroy completely the other on whom it feeds. Neither pole is ever pure; each is a tension within the other. And this, we may now see, is the root of the irony that permeates these issues. Inequality, the most basic of human necessities, is what will finally defeat every interpersonal situation. If I am merely "one with" what I apprehend, I do not grasp it at all but only live it; and therefore every cognition has its proper place on a continuum of relative inequality, from the sharply defined and distinctly outlined concept to the pain that overwhelms one. Moreover, for one person to deal with another they must be unequal. They cannot both talk at the same time; one must listen, take in, and receive, while the other gives, controls, holds, and directs. And this is true even of reflectiveness—for if I parrot another person, he gains no vantage point from which to build a reflective understanding of himself as a historical being. As the world is known through its resistance, so the other person is known by his being different and thus unequal. But in the end there is no guarantee that the resistance will be broken through or the differences dissolved in a common ecstasy. The world was not fashioned for any one of us. Therapist and patient are, in Jasper's words, "companions of destiny."

The Subject as Somnambulist

In the preceding pages which deal with the concrete clinical situation, the position I have advanced is that both members—therapist and client, or experimenter and subject, or tester and testee—are partners to it and therefore related indissolubly to each other. If either gives up the relationship, he thereby leaves the situation, and what will be left of it will be understood in some partial and ineffective way by the one who remains. If it is the patient or test subject who chooses to stay out of the situation, the psychologist will have to depend on inference and construction; lacking immediate information, he cannot say anything beyond what his experience has already gained for him from previous cases. On the other hand, if his own attitude and outlook effectively drives his subject out of the situation which they ought to share—for example, if he is incapable of seeing and meeting the subject as a person with whom he shares the session— he will arrive at his conclusions without benefit of the concrete data and deductively reach that kind of pigeonholing we call a diagnosis. The subject who is left in a situation from which the therapist or tester has abdicated will also be victimized in his understanding of what goes on in it. He will cast the session in the mold which best satisfies his needs or causes him least pain, and, regardless of the express purposes as stated formally by the psychologist, he will act as seems to him most appropriate to that partial or mistaken construction. Or, if he is completely hemmed in by the tester's stated demands, he will restrict himself to just these and thereby refrain from offering even the limited amount of useful information he might be prepared to give.

Both members of the clinical situation belong in it—and a consequence which follows immediately is that both of them, being persons, will act as though things make sense to them. This is a fundamental thesis of any psychology which claims to deal with clinical settings. But because it seems so simple, it is likely to be overlooked or taken at face value, in spite of evidence from all sides that, considered seriously, it provides our best starting point. Let us consider a problem which has been well studied experimentally, and therefore seems remote from the clinical setting—the question of suggestion and conformity. A discussion of it should lead us directly into the next major issue we will examine in this chapter.

There has been for many years in psychology a vaguely stated but pervasively influential doctrine to the effect that in his social interactions man is, as the French sociologist Tarde once put it, essentially a somnambulist. Though he may vehemently and foolishly deny it, parading his pride as though this substituted for reason, the doctrine states that he can be swayed by demagogues, emotionally aroused to perform irrational acts, and influenced by the stress of almost any chance circumstance. Raised to anger, he will say things that calmer men might regret; in the company of his equally foolish peers he will often generate a spurious courage and be carried to improbable heights of valor or else be swept by the hysteria of a crowd to join in unwonted acts of cruelty and violence; because of a moment of excitement he will become a totally untrustworthy witness; and when put under the pressure of opinion by an authority or the consensus of a group, he will go along with what is actually an arbitrary and baseless judgment. He may seem to conduct his everyday affairs in reasonable fashion, but in truth he waits to be swayed by every vagrant breeze of fashion, no matter how foolish or finagled it may really be.

This is the picture we are supposed to have of that praised, bedeviled, and harried creature, the common man—that is, if we take any stock in a string of experiments on testimony, on suggestibility, and on conformity. Now, the very structure of an experiment, particularly when the subjects comprise a large group whose individual members are necessarily reduced to the anonymity of integers adding up to a group average, sometimes makes it rather easy to effect a demonstration of these propositions. It is vastly more difficult—and given the structure of the psychological experiment, incomparably more demanding on the experimenter and his subjects—to develop a coherent proof of just the opposite, that most people will, if given half a chance, look at things as though they made sense and try to act coherently toward them.

One social psychologist who has studied the problem of suggestion and conformity in this light is Asch (1940); more recently Pastore and Horowitz (1955) have refined the method and made it even more evident that if one makes it possible for the subject to indicate his intent, his actions will be revealed as sensible rather than swayed and as intelligible rather than arbitrary. Summarizing studies by himself and others, Asch remarks that

. . . one must conclude that the description of socialization in terms of the blind adoption of beliefs and practices is both schematic and misleading. Generally practices are adopted on the basis of reasons that have the appearance of validity. Often there is a close coincidence between the face significance of action and the social evaluation it receives. Other beliefs come in the context of a relation of trust that has proven largely valid, a condition that paves the way for confidence in assertions and rules one cannot adequately comprehend. . . . We shall not make significant progress as long as we fail to see that from the standpoint of an individual who is capable of understanding others and entering into a common purpose with them social life is never mere conformity or imitation. . . . Viewed in wider perspective the idea of suggestion and the studies grouped around it touch upon a problem of deep importance. They refer to situations in which individuals are barred from relating themselves independently to data and are misled by the reliance they place in others (1952, pp. 415–416).

Elaborate provisions have at times been arranged in order to investigate the processes in question here. This itself should make us suspect that the results may not be as psychologically inevitable as some would have us believe, not if their production demands complex and artificial arrangements. One of the most intriguing of these experiments, and in its results most convincing, has been reported by

Crutchfield (1955), who used an elaborate arrangement of booths and control panels to present a spurious consensus to each subject. He tested fifty professional men, five at a time, on a series of tasks, interpolating among these a total of twenty-one critical instances in which, when ostensibly responding fifth in order, a subject was required to decide for or against the consensus planted by the experimenter. The "correct" responses had been obtained in advance from an equivalent group of forty subjects who had made their judgments without use of the conformity and panels. The results from the experimental subjects appeared to provide striking evidence for the extent to which even this select group of adults would conform to what seemed to them a unanimous group opinion. Between 30 and 79 per cent became conformists on at least one occasion. In general, "significant group pressure effects" were demonstrated on nineteen of the twenty-one critical items, at times even in the direction of an "arbitrarily chosen and irrational answer." Referring to those items having to do with views on pressing national issues, Crutchfield remarks in conclusion, "I think that no one would wish to deny that here we have evidence of the operation of powerful conformity influences in the expression of opinion on matters of critical social controversy" (p. 197).

My purpose in using this ingenious and plausible study as an example is not to argue, as Asch (1952) has done so well, that the results in such studies run counter to those obtained when subjects are allowed to be rational and not misled or constrained; nor to suggest, as a number of writers have recently pointed out in surveying this area, that the study fails to distinguish between naïve, rigid, "sincere" conformers and insincere, opportunistic, "public" ones— the hallmark being the extent to which the latter temper their answers to what the experimenter might think of them; nor, finally, to point out the disastrous human consequences for a social science which is based on the premise that intelligent adults are often vacillating or spineless in their most significant social judgments. Rather, I mean to use this example as a continuation of the discussion in the preceding chapters, where we considered a phenomenon that is all too rarely described in the contemporary literature of the clinical and social sciences: the phenomenon most simply stated as a meeting between two persons who together share their common situation. From the vantage point that either of the participants may assume, the situation has in large measure the character of beginning rather than ending; this was the thesis of an earlier chapter. From the scientist's standpoint, of course, other kinds of conceptions and propositions may be required to systematize his understanding. The studies of conformity, and particularly the excellent one by Crutchfield, provide us at this point with an opportunity to present the issues in simplest form.

It strikes us immediately, on examining the data of such conformity studies, that they tend to proceed in a vacuum. Since a vacuum, like any other spot of emptiness, will draw into itself whatever happens to lie in its vicinity, all sorts of odd and arbitrary ideas are sucked toward its theoretical center. We find that, as we noted above, otherwise responsible adults are assumed to sway with every transient influence—a proposition which is not only palpable nonsense but assumes as well that only the experimenter (and, of course, the readers of his published work) have the fortitude to withstand such powerful influences. If this judgment seems harsh, let the reader ask himself how many of his opinions on "matters of critical social controversy" he would change on discovering that four other test subjects disagreed with him. If the conclusions which seem inescapable from the data are themselves nonsensical, we are forced to conclude that the method by which these unexceptionable results are drawn must contain a fatal flaw. It will not be enough to remark that Crutchfield's experimental arrangement was quite complicated and artificial—although we should note in passing that the device by which he produced his results was, for perhaps very good reasons of policy, in no way like the situation arranged by Asch (1952, Chap. 16), who simply had a group of ten subjects, nine of whom were confederates of the experimenter, announce aloud their answers to a series of problems. Nor will our purpose be fully served by the general thesis that the experimental situation is by its nature always a very special one from which it may sometimes be dangerous to draw conclusions about nonexperimental behavior. Instead, we have to consider at this point the nature of the experiment as one form of a meeting between two persons. In what way does an experimenter like Crutchfield make of it a genuine encounter, and in what way does he so change the structure of the situation that the resultant data lead us in a new and different direction?

One of the ways in which Crutchfield extended the significance of his results on group pressure and conformity was to compare subjects' reactions to this kind of situation with the responses on conventional paper-and-pencil tests of authoritarianism and other personality traits. He found, as one might suppose, that those persons who tended to conform unthinkingly to group pressures also revealed themselves by other measures as compliant, moralistic, naïve, rigid, and so forth. The constellation is by now familiar to every student of the field. Now, there are two widely disparate ways of looking at these findings. Suppose that a subject who has already indicated that he will go along with the group on decisions as significant as those concerning his civil liberties or as transiently pressing as those concerning the relative sizes of circles, now answers affirmatively to the test item, "I am very careful about my manner of dress." One approach to understanding this correlation is to assume that the subject has in the latter response revealed how cautious he is. In this sort of approach the experimenter—at this point an elaborate metaphor is called for in order to explore the issues—acts just as though he had somehow managed to pry off the top of the subject's cranium, peer inside, and see a little bit of an entity called caution. The relationship subsisting between experimenter and subject, he claims, is in no way different from that between chemist and compound; in both cases the scientist inserts the proper probe and, when it wiggles or buzzes, judges that the expected entity is indeed present. Nor is the structure of the situation changed by virtue of the psychological experimenter's interest (as in this case) in what is called the subject's introspection rather than his externally observable behavior—that is, in the subject's report about himself rather than about another person's or a mechanical instrument's account of him. Regardless of the particular technique utilized or the specific content of the test items, the approach is one in which a device is deemed useful to the extent that it forces the revelation of some part or entity which is assumed to reside intradermally in that sack of drives and processes we call a person.

There is an alternative approach. Its basic term is *intentionality,* which refers to a phenomenon characteristic of every human act that we can apprehend and understand: the meaning of the act is to change the world as the world appears to the person who is acting, and therefore the act is so organized and carried out, within the necessary limits of person and circumstance, as to count and finally to be accountable. An act is directed toward whatever appears to the person as its appropriate object. When the person concerned is a subject in an experiment, his act is directed, as it inevitably must be, at least in part toward the experimenter himself. By this logic, the person who says of himself on a test item that he is very careful about his dress is not simply revealing his caution, though in the terms of a simplified scheme this may indeed be so. He is also, and more fundamentally, presenting himself in a certain light and as a certain kind of person, and he is making this presentation to himself as well as to the experimenter as representative of the world of relevant people. He is not so much *revealing* as *expressing;* and between these two terms, and the conceptions that they label, lies a gap which it is our task in this book to begin to bridge. Therefore, what a person reveals—a question which is supposed to be answered in some part each time that we pry off the lid of the cranial box and pull out a bit of its essential contents—and the corollary question of how this revelation may best be produced and consensually verified, are first steps on a trail which is without a useful end for a clinical science.

Again, there is an alternative. We will be able to discover what the person is, in this sense, only by approaching him to have some dealing with him. When we do so, what he does will inevitably be done toward us as well; so that what he is becomes inextricably tied to what we are, which must also be expressed through what we ourselves do. There is no escape from this completely human arena. Fortunately, the conformity studies, because they present in almost startling clarity the best and the worst of an approach which in these respects effectively dehumanizes the subject, provide us with a way of stating the basic alternatives. Let us now carry the argument a step forward by reviewing a closely allied and equally pertinent problem area, that of *malingering.*

Two Men in the Examiner's Seat

The problem involved in subjects' attempts to "fake" or otherwise deliberately distort their responses, usually to a paper-and-pencil type of test, has been studied for almost as long as there have been such test instruments. A definable concept of malingering took shape as such only during a period of intense activity in World War II. However, very soon after World War I, during the first decade of the development of personnel and aptitude tests, Laird (1925) first considered the question of how one can trust the results obtained. To prevent the subject from deliberately distorting his results, and to increase the trustworthiness of his data, he carefully refrained from phrasing a test question in a way that might "smack of goodness or badness." Further, in an excess of constructional naïveté, he supposed that the scores he did obtain would in any case be "self-correcting for these tendencies inasmuch as they have been determined by actual distributions and not by any arbitrary criteria" (p. 129). The idea that deceivers on tests will be automatically canceled out by the pure in heart did not, fortunately, gain general acceptance. Rather, as Steinmetz (1932) showed a few years later, some persons are simply able to answer a self-report type of inventory in any one of a number of ways. In an experiment which has since been repeated dozens of times, he had students try to reproduce the probable responses of a "teacher-administrator" to the Strong Vocational Interest Blank; and just as Strong himself had once demonstrated that some students could fake an interest in engineering, so Steinmetz discovered that those who have no "initial predilection" for an occupation but simply a kind of "social insight" are able to slant their results as needed.

From the very first, then, the question of malingering was studied in terms of the problem of whether answers to a structured test could be successfully faked. Initially, it appeared that the answer was yes. But then the influence of clinicians began to be felt, and their special methods swung the balance back toward the tester. In an intriguing report by Willoughby and Morse (1936) on the spontaneous comments made to an individually presented questionnaire, there was noted "a consistent warping of responses in the direction of least subjective pain" (p. 575). "A substantial minority of subjects," they remarked, "will misinterpret or rationalize their response to almost any item" (p. 574)—a finding which suggests that clinically sophisticated testers were now in a position to detect, and therefore defeat, subjects' attempts to fake their protocols. Evidence gathered by Bender (1938), in regard to subjects' attempts to simulate either mental deficiency or a Ganser syndrome, suggested quite strongly that such attempts with the Bender-Gestalt plates were easily caught. Similarly, Fosberg argued on the basis of two protocols (1938), and later (1941) with thirty-seven subjects, that the Rorschach cannot be successfully faked so as to present either a spuriously good or a spuriously bad impression. He attributed this result, as had Bender, to the fact that naïve subjects simply do not know what constitutes a specific kind of performance and therefore either respond inconsistently or else adopt incorrect criteria. Benton (1945), using the Rorschach with soldiers suspected of malingering physical defects, came to similar conclusions, as did William A. Hunt (1946); their subjects gave few responses, marked by slowed reaction times, a high rate of rejection, and even failure to perceive some Populars. Their general attitude was one of "perplexity . . . pained compliance" (Benton, p. 94), of "an insecure individual proceeding in a strange situation with great caution" (Hunt, p. 253). On the basis of this evidence, Gough (1947) felt that the clinician was warranted in claiming the ability to pick out the protocols of malingerers on the Rorschach and even on the MMPI.

Or could they? If the instrument was a sentence completion test, as Meltzoff (1951) showed, subjects could indeed "manipulate" their responses so as to appear either well or badly adjusted. Similarly, when TAT subjects were asked to make either a "best possible" or a "worst possible" impression on the examiner, they were quite successful in regard to the latter (Weisskopf and Dieppa, 1951).

The whole situation reminds one of the struggle which is raged back and forth between safecrackers and manufacturers of vaults. In this endless battle of diametrically opposed forces, the advantage shifts first to one side and then to another as new techniques are developed to overcome an advantage gained or a former method defeated. Thus, the rapid development of mechanized mass testing procedures, especially under the impact of wartime needs, soon made it necessary to develop built-in safeguards against faking. Large-scale testing opened the way to wholesale faking; and this in turn required automatic machinery for its detection. The general device by which the latter was to be accomplished had already been offered by Ruch (1942), who proposed an empirically derived key: each item on a test was to be given a weight based on how easily it could be faked; the weight in turn was determined by data concerning how frequently it was answered in a specific way by those who are able to fake successfully.

Apparently working independently, Goldstein (1945), who was faced with the concrete problem of detecting those who feigned "mental inaptitude" in order to avoid military service, now rediscovered the same method. His key was based on the materials in the Army Visual Classification Test but, as he noted, "the methods which were originated in its construction are applicable to psychological tests in general" (p. 104). He found, as had Hunt and Older (1943) in related work on military personnel who pretended to be feebleminded, that it was not too difficult to construct a useful key; for the malingerers failed too many easy items, passed some quite difficult items, and showed a suspicious inconsistency, or "internal scatter."

But the automatized approach, simple and plausible though it appeared at first sight, was fraught with unexpected difficulties, as indeed are most clinical areas when they are broached by the unwary experimentalist. Consider the obstacles which Goldstein had to surmount. It seemed to him, as it ought to seem to most reasoning persons, that there should be no trouble in trapping naïve subjects by the proper selection of test items, for they would not be likely to know how the items ought to be answered at each level of intellectual functioning. "An accurate subjective appraisal of the ease or difficulty of test items is a hazardous task even for test experts, certainly so for inexperienced selectees" (p. 105 n.). But the troubles now mount when, in order to develop a key, the experimentalist asks subjects to pretend for him that they are feebleminded. Since his key is not meant to detect mental deficiency—for the test itself, presumably, will do that—but rather the act of malingering, or simulated mental deficiency, he must ask his subjects to pretend to fail but to

do it in such a way that the examiner cannot catch on to their simulation. As might be expected, "the concept of simulated malingering
is difficult to grasp," so that on the first attempt "very few appeared
to have comprehended the task" (p. 112). Some subjects tried to pass
the test; some of these, by a strange twist of methodological irony,
were actually unsuccessful in their attempts to fail by passing and did
in fact fail, thereby raising the question of whether they should
receive passing credit for failing or simply be failed for failing to pass
as failures; and still others adopted the straightforward stratagem
of failing all the items. After a number of efforts, repeating the testing session with his subjects and explaining to them what he was
after, Goldstein was finally able to secure a sample of "good" malingerers. It should be added that although these malingerers were good
in the sense that they were successful, they were not good in the
sense of *true* (one hesitates to use the term *authentic*), for theirs
was a simulated or false malingering—a lie about a lie, so to speak.

The distinction is apparent to Goldstein too, for he takes up the
question of a possible difference in motive between "true" and experimental malingerers. His conclusion, that they do differ in regard to
motivation but that the difference could not change their mode of
performance, rests on the self-evident proposition that the two kinds
of malingerers are similar in that they both want to "fail-in-such-a-
fashion-as-to-deceive" (p. 116). A few years later, in the course
of a study along similar lines, Pollaczek (1952) argues in the same
fashion that "there is little reason to suspect that any other personality
or intellectual factors are operating in any important fashion to distinguish the behavior of the two types of malingerers" (p. 76). Here,
we see, is the first fruit of a program of test construction in which a
completely empirical approach substitutes for coming to terms with
the subject as a person. All that counts, apparently, is a final rating,
no matter how the subject has arrived at it. Therefore nothing odd is
seen in the claim that the man whose aim is to defeat the examiner
does not differ from the man who, after special coaching from the
examiner, has finally learned how to please him.

Such cavalier dismissal of simple common sense requires a theory
of some impressiveness to sustain and perhaps dignify it. This was
very soon furnished in an important paper by Meehl (1945), in which

he supplied the theoretical substructure while seeming only to deal with a criticism that had often been raised against the structured test. The criticism was to the effect that asking a person about himself was simply to assume too much; the procedure failed to take into account the subject's ignorance, his bias, and his repressive and suppressive tendencies. Meehl's answer was that one has to take the "verbal behavior" which is a subject's test protocol as data which are interesting and valuable in their own right; and following this, one goes on to discover empirically their "nontest correlates." The twin problems of the individual's accuracy or honesty and of the differences in individual interpretations of test items are therefore bypassed at one stroke. "It has not been sufficiently recognized by critics of structured personality tests that what a man says about himself may be a highly significant fact about him even though we do not entertain with any confidence the hypothesis that what he says would agree with what complete knowledge of him would lead others to say of him" (p. 299). The responses may always be "theoretically mysterious," but there need not for this reason be any limit to their usefulness.

By virtue of an approach in which the subject is always handled at this methodological distance, all the while claiming to deal fully and courageously with even the most "mysterious" of test data, Meehl both states the issue and fails to answer it. True, he lends strong support to an approach in test construction in which, similarly, the subject is never faced directly; but it is at the cost of mentioning the basic problems without solving them. Wherever one turns in his argument they crop up—for example, in his reference to "the actual relationships that hold between what a man says and what he *is* [italics in original]" (p. 297). If there is any meaning at all in the conception of such a relationship, and particularly if its separate terms make any sense, we should have some way of determining what a man really is—to use Meehl's phrase—and then of tracing out the relation of this finding to what he says about himself. An approach that accepts the latter as a fascinating datum in itself but which can do no more than compare it with other pieces of observable behavior has given up its claim to success. Moreover, a completely empirical approach must deny in principle the conception of "what a man is," for this essence comes into existence, for the empiricist, only by virtue of some technique for operating on it. Of itself, the empirical approach can never guarantee that what is elucidated by one or another of its tools is truly what a man *is;* such a guarantee requires an axiom concerning the nature of man—and what if two empiricists differ on the proper set of axioms? A final point: as we saw a few pages back, the problem is not solved but only muddled when the tester considers simply what a man reveals—that is, what he presumably shows of his inner traits or dispositions. An alternative view, taking into account as well the nature and mode of a man's expression, in all its intentional significance, might serve to broaden our whole approach to his responses in a clinical testing situation. To this issue, also, Meehl fails to address himself.

A major contribution, based solidly on the premises of Meehl's paper, soon followed in the form of a special key for controlling test-taking tendencies allied to malingering. As reported by Meehl and Hathaway (1946), this key is the K Factor for the MMPI, an instrument which is admittedly our current prototype of the structured personality inventory. Recognizing the fact that faking may occur in the best designed test, they suggest that one ought to meet the problem head on: The subject should be given a good chance to do his faking; he should be encouraged to present himself in an impossibly favorable light and allowed to reveal his own internal contradictions. A "faking" score is then derived on an empirical basis. Using this technique as a starting point, and recognizing also that one may "fake good" as well as "fake bad," Meehl and Hathaway developed a special scale by an elaborate process of combining items that were useful in a number of ways. Some of the items differentiated a special group of hospitalized patients—who had normal profiles when they should from their diagnoses have been abnormal, and who also had high L scores which pointed to a tendency to present themselves in an improbably good light—from a normal criterion group; and other items differentiated schizophrenics or depressed patients from normals but were not affected by attempts by normals to fake. The resultant scale is not meant to have any significance in a diagnostic sense, and in fact it does not serve to distinguish normals and abnormals in general. Rather, it acts to suppress certain "test-taking tendencies" found to some degree in all subjects, and in this way it serves as a corrective of the other scores. There is, these authors state, a set of "disturbing test-taking attitudes" which, if they are present to an appreciable degree, will throw off the more truly representative scores that the person might have otherwise obtained. The attitudes are related to malingering but are more broadly conceived, for they include both positive and negative distortion of "natural" scores.

It is clear that with the K Scale an important step forward had been taken, perhaps the logical end result of a strictly empirical approach to test usage. One weakness of the method of test construction by factor analytic methods had been corrected, that it was based essentially on internal consistency and therefore ruled out the chance of revealing such attitudes as made L and K Scales necessary. The best and the worst of the empirical approach are therefore clearly shown. On the one hand, if it is agreed that the tester or clinician can never know anything about another person except by a study of the ways in which restricted kinds of data fall out, then the use of a sophisticated method such as the full MMPI is beyond cavil. But if one holds to the hope that full knowledge of one person by another is sometimes, though rarely, given, and that it is the clinician's freighted challenge and duty to pursue this course, then the sophistication of the K Scale begins to seem empty and its successes shallow or trivial. Its procedure is seen as resting, finally, on a method by which the subject is outmaneuvered. Such a result can occur, in turn, only if the basic premise on which the tester operates is that the situation is one of struggle, the subject having hold of or concealing some inner thing which the clinician insists on getting for his own use. It is strange indeed that Meehl should arrive at this point after a brave beginning in which he was eager to make every possible use of the concrete clinical datum in its own right; strange that this should be the conclusion of an argument which began by noting that most test designers do not study the problem of faking because they are anxious to "get as far away from any unsanitary contact with the organism as possible" (Meehl and Hathaway, 1946, p. 527). It is even more ironic to note that in a careful study of the effectiveness of the K Scale in suppressing deliberate attempts to malinger, H. F. Hunt (1948) found that K was of little help to the examiner and that an even more elaborate index was required, the F raw score minus the

K raw score. Hunt concluded rather despairingly that the problem still exists, especially with "successful and subtle liars. . . . Deception, both conscious and unconscious, appears with disconcerting frequency in the populations conveniently available for normative purposes" (p. 401).

That deception is a function of the testing situation has been recognized as a basic premise by everyone who has tried to construct a key to detect or prevent faking. But strangely, the consequences have not been explored. For example, the string of studies which establish that self-report inventories can be faked successfully are usually based on artificial situations, subjects being asked as part of an experiment to pretend to fake or to imitate a specific kind of attitude. Some of the logical difficulties that might follow are suggested by the work of Goldstein, which we examined above. As it happens, studies which begin with a real-life situation, one in which the motives of the testee are taken into account, may often come to the same conclusion, that faking is possible. But the difference is that by the use of the real-life situation something has been learned about testing itself that was not known before.

There is a basic distinction here which is worth our while to explore further. On the one hand, the problem of faking may be handled as though it were a characteristic of a certain collection of test items, and therefore all the attempts to deal with it are based upon changes in or additions to the test itself. As one example, we have the special scales or keys built into so many inventories. On the other hand, the problem of faking may be approached by exploring those aspects of the test situation which seem relevant to its occurrence. Studies are then carried out to examine the aspects separately. Examples of this latter approach are neither numerous nor impressive, but taken together they are suggestive of alternative ways of understanding the clinical situation. In a very early study which was done as part of a distinguished series, Maller (1930) tested high school children on their group cooperation and helpfulness, and found a greater degree of helpfulness when names were signed to papers than when the work was done anonymously. "The signing of the name resulted in a higher score and greater persistence on the part of the children taking the cooperation tests" (p. 883). Even when ranking one another for cooperativeness, ratings of self as well as of others changed under conditions of anonymity. Examining the same variable more intensively, Spencer (1938) asked high school students who thought they had taken a test anonymously what they would have done if they had signed their names. He concluded from the results that only well-adjusted subjects are unconcerned about anonymity whereas those whom we would like to discover, the maladjusted, seem to need the cover of anonymity in order to be reasonably truthful in their responses. The conclusion to be drawn strikes us as reasonable—but more important is the finding that on many different kinds of material even naïve subjects will respond on the basis of two quite different bases. In part, their responses will be a measurable function of their enduring characteristics as individuals, just as a tester has a right to expect. But equally, their responses will vary in accordance with how they view the total testing situation and their own places in it—and this no tester can come prepared to measure, for it must always occur in spite of the test and must change from one situation to another. All that some examiners may achieve is to recover sufficiently from their surprise, and from the blow to their privileged status, to make some use of such results.

In sum, a small but impressive body of evidence which has been gathered in regard to faking under real life conditions (Olson, 1936; Gordon and Stapleton, 1956; Heron, 1956; Mayo and Guttman, 1959), bears out the conclusion drawn by Hunt: "What constitutes significant deception is probably relative to the specific group and its cultural background as well as to the situation" (1948, p. 401). A subject will always, on even the most structured test, do whatever seems to him the best thing to do under the circumstances as he sees them. And, as any clinician will quickly tell you, this is precisely what a subject will do on a projective test. To the subject, both kinds of tests are the same; they differ only in accordance with the aims, and the bag of tricks, brought to the testing room by the examiner.

This is not a conclusion which is likely to be drawn by an examiner who is committed to an endless struggle with every possible test subject. Nor can it be drawn if one's approach to the problem is restricted solely to such acts as manipulation, counter-manipulation, unmasking, and detecting—as, for example, in the thorough but one-sided review by Meltzer (1960). But the conclusion will certainly follow if we recall our fundamental proposition, that the act of a person can be understood only as directed toward changing the world that appears to him. When this is applied unreservedly to the subject in a testing situation, it becomes impossible to maintain that the situation is simply one person, the examiner, testing another, the subject. It is the situation which tests them both. In this context the word *test* has its ancient and literal meaning: E and S are tested by their situation just as metal is tested by the fire. It may be for just this reason that malingering was for the first time studied as a significant element in the testing situation at a time, during World War II, when the position of both examiner and subject was on trial in each session. It was the sworn duty of the tester to determine whether the subject was fit for military service; and the subject himself was either whole-heartedly engaged toward the same end, to prove his fitness for duty, or was equally determined in his effort to avoid the service at all costs. The efforts of both E and S swung around the same fulcrum, sometimes with both on one side or—and this became quite properly the definition of malingering—with the two facing each other from opposite sides of the same social demand. In such a setting, neither E nor S occupied that privileged position to which testers and other clinicians have recently made claim. Here may be the explanation for the unprecedented success of psychoneurotic inventories during the wartime period (Zubin, 1948), a happy result which has not been equaled since that time. When the two participants in a clinical situation are committed to the same overriding demand, whether for or against it, the performance of each, either in producing a protocol as subject or in understanding the protocol as examiner, is likely to be meaningful in any situation outside the clinician's office to which their efforts can be related. The question of how to extrapolate from test-protocol to nontest behavior becomes a vexing problem only when this condition is not met—when the subject's test performance is related to his nontest activities but the examiner's test actions are kept in an ideal realm of their own, related to nothing.

It was during the wartime emergency that a clinical examiner might honestly state a position which made sense in terms of an interaction with his subjects. He could declare that he meant to see that his subjects entered military service if that were at all possible; that he was by no means neutral as regards the desirability of this goal but that in fact his own worth as a tester depended on how loyally he carried out his duties; and that, therefore, he ran the constant risk of being bribed or threatened or fooled by a conspiratorial subject. The structure of the situation in which the military clinician did his work differs at just this point from that of the professional clinician today. It is the latter's expressed claim that he has no definable position at all. Though he may occasionally participate in a symposium in which the subject of values in psychotherapy is politely discussed, it is his claim that he has no stake at all in the values specifically appropriate to scientist, experimenter, or therapist. He is against sin—as Mowrer (1960) now uses the term to refer to the suffering and pathology of emotional disturbances—and in favor of the well-adjusted life for all, but beyond these unexceptionable sentiments, to which all citizens would subscribe, he makes but one concession to the need for taking a stand. He develops a theory of resistance and transference to encompass every instance of the subject's response to his supposedly nonexistent position.

If we view the examiner and his subject as engaged in a struggle, with E claiming to be above the struggle except during his military service, then we will have a kind of wartime malingering that we understand and, which is quite distinct from it, we will have a peacetime malingering with which we cannot cope. But if we view E and S as sharing and jointly exploring their common situation, we will be able to apply the lessons learned in war to the situation posed in peace. For in his malingering, however it occurs, the subject tells us something fundamental about the test, about the situation, and about his place in it, and it is always something that the test we give him does not allow him to say. He goes outside of the bounds of the test to say it; and we should not work to restrain him from this but listen as hard and as seriously as we can. His action is structurally very much like the familiar fraction of our subject population who do not support our experimental hypothesis. They are the people we should turn to first, for we will learn something new from them, whereas we will only be reinforced in something old by the subjects who verify our predictions.

The subject who malingers on a test is surely telling the examiner something, but only the examiner who is prepared to hear anything at all from his subject except the known answer to the prepared question will even be able to listen. He may take the view of one psychiatrist who, on the basis of extensive experience with malingerers in the military—from whom he had learned next to nothing—was able to tie his own thinking into this kind of impossible knot: "Every malingerer is really an unstable person, a psychopath, who by imitating a psychosis merely accentuates his own latent tendencies so that malingering is really pseudo-malingering" (Ossipov, 1944, p. 39). Or he may recognize, as did Vernon (1934) in the earliest days of personality testing, that there is "a fundamental difficulty which cannot be evaded, namely—the subject who knows that his personality is under investigation cannot react normally" (p. 174); that "the subject's answers are doubtless dictated, in part, not only by his notions about what the test is meant to measure (notions which may be more or less correct), but also by his relations to the people who are going to see these answers" (p. 166); and therefore that "his behavior will depend on his personal relations with the experimenter and his speculations about the object of the test" (p. 167).

The approach in which the tester abstracts a predetermined bit of data from his subject, or so constrains the latter that nothing new can happen in the testing situation, happily relieves the tester and experimenter of any trouble except that involved in the efficient use of their tools. But the alternative approach, spelled out in its fundamentals by Vernon, solves no problems at all. It states basic problems, some of them for the first time, and thereby only initiates the difficulties that the tester must face. He will have to recognize that the subject can never be fully understood except as a partner who has as much at stake in the testing situation as the tester himself—or if he has little at stake, then to that degree he is limited, and he can in any case be validly judged only against the norm of the subject who assumes full and continuing responsibility for what he does in the testing session. The tester will have to begin, as Vernon does, with the issue of the subject's relation to the examiner and his consequent concern with the purpose of the test. Basic to this issue is what must be recognized as the inevitable prejudice of subject against examiner.

Try as he may, the tester cannot keep the subject from inserting his own motives, so to speak, between question and response. If the subject is aware that it is his own personality being investigated, he will color his response to every question by his conception of the desirability of the trait he thinks is being measured. Unless the object of the test is somehow hidden from him, by one of the devices to which generations of testers have devoted their best efforts, he will then not be taking the same test that the tester is giving—and since the tester's test has not been devised to include the possibility being manifested by the subject, a large share of its results must, in their full psychological significance, fall outside the realm of data subsumed by the test questions. The tester will have looked for the molehill and found the mountain; and worse, he will not even be aware that this has happened.

Some years ago, Rosenzweig (1934) developed this point in a paper on what he had earlier (1933) called an "opinion-error" in all questionnaires—the error being that the subject is not usually completely naïve in regard to the examiner and his purposes. He therefore suggested that we openly recognize that the questionnaire is limited in this respect and then proceed to measure the "limiting factors," the results being used to apply a correction to the obtained test results. The procedure that he devised was to ask the subject what he thought he would like to be; and since this would be a rather "unconcealed" version of what the subject really was—which is what we are actually after—it could be used as a correction factor for the response usually obtained, which is the answer to our question of what the subject thinks he is. This device of asking the subject for his rating of his Ideal Self—as the approach is called today when it is used in connection with a Q-sort—may not solve in one stroke the problems that the tester faces from the knowing subject whom he considers even remotely as a partner. But for whatever it is worth, we should in all seriousness attempt to contrast it with the corrective factor introduced by Meehl and Hathaway for the MMPI. Theirs was a deliberate attempt to suppress the results of certain test-taking attitudes (the term *suppress* is of their own choosing). Rosenzweig's proposal moves in another direction entirely. It does not suppress but opens up even more the field of possibilities available to the test subject.

More recently, the direction proposed here was the topic of a study (Coplin, 1951) using a sentence completion test on the subjects of the VA assessment testing program (Kelly and Fiske, 1951). The author set himself the problem of discovering the pervasive verbal orientations that subjects might take toward such a test and therefore toward verbal test situations in general. For example, if the subject completed the sentence "I despise . . ." with the answer "No one," Coplin studied this as evidence "that he wishes to be perceived as being unbiased, altruistic, forgiving . . ." (p. 26). His concern was not with whether the subject's response was appropriate nor with what it revealed in regard to dynamics or psychopathology, but rather with the mode of response utilized; and he asked in regard to each such mode of response, or set, whether it was "a reflection of the person's true feelings or a product of . . . how he wishes to be perceived" (p. 7). In short, Coplin did not measure what a person *is* but of how he chose to appear to the examiner. That such an approach is indeed feasible is demonstrated by the fact that the author was able to extract three factors from his data which help greatly to organize our thinking about the responses to such test situations—fair-mindedness, willingness to risk committing oneself frankly to a point of view, and status drive. Similarly, when Mills (1955) compared the test results of students in abnormal psychology classes with those in other classes, not with a view to ascertaining degree of pathology, but in terms of the test responses as statements to the examiner, he came to related conclusions—that the "appropriate" situation of a class in abnormal psychology sets the stage for a "greater freedom" in seeing and talking about one's problems.

Set Versus Intention

It will be apparent that the term *set* is applicable to much of what I am implying in this discussion of malingering. This word has a long history in psychology (Gibson, 1941), but in the sense in which we use it in connection with test construction, we owe its current importance primarily to Cronbach. In two papers (1946, 1950) based partly on his earlier work on patterns of acquiescence in test-taking

(1942), he dealt with what he called *response set*. This he defined as "any tendency causing a person consistently to give different responses to test items than he would when the same content is presented in a different form" (1946, p. 476). What is most interesting is that by the use of this guiding conception, Cronbach came close to formulating an explicit theory of clinical testing. He began by including within the meaning of *form,* as the term is used in the definition just quoted, the manner in which the test question was phrased, the choices presented to the subjects, and the test instructions themselves. On this basis he was able to develop a broad definition of set which included such diverse aspects of test performance as caution, gambling, bias, or acquiescence; semantic issues, such as ways of defining key words in test instructions; styles in writing, particularly in essay-type examinations; and personal characteristics such as speed and accuracy. Response set, he stated, increases in significance as a test or an item is made less structured or more ambiguous; and because no test is completely unambiguous or objective in this sense, some set is bound to be induced in the subject. By this reasoning, the Rorschach is almost completely a response-set instrument; and elements of set are inescapable, if not pervasive, in other experimental phenomena, from the constant errors of psychophysical measurement to the "frame of reference" familiar to social psychologists.

Given the ubiquity of response set, Cronbach takes a middle ground as to what the experimenter should do about it. If the aim is to increase validity, such devices as multiple choice tests should be introduced to eliminate the effect of set; but there may be occasions when the experimenter chooses to capitalize on the phenomenon rather than try to undercut or bypass it. Indeed, a number of writers have recently argued ingeniously for just this latter course. Berg (1955) reasons that if the presence of some kinds of "response bias" is related to certain personality traits, the converse should also be demonstrable—that the opposing tendency, to deviate from the modal set for a population of subjects, should occur with an abnormal group. His reading of the evidence leads him to rule out almost completely the effect of specific item content; "deviant response patterns," he notes, "tend to be general" (p. 70). Pursuing a similar line, Jackson and Messick (1958) make a basic distinction between the *content* of needs and cognitive structures, which result in the "what" of a person's test response, and the *style* of his response and action. Both content and style, in their view, are constructs; and the latter means nothing but set, the term being changed so as to free the experimenter to capitalize on this sort of variance. Following Cronbach, they include as styles the sets to acquiesce, to overgeneralize, and to act well or acceptably, as well as the reverse of these. However, they make a stronger case than their predecessors for the significance of style. It is, they claim, the "major common factor" in responses to all true-false types of tests, including the famed MMPI.

The apparent extravagance of these claims becomes more understandable when we note that they are largely based on a series of studies with the F Scale of ethnocentricism (Adorno *et al.*, 1950). When this instrument was first introduced it seemed to herald a whole new era of objective personality testing. Here, in what looked like a major breakthrough, the insights of psychoanalytically oriented clinicians were to be fused with the theorems of social psychology, providing a soundly based testing device for a significant dimension of social functioning in the individual. Earlier studies seemed only to confirm the original findings, to the effect that adults could be clearly distinguished by means of the scale and that their scores were related to many other measures of rigidity, narrow-mindedness, and attitudes of prejudice. But then, following the discovery that F-scale scores signifying ethnocentrism were negatively correlated with intelligence, it occurred to a number of workers to examine the scale itself. No great acuity was needed to observe that it was worded in a specific and quite loaded way: the statements were extreme, clichés were extensively used, and the items were largely phrased in the same direction, so that any subject with a tendency to agree with a vehement, respectable-sounding platitude—especially if he were not cognizant of its full significance—might well score high on the dimension of authoritarianism. Studies in which the scale items were deliberately reversed (Bass, 1955; Jackson and Messick, 1957; Chapman and Campbell, 1957) were not entirely in agreement in demonstrating the effect of this set on item response, but they helped to tarnish the halo which had surrounded the test; and today most workers would probably agree that the set to acquiesce is sufficiently productive of response variance to make uncritical use of the F Scale somewhat suspect. Further doubt was then raised on the basis of studies on whether the F scale could be faked. Stotsky (1955), for example, found that subjects could change their responses significantly, either in the direction of "neurotic" protocols or if instructed to respond "as the normal person would"—although the latter, rather surprising result leaves one to wonder whether the subjects considered themselves somehow different from the "normal." Cohn (1952), too, showed that college students have no difficulty in faking the F Scale in order to respond either as "highly-educated, intelligent people" or as unskilled and uneducated laborers.

It is understandable that experimenters were led to make sweeping claims for the influence of style over content because of experimental developments indicating that the most promising "content" test of the structured type was largely the victim of the most common of the response sets. Perhaps we should not be too surprised, however, that this brave beginning, which repeated in essence the story of former workers who had come to believe in the limitless fakability of all structured tests, has not finally produced a full-fledged and soundly based clinical theory. The specific recommendations of Jackson and Messick (1958), as one instance, turn out to consist of no more than such suggestions as: techniques disguised as achievement tests should be used to evaluate style. A promise has somehow been lost, no doubt of it; the work on set, in all its guises, has not seemed to eventuate in constructive suggestions. One immediate explanation may be found simply in the unrecognized difficulties implicit in the use of the concept. As Jackson and Messick admit, it is extremely difficult to obtain measures of set that are "experimentally independent"—although they do not seem to recognize that the reason for this points directly at the self-defeating character of the concept itself. For if you are forced to measure style or set by the use of a test whose structure is essentially like that of the test in which set is to be detected, how do you rule out the effect of style in the subject's response to items in the experiment itself?

What is missing here? Clearly, it is the idea that set is a kind of relation between subject and examiner. In place of this, there is expressed unquestioningly, just as though it were self-evident, the idea that only the subject, and never the examiner, has a set. Like the term *diagnosis,* set is supposed to be applicable to only one of the two partners in the clinical situation. No mode of understanding exists which encompasses both subject and examiner, for there would be required for such an understanding a position in which the examiner gives up his claim to an exclusive and untouchable position in the clinical relationship—although interestingly enough, Cronbach (1946) did imply just such an orientation in his proposal that if the examiner joins forces, so to speak, with his subjects and coaches them so that they are test-wise, they will work to understand and eliminate their own sets. In spite of all the brave and impressive words to this effect, as is indicated by our investigation of a specific problem where this changed orientation might be shown, contemporary clinical theory, either of test construction or of test interpretation, has failed the tester who is most in need of it. Therefore those who see that at least some form of malingering is inevitable, that set is inescapable, and that style of response is productive of the largest amount of variance, will usually proceed with a free conscience to measure the subject's set and then use the results as a corrective and, quite probably, a suppressor of the unpleasant results otherwise obtainable. That each instance of set is itself a psychological problem ranking in significance with any answer the subject might offer in terms of his set, is a possibility that is never faced.

But as we have seen thus far, it simply must be faced; not at the end, when all the data are in and adjudged useful or not, revealing or lacking, but at the very beginning of testing in general and also repeatedly and continuously within each testing session. This, indeed, is the general conclusion to which I think we must be led by our examination of some of the ways of dealing with malingering. It is not, we can see, a particular unpleasantness or inconvenience which is sometimes superimposed on the testing procedure by a certain kind of badly motivated subject—and therefore becomes a phenomenon reproducible simply by asking people to behave as though they themselves were malingering. Rather, it is a general signal, like a fever in the body, which indicates a pervasive unsettling of normal and expected conditions and, by its very nature, points as a warning to those basic requirements which are necessary for sustaining even normal conditions. From a study of malingering we may gain initial entry into the complex field of events which compose the testing situation. For one thing, by its very occurrence it tells us that the possibility of testing rests on some difference in knowledge and leaning between examiner and subject. The place where the two meet must be in the vicinity of a common ground toward which both advance only by giving up some part of their own positions. The subject accedes, willy nilly, to the examiner's demands; the examiner agrees, perforce, to confide in the subject.

The malingerer, however, belongs to that special breed of test subject who chooses to overstep these agreed-upon bounds. He moves as far as he can toward the position occupied by the tester himself. He does this first of all by claiming some knowledge—which properly belongs only to the examiner—of the test's purpose and its specific methods; and he then applies this knowledge (whether validly or not is irrelevant) to presenting himself in a manner with which he is as familiar before the testing begins as the examiner will be after the testing ends. If his performance succeeds fully, his position throughout will then be indistinguishable from that of the examiner himself.

We have seen that the malingerer's attempt to sit side by side in the examiner's seat rests upon his knowledge of what it is that an examiner seeks to find out through his testing procedure. In order to change his responses in accordance with this aim in the test situation, he must know what the responses that he might choose to give will mean. All of the findings that we have surveyed in these pages combine to suggest that this is the central phenomenon of malingering and related issues in testing. The concept of set, for example, makes sense only if one implies, in using it, that the subject who shows a set to respond in one way or another knows what his own response might mean; for if he did not, how would one ever explain the consistency of his responses in a certain direction? In a discussion of his study of a "control factor in social adjustment," Wiener (1951) suggests two ways to account for his positive findings—one, "the hypothesis of a dynamic control factor tending to suppress indications of obvious symptoms," and the other the "suggestion of a simple continuum of subtlety to obviousness in items;" and the latter was suggested also by Seeman's (1952) independent study of "subtle" and "obvious" items on the MMPI. Again, both the hypothesis of a control factor and the concept of subtle and obvious test items require that the subject know something about his response which is not contained in the item's score; a kind of knowledge which is strikingly like that which the subject in a subception experiment must also have. He cannot suppress indications unless he has some knowledge of what to suppress; and he cannot pick out subtle from obvious items unless he has some basis for choosing between them. In a sense, the test measures nothing but the extent of this particular and hidden knowledge that every subject shares with the examiner himself—yet at the same time no test can ever be constructed to measure it.

THE
SCHIZOPHRENIC:
PROTOCOL
AND INTERPRETATION

I've never done anything at no time to nobody. Until I do something
to someone at some time I expect nothing from nobody.
                                                    —A PATIENT

THE RECENT SURGE OF INTEREST, BY LAYMAN AND PROFESSIONAL
alike, in what is called "the problem of mental illness," has brought
into the field an army of enthusiasts. One of the less fortunate consequences of enthusiasm is that it gives rise to the belief that the impossible can be accomplished and that the improbable is not really
so. The prevailing view of the schizophrenic way of life has thus been
colored by a quite unfounded conviction that schizophrenia can be
cured, an attitude which is based, in turn, on the unwarranted premise
that it is an illness to which the concept of cure is applicable. Test-

246

ing of the schizophrenic, either inside or outside the mental hospital, has most often taken place within the context of accepting both these propositions.

The Schizophrenic Position

The orientation toward testing which has been expounded in these pages stresses the importance of the total situation within which both tester and testee find themselves. This is more than ever true in regard to the schizophrenic, whose position is extreme in so many different ways. If the examiner takes for granted, as does the hospital admini- stration, the rest of the professional staff, and the interested portion of the community, that schizophrenia is a disease with causes, symp- toms, methods of treatment, and modes of cure—or even if he pre- tends to a more sophisticated view and refers to "the schizophrenias" —he will inevitably test in such a way as to discover only what will benefit his view. The questions that he will ask by means of his test will be limited in number and kind—for example, "What is the matter with this person?" or "What are the characteristics of this person which are related to whatever is the matter with him?" or perhaps "What procedures on our part are indicated so as to change or elimi- nate whatever is the matter with him?" These questions are familiar to us in the form of test referrals concerning diagnosis, personality evaluation, and treatment possibilities.

The trouble with this way of using the test material is not that it asks the wrong questions and therefore is bound to come out with inconsequential answers. More fundamentally, it is based on a view which seems, to the tester and his associates, completely self-evident. There is no possibility, within the view itself, of arriving at the notion that it is not self-evident; nor of arriving at the further notion, which would follow on the first, that nothing at all is ever self-evident within a meaningful relation with another person. This self-preservative tendency helps to explain the remarkable circumstance that the ob- vious logical alternative has simply never occurred to those who determine the treatment of hospitalized schizophrenics. In place of the conviction that the schizophrenic is a victim of some disease which has happened to him, the alternative has not been seriously considered that he is no more a victim of schizophrenia than you and I are victims of normalcy. Both conditions are no more and no less than the totality of the ways in which certain persons live out their lives. The degree to which the person may be "victimized" will have to be determined in each case, primarily through a study of the number and range of choices still open to him. The person who has no choices at all left to him for altering his condition is bound to be a victim and quite probably to feel like one as well, whether he is asymptomatic, a neurotic in treatment, or acutely psychotic; but the presence of even one choice that represents some alternative to his current way of life defines him as a nonvictim.

Strangely, we have no term for the nonvictim. Our contemporary theory makes no place for the act which is based on a decision, the deed which is free and therefore nonpredictable. The theory, the orientation, the approach, and the method all combine in the clinical situation to view the schizophrenic as a sort of reactive mechanism which, if we manage to pull the right strings, will move in other and more desirable directions. And because the entire business of clinical testing is built unthinkingly on this kind of premise, the true nature of the situation between examiner and patient is never explored. Even the logical possibility that it might be explored is ruled out. A psychology of testing, nestling fairly comfortably within the confines dictated by a limited theoretical view, inevitably develops practices in which power is exercised unknowingly and the results of its exercise are considered the only possible means of carrying out the procedure. No psychology of situations is even conceivable under such an arrangement; no way of understanding schizophrenia as a problem in choice and decision; and above all no basis for judging and acting upon the concrete situation in which normal and schizophrenic meet.

The alternative implied in the present work is that the schizophrenic is understandable as a man in a special position, and that regardless of the view that is proposed as a definition of this condition, the very act of defining demands a stand on human possibilities in general. We will never be able to ask "What is schizophrenia?" unless we are also prepared to face such questions as "What is man?" The two questions are on the same level; it is in this sense alone that we have a right to claim that we may use a knowledge of the norm in order to judge the schizophrenic variant. The specific view offered in the following sentences is presented as a basis for dealing with certain clinical material, rather than as a definitive position to be discussed for its own sake; that is a task far larger than can be accomplished in the present work. Briefly, we will offer that schizophrenia is a state chosen by the person as a way out of the fundamental demand for responsible action and the fundamental characteristic of reflectiveness. Once the schizophrenic condition has been achieved—usually by means of passing through an agonizing period of transition which we know as *psychosis*—it is marked by certain enduring characteristics, which will change only temporarily and only under pressures imposed on the schizophrenic by others. These characteristics center around a core of apathy, timelessness, and the absence of responsible or reflective action. When alien pressures do occur, the schizophrenic will respond either by reinstituting the symptoms which defined his period of psychosis, by acting in some other way that will increase the distance between himself and the task, or even on occasion by going along with the demands. But in every case, by the nature of his extreme position, the act that he can be brought to perform will be nonresponsible and unreflective; it will produce no true change in his history or his destiny.

The world in which a person in this position lives is radically altered from our own—perhaps altered beyond our capacity to apprehend it. We can, however, trace out some of its boundaries—for example, the awful terror with which the schizophrenic must confront the possibility of any drastic change in the concrete arrangements of his life pattern. Other aspects are revealed, if dimly, when we obtain material spontaneously produced by the schizophrenic. The following "essay," given to his therapist by a young male patient, tells us about a clinical entity that our theory would never have allowed us to suspect. The patient entitled his essay "Nothingness."

Is just plain blank. Its void. It has no affiliations with anything. It has nothing to do with anything. It doesn't involve competition or undue association. It involves a system of taking care of ones own affairs. It forms protection. It involves staying out of people's way. It concerns correct concern for ones self. It has nothing to do with science or engineering.

It is a truism. If any undue stress is placed on anyone sometimes its nothing and sometimes it isn't. Various types of nothingness can be pushed out. It can be used for all sorts of things. Once one uses any sort of substitution it ain't nothing. It eliminates all abstract faults. Different things can blank people out. It concerns no undue affiliation with any mens clubs or front organizations. It allows membership in the YMCA. It means schizophrenia releif [sic] permanent. That is the thing called void. It means the use of positive force. It maintains no classifications of leadership. It means no intermixture. It means straightness. It is the space between the seperation [sic].

As with every authentic human expression, this one can be perceived and understood in many ways. There may be some virtue in a single-minded tracing out of the diagnostic and psychodynamic clues in this passage—in particular a grossly homosexual association which the reader might amuse himself by tracking down. But whatever else this essay is, it is the statement of a position; it tells how things seem to the patient himself. Before we pass diagnostic judgment on it, we have to accept it as this and then to consider carefully the nature of the situation in which it became the clinician's property. This much is true of every expression. The angry look, for example, is understandable as such only because reception or perception of it is possible for some persons; and for those who cannot enter a situation marked by anger, perhaps because as far as they are concerned this expression is ruled out, this kind of look will not be received by them at all. The essay we have quoted was typed by a patient whose productions were rarely coherent, and it is was given to his therapist as part of a pack of drawings and other writings which concerned vague, delusional plans for organization of the hospital's bureaucracy.

The essay itself seems to fall into the same category—that is, it appears to be not a missive directed to the therapist personally, nor even a report about the patient himself. Rather, it is an attempt to attend to a problem and to resolve it. The writer of the essay, one might say, is not pouring out his feelings nor writing a diary nor speaking directly to a second person; his writing is not an expression in this sense. He is task-oriented, and like any writer who is directed primarily toward his task, he has managed to achieve some distance from what we know as his condition. It is for this reason, most probably, that this relatively "unreachable" patient has been able to produce a coherent document which might almost pass for a theoretical exposition. And this may also be the reason that his production of this and similar pieces over the course of a year or more of psychotherapy seemed to bear no relation to the degree of therapeutic success nor to the closeness that the therapist was able to attain with him. Recognizing this, the therapist finally came to realize that the patient actually saw himself as a kind of philosopher of schizophrenia, a man uniquely gifted to explain to strangers what his unique world was like. This recognition led to a significant forward step in treatment, for it made possible the therapist's realization and acceptance of another way of understanding the patient's episodes of coherence: that they were not indicators of lucidity or normalcy but exactly the opposite. They were warnings that essential change was precluded. Viewed in this new light, the patient's communications were to the effect that his position was impregnable. Like a native guide in a strange country, he was occasionally willing to take the visitor on a tour, but this was never an invitation to the latter to begin an attempt to have him change his place of residence. And since this proposition was clearly a free choice on the patient's part, the therapist was morally bound to respect it.

Note again that all this does not constitute an "interpretation" of the patient's essay on nothingness; nor will it lead to a diagnosis nor an elucidation of the dynamics of the patient's personality organization. These may be worthy endeavors, but they are second steps rather than first. To undertake them is to ignore and thus to bypass the nature of the situation as an encounter. The clinician whose activities begin with interpretation of this sort never becomes aware that he and the patient are independent powers, that each is engaged in preserving his sovereignty, and that their meeting constitutes no more than a transient agreement to meet and test each other out. Unknowing, and therefore ignorant in the most harmful sense, the clinician bent on interpretation assumes without question that it is his place to pre-empt the situation for his own purposes. Clinical data which ought to become the test protocol, and in this way lead one or both of them toward an understanding of a situation because they both find themselves in it, are transmuted instead into a set of more or less provable statements of fact. What should be the conclusion of an inquiry is utilized as the basis for a deductive argument, and the result is that nothing new can be revealed, only demonstrations of known and familiar patterns. It is highly improbable that a clinical approach which has as its aim an interpretive endeavor would be able to see the essay on nothingness as other than a sign of rapprochement with the therapist; whereas an approach which first establishes a situational context for interpretation will claim exactly the reverse. The practical difference between the two is seen in the fact that the latter approach enables the therapist to begin planning some asymptomatic life arrangement for the patient in which his chosen position can be maintained with the least inroads on his own dignity and with minimal stress on his surroundings.

The Problem of the Test Rationale

All of us, I am sure, would agree that one of the psychologist's first tasks is to understand and then make use of the data he obtains by means of his testing. Some of these data are easy to handle. The so-called nontest behavior, which may range from smiles to seizures, from shuffling to masturbation, covering the gamut of human expressive movement as well as of other activities made meaningful chiefly by the clinician's interpretive zeal, seems to be understandable to everyone with clinical skill and experience. But what of the actual test responses? They are the reason for getting the nontest behavior, for the latter would not even be obtained if the former were not sought. Yet these test data are rarely dealt with as though they were immediately understandable.

The link between test response and something other is the *test rationale;* and it is apparent that although it takes many forms, and may even be partly hidden behind some attractive alternative, it usually serves a single purpose. Notice that a rationale, in this usage at least, is not the same as a theory. Rather, it is an expression of the relationship posited between a theory and the particular set of facts given to the clinician in a test protocol. To the extent that the protocol is considered a kind of unique and special example of the subject's behavior, which seems to hold true to some extent for every writer in the field, a theory is not in itself sufficient to explain the test data. These require a rationale as a special kind of link, or translator, between test data and theoretical formulation. At one end of the chain of reasoning is the subject as he gives his test response; the response is then tied, by means of the test rationale, to a theory; and the theory in turn serves to describe the very same subject as he might appear in some other situation outside the testing room. In this sense the test protocol is looked upon as analogous to the results of an experiment, and the test situation is like the experiment itself. It is a special and contrived arrangement out of which the psychologist hopes to learn something about the real, or true, version of the person who faces him across the desk. In brief, the person who faces the psychologist, insofar as he is a test subject, is somehow not really real; he is at best a valuable or useful representative of his own true self.

Only rarely, or hesitantly, have writers and experimenters in this field considered an alternative proposition, which is that the test behavior—that is, the test responses—may be described and examined in its own right. To do this would require a number of changes in our present mode of understanding the data from projective tests. We would have to affirm, for example, that there is never more than one kind of data; that it is always given to us in the course of the concrete interpersonal situation; and that it is real because it is all there is. This multiple proposition was examined in some detail in an earlier chapter. In addition, we would be required to have what we do not now have in spite of all our psychological theorizing, some coherent psychology of social perception. For test interpretation rests, finally, on the interpreting of tests; and to aid in our comprehension of behavior of this sort, we will have to be able to elucidate the principles by which one person looks at another and arrives at an understanding of him. This psychology must come before test interpretation, preceding it as learning a language precedes writing a sentence in that language. Interpreting test material cannot furnish us with a psychology of social perception, any more than ignorantly putting one word after another, like the chimpanzee typists in the well-known story, can produce more than accidental sequences which happen to imitate the contents of a novel.

The general line of argument offered here is hardly new; it has been presented in some detail by various writers who have concerned themselves with the problem of validating clinical tests. In discussing the experimenter or judge as a "transmuter" of nonquantified into quantified data, Soskin (1954) has remarked that when we do research on validating nonquantitative techniques, we are more likely to find ourselves validating, not the instrument itself, but the "inference-making characteristics of a variety of human observers based on their interpretations of the performance record" (p. 113). It is these characteristics, we may add, which form the basis for a psychology of social perception. Similarly, Tomkins (1947) suggests that our aim should be to "study the conditions under which the individual is likely to rate himself accurately and the conditions under which he will deceive himself" (p. 19) when he takes a test of the questionnaire type; and that this approach, rather than one in which we attempt to test the validity of the questionnaire, will in the long run be of the greatest value. The validity of inferences drawn from projective tests, he adds, is a characteristic of the inferences, not of the tests, and it depends finally on the current level of development of psychology as a science.

The moral to be drawn at this point is this: in the absence of a coherent system for understanding by way of perception, we are likely to have nothing better than partial and even irrelevant substitutes for understanding. Standardized tests have often been offered as a substitute, with the result that they have all had to lean upon some sort of rationale to connect them with a theory which, in turn, purports to supply that understanding, or at least a way of achieving it, which was needed at the outset. The tests have therefore been at worst busy work, at best devices by which the psychologist-clinician might demonstrate that he is both more skilled than the layman and more impressive than the psychiatrist. Projective tests have been of some use largely to the extent that they enabled the clinician to apply whatever understanding he would have been able to muster without them; and since he soon became aware, if he was at all adept in this work, that he could use the same techniques and skills more directly and profitably by meeting the patient or client in a face-to-face treatment situation, he has tended to drop the tests in favor of the practice of psychotherapy, demonstrating thereby an embarrassing lack of sustained confidence in the very instruments which defined his own calling. If the client or patient was ever understood as a human being who was functioning in terms of his unique distress, this was because the clinician himself brought to the test situation some ability to achieve this understanding. Some psychologists, indeed, have even gone so far as to consider the testing session simply as a sort of license to spend time with a subject—although admittedly, and fortunately, with the special value that in such a session the tester is probably less anxious than the testee. Others, less radical, have expressed the two sides of the split by maintaining in their test reports a careful division between the paragraph "describing" the subject's test behavior and the remainder devoted to "interpreting" his test responses.

The trouble with this line of reasoning, of course, is that it, too, is reduced to absurdity if carried far enough. It is at least probable that there is no point at all in the use of specialized instruments in the hands of a clinician; that the radicals are in this instance quite right in denying any value to the tests except perhaps as symbols of a vocation, something like the red and white striped pole one sees in front of a barber shop. That is, it may be argued that in a discipline which aims at human understanding of human beings the only useful instrument is the clinician himself, and the only possible content a theory of social perception. It is easy to see the scope of this question. It points to the problem of the relation between the perceiver as ego and the perceiver as user of his own perceptual processes; or, if you like, to the relation between the person and his own mode of functioning. For undeniably, if the clinician is both perceiver of his test subject, which he is, and scientist who systematically organizes his own perceptions of his test subject, which he ought to be, then a psychology that provides principles to understand the work of the clinician must also have this dual aspect. If the clinician fails in one respect, as do those who look on themselves as no more than sensitive strings vibrating to the rhythm and tune of each session, he will be at best an unknowing partner and at worst a fascinating figure who remains unreachable. If his failure is in the other direction, toward the depersonalized mechanization of the test approach, he will be no partner at all, although he may be competent and willing, intelligent and receptive, acute as well as serious in his calling.

"Gregor" Again

We would have difficulty in finding any category of test subject who is less likely than the chronic schizophrenic to share as full partner in the testing situation. If anything, he will usually be found at the other extreme, refraining almost completely from committing himself as a person. Perhaps this is why the practitioners of a science of Others have chosen him so often as a target for the public display of their skills, for he surely appears to exemplify just the impersonal Other with whom they are best equipped to deal. Our thesis in these pages, on the contrary, is that the schizophrenic, too—perhaps particularly so—has a position, and that he is committed to it as fundamentally and as desperately as the examiner is, or ought to be, to his own. It will, therefore, be especially instructive to rereview, at this point, an elaborate set of published clinical data on just such a case.

At the meetings of the American Psychological Association in September, 1949, there was presented a "diagnostic case symposium," sponsored jointly by the Society for Projective Techniques and the then Division of Clinical and Abnormal Psychology and its Committee on Diagnostic Devices. An extensive series of test results on a single patient, a hospitalized male schizophrenic, had been distributed among well-known clinicians, each of whom agreed to do a purblind diagnosis using only the test that was his specialty plus a minimal amount of material from the case history. The chairman of the symposium was John E. Bell (1949a, 1949b), and the discussant at its conclusion Frederick Wyatt. The specialists were Susan K. Deri (Szondi test), Max L. Hutt (Bender-Gestalt), Bruno Klopfer (Rorschach), Karen Machover (Human Figure Drawings), Roy Schafer (Wechsler-Bellevue and Word Association Test), and Morris I. Stein (Thematic Apperception Test), joined during the discussion by Edwin S. Shneidman (MAPS Test) and Elizabeth F. Hellersberg (Horn-

Hellersberg Test). In addition, a large number of other tests were given to the patient, the results of which were reported (Bell, 1949a) but not included in the discussion: The Ball and Field Test from the Stanford-Binet; the Franck Sex Symbol Test; freehand drawings of a house, a face liked, a face disliked, and self-portrait; the Rotter-Willerman Sentence Completion Test; the Lowenfeld Mosaic Test; the Elkisch scribbling drawing; drawings of squares and circles, estimation of distances outward and inward, drawing of money, estimation of weights, and estimation of handshake, taken from the Allport-Vernon studies of expressive movement (1933); the Harms Line Analysis; the Mayer and Mayer Dynamic Concept Test; the Rosenzweig Picture-Frustration Study; the Mira Myokinetic Diagnosis; Mirror Drawing; Finger Painting; the Van Lennep Four-Picture Test; and the Stein Sentence Completion Test.

The total is impressive, even frightening—twenty-seven different tests in at least ten sessions by four examiners. The inevitable first question that occurs to anyone who has had to cope with the problem of motivation in one subject during the administration of a single test is how this all-out program was presented to the patient. Was he given an explanation? Did he ask for one? What did he offer in regard to the reasons? How was this taken by the examiner(s)? Now, the answers to these and similar questions, as reported by Bell, are curious, to say the least. At one point Bell (1949a) states: "He spoke spontaneously of his vocational plans, interpreting for himself that the tests had something to do with vocational guidance" (p. 156)— and presumably he was not disabused of this notion. Yet in another place, Bell (1949b) gives us a different story: "You may expect from me some apology for subjecting an hospitalized patient to such a tremendous battery of methods as is recorded in 'The Case of Gregor.' Let me reassure you that I was not unacquainted with the possible consequences of such a request from Gregor. The testing was undertaken with the full cooperation of the Neuropsychiatric Staff of the Hospital. Gregor expressed a belief that the testing was associated with his returning home for Christmas, and accepted it as such" (p. 433).

Whatever their divergent orientations, the clinicians who participated in this project, as well as the majority of their listeners, probably had in common a bias toward a "dynamic" psychology—that is, a system in which needs, wants, and wishes assume a dominant theoretical role and in which motivation is given priority as a determinant of action. Also, all of them would have been in general agreement that full understanding of another person requires gaining access in some way to his viewpoint and world outlook. These ideas are the commonplaces of a clinical psychology. It is all the more wonder, then, that the ideas should have been so thoroughly eliminated from the results of a large-scale project which presumed to display the professional capabilities of representative experts in test interpretation. It seems clear, if only by omission of the fact, that Gregor was never really told the purpose of the testing. Consider what this means. He had been hospitalized for something over two years, during which time he had been the recipient of the full armamentarium of modern psychiatric practice—insulin coma therapy, group and individual psychotherapy, prefrontal lobotomy, and quite possibly all the host of planned activities which today are dignified as types of ancillary therapy. In all probability he was fairly well acquainted with the hospital routine and with the practices associated with psychological testing, particularly in view of the fact that he had achieved a sufficient remission of his condition to be considered a candidate for a visit to his home over the Christmas holidays. As far as he would have known, he was almost the only patient to have been treated in this way. What did it mean to him, then, that he was singled out of a large population of similar patients and tested to a degree far exceeding the requirements of any treatment plan known to him? The specialists who parade their skills do not tell us. Moreover, they fail even to wonder about it. But if one pays no attention to the motives that the subject might have in taking a test, and if one fails to seek access to the subject's personal view of the whole testing procedure, how "dynamic" can be the psychology which is built on the findings?

It would be easy to press this point still further, noting that the two reasons Gregor himself offered for the testing—that it was for vocational guidance, and that it was "associated" with his going home—do not coincide and in fact are slightly at odds in their implications; for the first asks that the subject display his specific aptitudes even at the cost of also showing some pathology, whereas the second calls for a relatively bland and asymptomatic performance which is not marked by effort or strain. But without belaboring the issue, it may be concluded that here again the test data are interpreted, this time on a massive scale, in the total absence of a relevant context or of an understanding of the situation in which the data were obtained.

In view of the fact that one rarely has the opportunity of leisurely studying the public statements of a conclave of clinicians, the reports quoted in full (Bell, 1949b) are worth our attention. One begins by trying to fit these separate contributions into one unified whole, or at least to discover a key to the way in which they both agree and disagree. But it turns out to be surprisingly difficult to organize them in such a way as to make meaningful comparisons. Each of the expositors displays a superlative skill in so phrasing a contribution that he leaves it, with but rare exceptions, essentially unrelated to the definitive findings so confidently proclaimed by one of the others. This is not to say that the interpretive efforts are vague or unscientific. On the contrary, they are—again almost without exception—clearcut, definite, and declamatory; humility is not one of the more common virtues of experts in any field. Nevertheless, the separate essays are unrelated, and there seems to be no way that one might organize them into a many-faceted whole.

To complicate the matter even more, the diagnostic formulations which are arrived at independently by the six clinicians do converge on a common clinical picture. It is that of a bland and/or stabilized schizophrenic-like condition which was at the time of testing either in transition or in temporary remission; and there are also indications of previous psychotic episodes, marked mostly by catatonic features, of strong homosexual elements and of some depressive aspects. The convergence is evidence enough that clinical psychologists have come of age, and that in a crucial test of their worth—their ability to approximate the psychiatrist's diagnosis in reliable fashion—they have nothing to be ashamed of. But does their collective performance show more than this? It is quite doubtful whether all the contributions, taken together, tell us anything about the patient that might not have been gained from reading the case history and formulating a diagnostic picture in psychoanalytic terms. The troublesome question which is raised by this situation is whether these contributions do in fact bear any relation to a unique individual, that is, to a living person. The experts agree—but almost without exception their agreement is in a realm at least once removed from the person who is supposed to be their concern. It is the thesis of the present chapter, and of this book as well, that unless the clinician takes a stand by which he, too, risks himself in the testing situation, he will always remain thus removed from his patient. If he stands immovably on a vantage ground marked by the exercise of power, he will only parade his knowledge and will see his subject only as a kind of subject matter.

What the clinician ought to look for in every testing session is a contribution by the test material to his own understanding. If he has learned nothing in the session, he has wasted both his and the patient's time. Now, the case of Gregor, beyond merely reinforcing the experts' convictions as to their own nosological acuity or psychodynamic omniscience, has an almost inexhaustible amount of data to help us in our attempts to understand the schizophrenic position. Even the simple fact that the patient displayed no essential difference in the level of his performance over a period of at least ten sessions, or during the time from the beginning to the end of a lengthy testing session, should strike us as provocative. Like so many schizophrenics, Gregor seems "tireless"—yet in common with many patients in his position he will often state that he is tired, he will show many overt indications of lack of energy, and his history will usually contain references to critical periods in his life when he was continually fatigued. How can one be both tired and tireless?

One possible answer is worth considering for the implications that it has for the entire dimension of activity-passivity along which so much of Gregor's behavior was scaled by these experts. It is that he is neither tired nor tireless but beyond both conditions. He has declared himself at a position which involves refraining from acting in the world; and thus when we bring him to the point where action seems required, by making a demand on him to perform an act which is intelligible to us, he finds himself pushed up against the world's resistance, as it were. Held at this place because of our demand on him, his experience is one of wearing himself out against a purely resistive manifold, and his report is that he is tired. Yet because his doing is in fact no real doing at all, he can continue wearing himself out, so to speak, for an indefinite time. In this way he can be both tired and tireless. The catatonic, who epitomizes concretely and bodily the position of the schizophrenic, depicts in its most stark and observable form the consequences that ensue when we impose on him a requirement that he make a move. He will either maintain his pose, so that our impression is of negativism or refusal, or he will follow our demand as though the very air and space around him were tangible. The action that he carries through under continuing pressure from us has all the quality of a movement made right in the teeth of a world of pure resistance.

It is clear, however, that the tester whose approach to his work is dominated by a tacit conviction about his own flawless clinical rectitude will hardly raise such questions, let alone allow the test material to provide tentative answers. Instead, he may utilize the tests in the service of a predetermined set of convictions; perhaps—to take an example with which we are all familiar—to enable him to spell out, with flourishes, the drama of the patient's inner life. This is the method of choice of many clinicians who show a great natural talent as playwrights, although their case of characters is usually severely limited and repetitive, and they, themselves, are restricted to standing well outside the patient in order to peer in. Or the tester may prefer to use the test material simply and primitively as a set of facts which need only a practiced hand to fit them to a prearranged scheme, as a mechanically adept subject might fit blocks of different shapes into precut holes. A radically different kind of method, however, will begin and end within the vital situation of two protagonists at odds in a situation that encompasses them both. An immediate consequence will be the recognition that clinical tests differ in the ways in which possibilities are offered the subject to state where he stands in relation to the test situation and examiner. This central characteristic of clinical testing is particularly relevant as regards the total performance of Gregor; and we may therefore go through the material in some detail to trace it out.

It would seem that if a test is to be of use at all, the examiner should be able to guess in advance what his subject's answer might conceivably be. If it is the kind of a test in which he can make no such guess and the subject's answer is always to some degree a surprise, then the resulting interpretation will have to consist entirely of the examiner's own educated fantasy. One of the tests used with Gregor, the "scribbling drawing" technique of Elkisch (1948), brings us very close to the "fantasy" end of a continuum, of which the other end might be constituted, for example, of the examiner's organized theory concerning a structured and objective test. Now, it is of great interest that Gregor's ease, freedom, and lack of hesitation are directly proportional to the extent to which a particular test lies toward the "fantasy" end of this continuum. The examiner's comment to the Scribbling test was: "The subject did the original scribbling with considerable freedom and no hesitation" (Bell, 1949a, p. 165). Similarly, when he began to fingerpaint, "the subject showed no hesitation" (p. 187), and on the Horn-Hellersberg Picture-Completion Test (Hellersberg, 1945) he "worked rapidly and with confidence" (Bell, 1949a, p. 170).

Of the twenty-seven tests in the battery, these three are probably the least "structured," if we use this term to mean that it makes no sense to refer to an answer as right or wrong and that the number and range of possible answers to the test instructions are practically unlimited. On these, Gregor's mode of response, or approach to the task, was close to that of the creative, normal adult, whom we expect to enter into such wholly projective tasks with a sense of spontaneous freedom and pleasure. But as we begin to move along our continuum, we find that Gregor's discomfort, his tendency to back away and disclaim, his mannerisms, and the degree of disturbance manifested in his test productions increase correspondingly. In the Drawing test, for example, where a continuum of structuredness is exemplified in the separate tasks required, he was asked first to draw a person; and the figure he drew, which was of a definitely outlined woman, was done with no resistive or evasive comment. Next, he was asked to draw a person of the opposite sex, and to this more structured request he responded with a much vaguer figure, asking when he was more or less finished, "Is that enough?" The third request, to draw a house, resulted in a very sketchy and primitive outline; to the fourth request, to draw a face he liked, he could only make a start and then quit; and to the last two, a face disliked and a self-portrait, he confessed that he was unable to do it at all. The sequence of tasks in this test is, for technically important reasons, graded so as to produce material of an increasing personal relevance; but it may also be noted that the sequence corresponds just as much to one of increasing specificity—that is, to an increasing extent to which the result can be judged by standards already available to the examiner. Thus, as the test became more structured, Gregor's performance deteriorated.

Because the test situation is ultimately one that involves both patient and examiner, what we find to be true of one will turn out to refer to the other as well. We have just noted that the more "projective" a test is, the freer, in general, is the subject; and this is perfectly correlated with the fact that in such tests the examiner, too, is less restricted by a structure. Each of them, examiner and patient, find a greater freedom to express in fantasy the possibilities opened by their shared situation. But in a more structured test like the Wechsler-Bellevue—again, by the use of *structured* we refer to the extent to which the subject's answers can be judged and graded by an examiner—the subject is literally forced to stick with the question and to answer it in an all-or-none manner. Most of the items on this test, for technically good reasons related to its original use as a test of intelligence, may be scored either right or wrong; or they may at least be scored as poor, fair, or good. Because of this specific and univocal character of the questions, the examiner is always in a position to state whether the subject does in fact stick with the task.

Faced with such questions as those of the Wechsler-Bellevue, then, Gregor adopts a number of different ways of responding. If the answer is easily available to him, as in the simpler items of a test, he gives it; but if, for some reason, he does not have a fairly good answer at his fingertips, he slides away, he gives up, he says he does not know, he guesses vaguely and ineffectively, or his response is clearly inappropriate and suggestive of a thought disorder. With the exception of his skill at constructing patterns—for example, he did the Block Design items with ease, which may be related to his ability in drawing—his talents are revealed as entirely glib and superficially verbal, and they perform no service in enabling him to come to grips with a problem. He even goes so far as to give a fairly good answer and then decide in favor of backing away from it, as in his response to the "Land in City" item on the Comprehension subtest: "—there's more people on it—wait I'll give that over again. I don't know." In addition, he has one other technique by which he attempts to hold off the specific demands of the test: he offers a random, and therefore incorrect, answer to the first item of a subtest, in this way resisting at least initially the change in set required for a new task. Thus, his most extreme errors occurred as responses to an initial item—for example, he could not repeat the digits 582 forward nor 629 backward, although he succeeded with five digits forward and on a second trial with three digits reversed; he added 5 and 4 incorrectly on the Arithmetic test; he responded to the Envelope item of the Comprehension subtest with "—put it in the post box," apparently a contamination of "post office" and "mail box"; and his answer to the first item of the Picture Completion subtest was "Signature."

Clinical tests differ, we noted above, in regard to the possibilities offered to both S and E. In terms of a continuum running from fantasy to structure—which embraces one set of possibilities offered to Gregor—we have seen that he displays both freedom and confidence at one end of the continuum, and a particular pattern of "holding off" and backing away at the other end. One result is that he appears to be more clearly psychotic on the Wechsler-Bellevue than on the less structured tests; on the latter, it is his characterological traits or areas of distress which are usually revealed.

These conclusions are, of course, not offered as a diagnostic formulation, for our task here is not to establish a diagnosis. With regard to the hospitalized schizophrenic, that has usually been accomplished repeatedly, over the years, and could in most cases be done again by an experienced ward attendant. In Gregor's case the question is not whether he is schizophrenic but in what way he is, what this means for the structure of his own world, and how we may use our understanding of his condition both to help him in his life adjustment and to increase our grasp of human problems in general. When we look at his test productions in this light, we see, not a continuum of passivity-aggressiveness nor a deteriorating process, but first of all a pervasive quality of ineptness. He simply fails to meet a problem or a demand. We have seen that this quality varies in accordance with the degree of structuredness of the tests, from a blithe and careless freedom in the purely projective measures to an evasive backing away in the more organized tasks. The content as well as the style of his responses on tests falling between these extremes reveals without exception his overriding quality. Having offered this, however, we must emphasize again that as a generalization concerning a particular test subject it differs significantly from the kind of descriptive statement contained in a diagnosis. Recall that we arrived at it, not by the application of a theoretical framework to some test data considered abstractly, but by considering one of the fundamental characteristics which unites examiner and subject in a test situation; by reviewing our own contributions as well as those of Gregor in this light; and then by fitting to the resultant picture the kind of totally descriptive term that one might require in a task of social perception.

As so often occurs with the stabilized and relatively test-wise schizophrenic, the patient himself offers the best single description of the stance that he takes in this situation. In answer to the question of what the man that he has drawn is thinking, he says: "Well, he's not—he seems to be—he knows that he has to—he's purposely keeping a blank mind—as though you told him to stand there only—no! that's wrong as I look at the picture—he just doesn't know what's happening" (Bell, 1949a, p. 9). Perhaps one should not pick out one remark from the responses to an entire battery of tests and claim that it alone is representative. However, our choice is justified in part by the fact that Machover does just this in her dramatic interpretation of Gregor's Human Figure Drawings. She quotes a part of his association to the drawing of the male figure: "as though you told him to stand there—he just doesn't know what's happening." To this she comments, "The latter association is a perfect self description. Gregor is virtually holding his breath because someone told him to and he will resume life again soon, he hopes" (Bell, 1949b, p. 449). Here is a most instructive point of agreement as well as difference. We agree with Machover that in describing the drawing of a male figure in this way Gregor provides an apt appraisal of himself; but it should be noted that we do not agree on the conclusions to be drawn from it. What is perhaps most interesting is that Machover chooses to pass over the patient's revealing term "purposely." Only by ignoring his use of this word can she conclude that Gregor is almost holding fast "because someone told him to." The fact is that he, himself, offers even this interpretation only as a weak alternative which he then quickly withdraws in favor of no interpretation at all. This is consistent with his entire test performance. Contrary to Machover's moving portrayal of a "crisis in the struggle against disintegration" (p. 447), the inescapable impression, if one comes to the material with no presuppositions about the stark intensity of the schizophrenic's inner turmoil, is that he manages to cope with an overwhelming clinical assault with no more than mild distress, embarrassment, occasional confusion, and retreat to some habitual psychotic mechanisms.

In addition to the rather negative finding concerning his emptiness, however, some positive conclusions may now be drawn from certain consistencies in the test record. If we are justified in pointing to the expression "purposely keeping a blank mind" as a fitting summary of his condition, and if we have correctly understood the way in which his performance varies from free to evasive in accordance with the "openness" or "closedness" of the task, then the conclusion is forced on us that in some sense Gregor knows the significance of what he offers on the tests. His decision, whatever it may be, was made before the test began, so to speak; and by virtue of it he follows a certain pattern through the range of test demands. If we were to try to state in one word what that decision might be, we would offer that its direction is to inspire the examiner rather than inform him. This is the sum total of whatever meaningful or understandable acts Gregor carries out in the testing.

We can now learn something further about the schizophrenic position if we study Gregor's test performance in these terms. Like all chronic schizophrenics, he has passed beyond the turmoil that is popularly supposed to characterize his state; that was left behind at the close of a period marked by psychotic symptomatology, and he will rediscover the turmoil only when he is pushed back to this period by our attempts to have him revert to his premorbid state. Our attempts toward this end usually go by the name of cure—and, therefore, both his impenetrable resistance to our efforts and his horror at the prospect of reliving the psychotic period are perfectly understandable. The schizophrenic has, by this means or occasionally by others, arrived at a position; and if he were able to achieve a reflective understanding of it so that he could state for our benefit what it involves, he might tell us that it requires him to act as though nothing mattered. No act is consequential; therefore, none points ahead; and as a necessary consequence, all acts take place in the immediate present or else by virtue of gains retained from the past. Thus, when left to himself he will appear to go through an endless series of pointless movements or else he will seem to do nothing. The pattern will change only when we approach him, particularly when we come armed with those tools which define a trade bent on effecting some change in his declared position. If he is at all wise in the ways of the institution—as Gregor most certainly was—he will be able to take the tests rather than appear untestable; and what will then be revealed is not the fact of his schizophrenic position, which preceded the testing session as a decision precedes an act, but the habitual or characterological modes by which he effectuates the decision.

In Gregor's case, as we have seen, these modes consist of a limp and self-disclaiming ineptness, a naïvely ingratiating pleasantness, and the overt denial of any exercise of power. That these are typical characteristics in his case is suggested by the very fact that he was chosen as a subject for the study. It is improbable indeed that a patient would have been picked for such exhaustive testing if he had given any indication that he would fail to "give his all" for the cause of research. Once he enters the testing situation, and then remains in it long enough for clinicians to obtain their data from him, it becomes possible to take an uninterrupted look at the interplay of his modes—and here lies the special value of the clinical tests. The point that we have made about Gregor, however, and by extension about every other test subject to whom these pages refer, is that the use of the tests in this way depends on our first establishing a context for understanding the data we obtain. Every judgment that we pass in regard to another person, if we take it seriously, is a declaration of our commitment to him in his full worth as a person. But this can hardly be achieved if we pretend to no stake in the situation; this is a commitment which is false to its premises. However we conclude our meeting with him, then, we should at least begin it by establishing a context of understanding rather than exploitation. The clinical patient, whether schizo-phrenic or not, and whether in or out of the hospital, is not a collection of evidence in regard to our predetermined theory, but the very life of our practice; not the target for our technique, but the living source of our method. Our problem, given anew at each session, is to judge the situation that tests both examiner and patient; to establish the quality of the encounter; to state a context by declaring a specific resultant of social perception; and only then to begin to constrain both partners by explanatory propositions fitted to the social or insti-tutional demands of the situation.

SOCIAL
PERCEPTION

The Interpretation of Style

OUR TRAINING AS CLINICIANS AS WELL AS OUR ORIENTATION AS
scientists often combine to prevent us from realizing how much of
the processes of social perception, as these are spontaneously and even
naïvely accomplished, enters into our test interpretations. Examples
can be multiplied in the experience of any psychologist who uses
tests; they range from simple judgments of a subject's emotional state
to such complex evaluations as are exemplified in our tendency to
overrate the intelligence of the paranoid and underrate the intelligence
of the hysteric. On occasion, too, the phenomena which are grasped

269

in social perception form the significant core of a subject's test productions. The TAT stories that follow, as a demonstration of the
latter point, were written in longhand by a young male subject, probably schizophrenic, who was in prison for multiple murder. His own
life history had been an unrelieved tale of brutality, neglect, and crime.

Card 3BM. Arey is in a daze he has been for the last 2 or 3 days
since the police picked him up. He has been trying to tell them he doesnt
know anything about a robbery but everytime they take him out they beat
him and throw him in his cell. He wonders if they will call his mother.

Card 18 BM. Johnny had been needing money pretty bad to take care
of his family. He had tried for 2 weeks now to find a Job but couldnt.
So he got his gun and tryed to rob a store. but the police run in and
caught him. he is thinking what will my wife think what will happen to
them now they send him to prison for 5 yr. his wife gets a divorce and
marries another guy and adopts his kids out. So he hangs himself in his
cell one night.

Card 4. George had made up his mind to go to the new hore house
he had been thinking of going for a week now. He picks the first girl
he sees and he is through and some woman bangs on the doar and says
come on out or pay more money your time is up. George puts his cloths
on and opens the door and there stands his sister he hasn't seen her for
6 years she begs him not to tell their Mother he is stunded and wonders
out in a daze. he desides not to ever go in a hore house again.

Card 6BM. Charlie had had his draft call for a week now but had'int
told his mother yet on the day he was to leave he told her she said she
felt sick and was goring to bed for him to write her and take care of himself. after he got in camp he wrote his Mother every day.

Card 17BM. George was doing life and had served 6 years allready
he had been planing to excape since first day he was hear. Now the time
was hear he had disided not to wear his cloths as he had to swim the
river. When he was sliding down the rope on the out side he wondered
if he could swim that far it looked a lot wider than he had expected. he
had swum about half way when the cramps took him and he sunk out of
site.

Card 7BM. James had served his time and had started out the front
gate when the warden called him back and told him he would like to
talk to him in his office. The warden talked on and on. James thinks to
him self i wish this bastard would get unwound. he felt irotated. he wanted
to be going. the warden finely shook hands with him and wished him

good luck. James was out in front of the prison now and starts across the street when a car swings around the corner and hits him. a man said and he just got out of prison to hear is his release.

Card 13MF. Pauls wife had been feeling pretty bad lately and that in turn made paul feel bad. he had been staying out late at night for a couple of weeks this time when he came home his wife had taken a bunch of poison and was laying dead on a cot. he stood their and wondered what she did it for. After that he wondered around the country a while then joined the army and got killed.

Card 13B. Homer's mother and dad had been on a drunk for 3 or 4 days, they started fighting and the police came out and got them and put them in jail. he set in the doar way for a long time and wondered when his mother was coming home. a big car drove up in the yard and took him to a place whear their was a lot of kids and he never saw his mother or dad again.

Suppose that we attempt to discover and make explicit just what it is in these stories which makes them a moving document. We would certainly point to the actual content—to the sadly repeated theme of a moment's happiness or privilege which is followed by some blow or perverse turn of fate. Even when the story does not directly touch on this plot, it states some of the associated conditions, as it were: the innocent man wrongfully accused and therefore torn from his mother (3BM), or the young man holding to a last tie with his mother (6BM). In addition to the bare content of the stories, however, there is an atmosphere which permeates them. One might tell a story of a man who was drowned while trying to escape from prison—as in fact many convicts do on this and similar tests—in a wide variety of styles and approaches. The subject may present it to the examiner as a little bribe, offering a morally tinged tale of deserved punishment as a way of showing the examiner that he himself realizes the consequences of wrongdoing; or he may add the unhappy ending as an ironic tagline to a story of adventure and drama; or he may restrict himself to a rather plain recital of well-known facts.

But none of these alternatives describes any of the stories in this group. The death which comes at the end has about it the quality of inevitability; and added to this is the storyteller's conviction of the pointlessness of it all. If only the first of these qualities were evident, the stories would sum up to tragedy; but with the addition of the second, they take on the character of horror. Yet it is horror related in the flat and toneless voice of one who is beyond it because he has learned to live with it and with nothing else. All that remains as relief from the dead atmosphere is a faintly realized wish for the figure of a mother, and even with this to cling to, there is depicted a world which, as in the story told on Card 4, has much of the disconnected and unreal quality of a nightmare.

Much more might be said about these stories and thus about the subject who tells them. But if we stick to an attempt to understand their unique quality, as we have done in the preceding paragraphs, we will find that the task is uncommonly difficult. We can easily point to the formal aspects of the stories—the heroes used, the types of endings, the relationships with male figures which are depicted, the primitive affect displayed, and so on. But all of this would not capture for us the atmosphere in which they are steeped. Yet it is this atmosphere which may well be the key element in our understanding of this particular criminal. The distinctive aspect of these stories lies in a kind of "coloring," which is a phenomenon with its own structure; we can sense it, but we cannot grasp it so fully as to be able to restate it in the formal terms of an independent schema. Though we apprehend it, and thus would probably have little difficulty in picking out this subject's stories from those of a dozen other young, schizophrenic criminals, we find that our only recourse in handling it is the unsatisfactory one of restating it in a semiliterary description.

A term that might be applied to the subject himself, to match the word *coloring* that we have applied to his stories, is *mood*. By this we refer to the total quality of his social presence, insofar as we are able to apprehend it. It is more than simply his emotional state, although this is an essential contributing element, and more than the "what" of his communication with us. As Heidegger (1962) has argued in analyzing the concept of mood, it refers to the way in which one is "tuned," and therefore it is an intrinsic part of how one is perceived in a shared situation. The method that we use, because we can have no other, is our spontaneous social perception with its gains as well as its losses. We find, on doing this, that we have already grasped the phenomenon, but we discover also that we can often only point dumbly to it, asking that another viewer join us and look in the same direction.

The terms that we have just used—*atmosphere, coloring, mood*—seem to refer to different varieties of the same kind of phenomenon. A more general term, perhaps no more satisfactory but at least broader in scope and more neutral in its connotations, might be *style*. We will, therefore, use it here to suggest that aspect of a person's social presence which is grasped originally, and usually unthinkingly, in the course of spontaneous perception. A common example may be found in our sure sense of someone's charm, or perhaps his coldness—and indeed, it is probable that the adjectives that we use to describe other persons, based upon our perception of them in ongoing situations, do not refer at all to static characteristics but rather to varieties of the one original phenomenon we have called style. Thus, to say that a mountain is high, on viewing it, is not at all the same as to say, on meeting a person, that he is charming or cold. The former refers to an analyzable characteristic which forms part of a given condition, the latter to one facet of a shared situation, in this case the facet based upon one of the participant's social perceptual processes.

These generalities may be spelled out in another, more complex set of TAT stories. They were written, as part of the complete series, by a 27-year-old subject who had had almost four years of college and was referred for counseling.

Card 1. The boy's father, who comes from the lower socio-economic levels and has always prided himself on having tendencies toward the "finer" things (say he manufactures dresses but reads Modern Library editions of the philosophers), has bought the poor kid a violin. Come what may, the boy will be a second Menuhin. He's a quiet kid, respectful and pretty well trained, so he makes no overt objection—and besides, he's impressed by his father's glowing pictures: "$10,000 a concert, just imagine! No factory work for you, no sir." Some vague dreams are beginning to form in the boy's mind, and the dreams (plus family pressure) will carry him through the first few lessons. Then there will be a plateau of drudgery, and he will finally drop the whole thing when he gets old enough to rebel openly. When he grows up and has a son of his own, he will give *his* son a violin and, though a successful and wealthy manufacturer of zippers himself, he will tell his son: "$25,000 a concert! No working in a factory for you."

The identifying characteristics we listed did not mention whether the subject is male or female. Nevertheless, it is most probable that readers of this production, whether clinically trained or not, would have no difficulty in arriving at the consensus that the subject is male —and further, they would quite probably agree on some other relevant facets of the personality which seem to be revealed in the story. The subject is clearly fluent, verbally gifted, intelligent, and at ease in the situation of being tested. Whether or not he is as clever as he tries to be or thinks he is, it is evident that he is motivated to display a kind of flip and cynical cleverness as his salient attitude toward the task given to him in the testing situation. Equally clearly, he is not moved in the direction of constriction, or confusion, or worrisome concern with detail; of the many possible ways which might define his overriding attitude, he has given us this one.

We have not yet arrived at a picture of a personality; nor of course have we said anything beyond the most elementary of statements about the subject's psychological functioning, diagnostic category, psychodynamics, or defensive structure. Yet in some way we have already described a person. We know—or at least we are more than reasonably certain—that the person is male rather than female; yet this is the sort of *prediction,* as it is often mistakenly termed, which cannot be arrived at by any of the rules or principles which might give us defenses, diagnosis, or dynamics. There is a certain kind of data that we have managed to gather even in this preliminary survey of the subject's story. It is clearly not the same sort that we obtain when we go about interpreting a TAT story, or a set of Rorschach responses, or, for that matter, any test production susceptible to use as a projective instrument. The data we have gathered here are apparently available to almost anyone who will take the test production seriously; and therefore the examiner is, at least initially, not much better off than his nonclinical associates or even the subject himself. In addition, our data have the quality of seeming self-evident; and they were apparently obtained immediately, almost directly, rather than by the application of a chain of reasoning to some carefully stated axioms.

These are, as the reader will already have recognized, just the characteristics which would appear to belong to social perception. This is what happens if we approach a test production with no claim to limiting the subject, with no goal of diagnosing or categorizing him, guided by nothing other than the spontaneous interest with which we go through an act of social perception. Even the sketchy example that we have discussed thus far is sufficiently clear to allow us to offer some generalizations about this process of deliberate social perception. First, it is evident that this is not a process of intuition; there is nothing at all that is mysterious, magical, subjective in a derogatory sense, or unreliable about it. The fact that most of us can do it should hardly be cause for professional jealousy on the part of trained clinicians, but rather for joy in discovering that their own central activity is so solidly grounded in a meaningful human act. Further, it is apparent that a method based on the conscious utilization of the miracle of social perception does not constitute an alternative system of interpretation; it does not furnish still another set of interpretive statements, a new way of obtaining a diagnosis, nor a fresh system for categorizing its subjects. Its relation to existing approaches is, rather, that it provides a test protocol, as we may define this term—that is, it organizes the test data in such a way that it enables us to discover differences between persons without committing ourselves to expressing power in relation to them. For this reason the method of social perception offers a context within which existing interpretive approaches may freely find their respective places. Every such method of interpretation will of necessity be limiting and thus limited; and our further task as clinicians is to determine just how the test protocol, as we have derived it, can best be utilized by means of one or another interpretive system.

Two more stories from the same subject will provide material for developing these points.

Card 9BM. Collection of laborers resting on the grass when the boss left for a while. They've been busy repairing a section of railroad track, it's August, and the foreman is a couple of miles away on the handcar, so they're taking a break. But it doesn't last long—they hear the handcar approaching, get up in a hurry, and grab their tools. What they don't know is that the foreman had gone down the track to take a nap himself and would have stayed there except that he heard *his* boss approaching.

Card 10. Mother and father (they look too old to be a young couple) have just had a pretty rugged session with their son, who insists on leaving home, marrying the girl that he wants, and setting up for himself. The son has stormed out of the house in what he thinks is a dramatic exit, though unfortunately he has had to stop to pick up his galoshes, and the father is comforting the mother. She thinks she's lost a son forever, he feels the same way but has to display some fortitude and comforting. They both recover from the episode, though it leaves an empty spot, since both parents and son are too proud to give in. Finally the kids have a baby and he sends them a card congratulating them on being grandparents, there's a grand reconciliation, they all have a couple of drinks, the father magnanimously offers to take the son into business, the son refuses, there's another scene—it's a hell of a life.

We would in all likelihood have no difficulty in assigning these three stories to the same author, and we would probably be able to state our reasons quite easily. What they have in common, it strikes us, is a *style*—and by this term we mean to include the characteristics mentioned above in regard to the first story alone: its maleness, its fluent and flip attitude, and its ease, as well as a more general quality that we might sum up as a way of handling the story-telling task. In each case the subject seems to accede actively to the test instructions and to do so without straining. He describes what is going on in the picture, then what led up to it, and he appends an ending which tells what the outcome will be. But in another sense this is not quite what he does. He certainly does not go through a sequence of past-present-future, as some subjects do who denote the temporal transitions in their stories by saying, "And then he . . ." or "What will happen is . . ." The method our subject chooses of conforming to the rather artificial instructions of the test is unique, but it is also consistent and, therefore, we are justified in seeing it as an indicator of his style. In essence, he never leaves the present tense. The past is given in a series of flashbacks, the future as a mere logical consequence with the character of inevitability.

We may compare this way of handling the formal test instructions with a number of other approaches: the more usual one of simply relating a sequence of events, or the one of restricting the story to a description of the situation as depicted on the card. The procedure based on a sequence does appear to depict a past, present, and future, but these temporal dimensions have an impersonal quality. In the terms used by technicians who work with electronic computer programs, this kind of TAT story is not placed in "real" time; that is, the time represented in the story has no sensible relation to the actual time in which the test situation takes place. Equally, a procedure in which the subject can do no more than talk about the situation shown on the card is not a description of a "real present" but again of an impersonal and fictive time. By contrast, our subject's response to the test situation is unique. The stories that he tells all take place in a living present; it is almost as though he were so involved in them as to be caught up within their time, filling us in on the background by means of flashbacks, predicting for us what the inevitable outcome will be. As nearly as such calculated stories can be, these would seem to be openly autobiographical.

Our first attempt at examining the subject's style, when it is viewed as the pervasive expression of his adjustment to the test situation, has led us to this conclusion concerning his involvement in the test. Note that this conclusion is not stated in the form of a diagnostic formulation or an interpretation of his defensive structure. Rather, it is meant as a way of describing the position he chooses to take in the contrived and complex situation that is the clinical encounter. Our conclusion, then, becomes a first sentence in the test protocol—that form of organization of the data when they are approached with no commitment to limiting or defining the subject. We can now add to our first statement the ones that we made above, concerning the subject's glib, flippant, yet fluent and relatively relaxed attitude toward the task. The combination of these statements gives us what seems like a contradiction, which we may put in the form of a question: How are we to understand a test subject who is on the one hand relaxed and casual, almost flippant, and in full control of his verbal gifts, yet at the same time so involved in the test situation as to offer a series of clearly autobiographical stories? The answer will not be forthcoming without further study of these three stories and of the remainder of the series as well. However, one point should now be clear: that by means of an approach which approximates social perception—foregoing interpretation, accepting without question just what the subject attempts to do, refraining from diagnosing or categorizing, and simply apprehending his style as figure against the known background of the test encounter—it is possible to develop a protocol as *a context within which specific interpretive interests may be pursued*. The sketch of a protocol which we have developed on the basis of these three stories tells us a great deal about the subject's chosen relation to all situations which are similar to a testing session. In this particular case, it tells us much about his range of possible responses to a contemplated course of psychotherapy—which happens to have been the reason for testing him. He has obviously come to the point where he will give at least as much as he is presently capable; he will go along with it and work at it; he will be involved, whether he appears to be happy about the involvement or not; and he will persistently cover this response with an elaborate cloud of glib, flippant, often wry maneuvers which he, at least, will tend to perceive as rather successful evasions.

With this much gained—but only after this point has been reached in regard to organizing a test protocol—we will then be in position to pursue whatever directions of interpretation are suggested to us by the theoretical and nosological scheme to which we may individually subscribe. One possibility might be to examine more closely the theme of parent-child relations, and in particular father-son relations, which appears so clearly as a focus in the three stories. Of equal interest, and not unrelated to this first theme, is the curious thematic trick of repeating the plot within the plot. In each of the three stories the trick appears: in the first story, the specific conflict between father and son is repeated without change as a conflict between the son and his own son in later years; in the second, the attitude of the laborers toward their foreman is mirrored in the attitude of the foreman toward his own superior; and in the third, the quarrel between parents and son is patched up but renewed in the same manner after the son has himself become a parent. The moral that our subject seems to be suggesting, by means of this twist of plot, is twofold: the eternal quarrel with parental figures may be resolved by one's becoming a parent oneself, but in the long run this is but a temporary solution; the quarrel is really eternal. On this basis alone, it would not be at all farfetched to entertain such formulations as "identification with the aggressor" and "depressive underlay."

Reflectiveness and Social Perception

A clinical science has to start with the straightforward statement that its concern is with people and their actions in relation to one another. In such a case, as we noted in Chapter Two's discussion of defining behavior, its data are nothing other than perceptions of other persons, either in the form of the data gathered by one subject about another, or those apprehended by the scientist, as experimenter or examiner or therapist, about his opposite number in the clinical setting. When Burns wrote,

> O wad some Power the giftie gie us
> To see oursels as ithers see us!

he sketched out the field of the clinical sciences—they look for some understanding of persons, and for this they depend on knowledge of "how ithers see us." The general problem of how we know other people and how they know us is hardly new. Yet interestingly, when serious attempts are made to consider this question, the results turn out to add little to our understanding. Consider, for example, Bakan's (1956) argument that "knowledge of the other one is somehow to take place by reference to one's own experience" (p. 660). This, he says, is based on "the assumption that, after all, we are all pretty much alike. And insofar as we are all alike we might be able to 'understand' one another by referring each other's expressions to our own experiences; and by some process which, we will say, is very much like the logical process of inference, we predict and thereby control the behavior of the other person" (p. 658). Plausible as this appears, it has the defect of understanding uniqueness by way of a proposition about communality, a logic which is bound to lead to either an illicit or a circular argument. Further, it must assume some process of inference, by whatever name one calls it, to account for the recognition and utilization of similarity. Most important, it says nothing about what is really the key element in the involved process

—the way that a person is supposed to know about his own experience.

Can we, as Bakan argues, rest the case for social perception—and ultimately a theory of the clinical sciences—on this kind of knowing? Or may there not be another kind of knowing, both of oneself and of the other, which does not require a "logical process of inferring" or indeed any chain of logic at all? One possibility has been generally ignored in a discipline bent on the conquest of thing-like data. It is that two kinds of data, the social and nonsocial, must be included in the findings of a psychological science. The relation between them cannot be stated *a priori*, but will only become clear as we develop a theory that enables us to deal with both kinds of data. For a most useful beginning, then, our aim should be, not to assume that there are no distinctions that can be made between the two, but to devote our efforts to discerning the ways in which they do in fact differ.

I propose that there are five important ways in which data of social perception differ from data of nonsocial preception. First, social perceptual data cannot—with one exception to be discussed below—be gathered by a person in reference to himself. It is, of course, true that a person can look at himself and then deliver, either to himself or to someone else, a report about himself; and it may appear that these are the data of social perception. But this report arises from the person's ability to hold himself for a period as a kind of object, and what is social in this instance is therefore not the target but the origin of the perception; the report, then, is an instance of social perception rather than its results. Second, the possibility of an experiment in social perception—which depends, like all experiments, on the experimenter having at his disposal a means of posing both dependent and independent variables—is ruled out because the experimenter can never be any better off than his subjects. The requirement, as we have noted previously, has been well stated by Bruner: "It is of the essence in any given experiment that we define in advance what we as experimenters mean by relevant information and do not depend upon the subject's response to do it for us; otherwise we would be in a complete circle" (1951, p. 131). But since the experimenter's version of the target in social perception is intrinsically no different from that of his subjects, there is no way he can satisfy this initial requirement; he has no guarantee that he is not in fact caught in the circle to which Bruner refers. Herein lies the source of the impenetrable difficulties surrounding experiments in this field, difficulties not solved but only brushed over by such devices as bringing in still a third group of equally similar persons, known as judges, and trusting that their majority vote will end the methodological filibuster to which the experimenter has of necessity committed himself.

A third characteristic unique to the data of social perception is that such data have an insistent and ubiquitous logic which is not met with in the data of nonsocial perception. In an early experiment, using facial parts based on Piderit's "geometry of expression" to make up various expressions, Boring and Titchener (1923) found that they could not fit together a face, even of apparently contradictory elements, which did not turn out to be "sensible" to their subjects. The phenomena of social perception are universal, self-evident to a very great degree, and seemingly grasped as such without specific training. The infant, for example, who has barely reached the stage when he can respond to the difference between a square and a circle—surely a perceptually simple distinction in the nonsocial realm—will easily react differentially to social perception stimuli of much greater complexity, such as smiling as against frowning faces or harsh as against tender voices.

This characteristic of social perceptual data is closely related to a fourth, that these data when apprehended lead to a specific and unique experience on the part of the perceiver himself. Social perception, as an act, is not a form of cognition; the one who has it does not know but grasps—or rather, what he knows is known immediately, completely, and without an aura of the probable. Suppose a person approaches me with a broad grin on his face and his arms outstretched in a greeting. In an instant I know that this person is friendly, and with this I know that he is not angry, not sad, not afraid, not disgusted, not bored, not horrified. Moreover, there is a special way in which I know this. Most knowledge, either of facts or of details, is of a probabilistic kind; having the knowledge, we are always aware that more knowledge is possible. This is its nature. If I say that I have a knowledge of linoleum installation, or glass blowing, or the history of architecture, I mean by this that I am in possession of a certain portion out of the sum total of facts in each area. Quite probably there is never a case in which our factual knowledge of an area is complete. What would this be like? The experience would probably be one, not of knowledge as we know it, but of intuition— for having complete knowledge of something, any idea that I might have about it would have the character of completeness and inevitability; it would seem self-evident, like the knowledge held by poets or angels.

Now this, of course, simply never occurs in any instance in which ordinary knowledge is possible. For first of all, complete knowledge of any area is probably beyond human capacity. It is inconceivable that the total range of facts about architecture, even though that total is certainly finite in number, could ever be encompassed by one person. Too, there are practical reasons why none of us ever even approach this ideal—reasons that point to the fact that total knowledge, or even impressively partial knowledge, is rarely required except by those specialists who are deviant even in their own fields. Recall, for example, our naïve awe in the face of quiz contestants who appeared to have mastered what to the rest of us seemed an impossibly large portion of the available facts in their field of specialization. For both these reasons, then, total knowledge is unknown in any situation where the knowledge is one of pre-existing facts. But the difference is striking in even the most common instance of the perception of expressive behavior in another person, for here our experience is one of absolute and complete knowledge. When the other person approaches me in what I take to be a move of friendly welcome, I know this in a way that would make the addition of any facts a superfluity. There is nothing that could be added, not a single additional fact that I could know, which would serve to change the character of my knowledge of his relationship to me. In this instance there is only one fact: he likes me. Therefore, the social perceptual data are grasped wholly and unthinkingly; and calling any of my experiences into question—for example, by asking me, "How do you know?"—is felt as superfluous and unanswerable because it introduces issues which have no place in my perceptual experience. And it is for just this reason that experience in situations of social perception often has the character of an intuition. It is not because any magical process is involved; on the contrary, nothing appears to us as so natural, so little artificial, as an instance of social perception. Rather, the experience reminds us of an intuition because complete knowledge of the relevant situation always appears to the perceiver in this way.

The last characteristic to be proposed about the data of social perception is that for each datum at least two possibilities always appear. The choice between them is made completely and unthinkingly, but it is also made in the awareness that what is presented both hides and suggests at least one other full and complete possibility. In social perception both overt and covert appear, each somehow residing in the other, the former enriched and brought alive by the latter, the latter lying behind and stating the source of the mystery of the former. For this reason we always know that we can never fully grasp or master the datum of social perception, that if we could, it would change its character and harden into the nonsocial entity we may handle without risk to ourselves. It is this characteristic of the data of social perception which is, so to speak, imitated by the ambiguous stimulus when the latter is presented to the subject in the course of clinical testing.

In discussing the first of the characteristics which are unique to social perception, we noted a few pages back that the person cannot make himself a target. If he apprehends social perceptual data, it must be of a social perceptual object; but when he serves as object, he leans toward the nonsocial and thereby stands in the way of the social perceptual act on his own part. The self-knowledge gained by turning the perceptual act on oneself is therefore almost bound to become a trap for the unreflective, for it pretends to just that kind of understanding which it must, by definition, rule out. The attempt at self-knowledge must lead to a dilemma, for no matter how much the person wants to know himself as something other than an object, his own act allows him no alternative. As Sartre (1953) points out, an attempt at knowledge about myself "can succeed only if I distrust every kind of intuition, only if I apply to my case from without, abstract schemes and rules already learned. As for the results, whether they are obtained by my efforts alone or with the co-operation of a technician, they will never have the certainty which intuition confers; they will possess simply the always increasing probability of scientific hypotheses" (pp. 214–215). Indeed, this may be just why those who parade so proudly their presumed insight into their problems and motives thereby advertise their true inability to see themselves as they really are. And it is probably also why the most awful results in psychotherapy are seen when the patient achieves nothing more than what is called *intellectual insight,* by which we mean a kind of relatively complete knowledge that one might have in regard to nonsocial perceptual data.

At the other extreme from such persons, whose tragedy is that they are able to know themselves too well, is the patient—for we see him most frequently in this role—who is incapable of knowing himself at all unless he sees himself in the light reflected from other persons. As the hyperknower tends toward the diagnostic category called *the character disorder,* so the man who knows himself only by reflection, whose world is totally a world of people, may be placed in the broad group called *hysteric.* The difference between the two is seen in almost every aspect of their behavior as patients—for example, whereas the character disorder, when he is also psychotic, acts quite well until he comes in contact with a staff member and only then shows his symptomatology, the hysteric, when he is psychotic, seems disturbed on the ward but becomes much less so when face to face with the staff personnel. It is the hysteric who responds so encouragingly to a program of "total push," in which all the resources of a world of people are brought to bear on him to change him in directions that other people would wish. When one talks to such a patient to try to find out how things appear to him during the time that he seems, to others, to be acutely disturbed, he is likely to describe a static world, a void without life. He has no direct knowledge of his psychotic behavior; because he is alone, "it" simply happens. Alone, he is incapable of knowing himself and thus of knowing what he is doing, for the "what" has no reality. It is the presence of other persons which makes this world come alive—just as it does, in fact, for the nonpsychotic member of the same diagnostic grouping whom we know so well in the role of actor. The actor knows, far better than we can ever tell him, what it means for the world to change, magically and instantly, when he steps on a stage to confront the pure presence of people incarnate; for is not an audience such a distillation of social reality, with its hum and applause and hush and warmth, its meaning and sense and whispers, its secrets and expectancies, individually faceless but totally human? The hysteric, lost in a world of social reality, is as much a victim of the dilemma of knowing as is the character disorder, who can know nothing but the nonsocial realm.

In this sense, it would seem, every person will be defeated in the attempt to look at himself, to know something of himself, or to assess his situation and prospects. Yet, as we all know, constructive knowledge of oneself is in some way possible. Psychotherapy would be a painful trick and a fraud if this were not so. Beyond the dilemma to which we have pointed, there must then be another phenomenon —and indeed, it turns out that it is something that all of us have known for as far back as our significant, as opposed to our merely factual, memories extend. This phenomenon we will call *reflectiveness*. Its definition is found in each situation of the person who recognizes his present position in its relation to his own history. Its source lies in the distinctive character of man whereby he can find ways to surpass the limits of his own experience. In reflectiveness we hold in abeyance what we are at the moment, and apprehend the time-boundedness of our present state; and in this way we attain a vantage point from which to view, in small measure or great, the fated course of our life which constitutes our unique destiny.

Because the basis of reflectiveness is in this tie to the significance of our lives, it is usually revealed as a phenomenon freighted with import; our moments of drama or crisis are the most familiar manifestations of a continuous current of reflectiveness that marks and colors our lives. The man who asks, "What have I done?" in this question expresses fully his recognition that one act is highlighted against the pattern of all his actions; the child who for the first time shows guilt when confronted, by an outraged parent, with the result of his latest foray; the person who leaps for joy at achieving a long-sought goal; anyone who asks himself, or someone else, "Should I?"; the citizen who considers how he ought to vote and then acts in accordance with that decision; the student who says, "I'd better not—I have to study tonight," and thereby gives up an immediate and inconsequential pleasure; the one who declares his love, and the one who freely accepts it as well. The list and variety are infinite, for they comprise every act for which we are prepared to acknowledge consequences. They are limited in actuality only by our habit, by our thoughtless activities of the moment, by the rush of our trivial and momentary delights, and by those psychopathic traits of character which lead some of us to act much of the time (and all of us to act some of the time) as though the past had no present force, the future no power, and ourselves no history at all.

There are many instances, both customary and pathological, in which we are constrained within some nonreflective experiential state. These moments, when recalled later, have a unitary quality about them: what we remember is the totality of the moment as an occasion rather than any of its distinctive or differentiated details; and what we also remember is an overriding quality, a color, that permeates the total experience. When the event is not only permeated but suffused with this single quality, the state is one of pure emotionality—as in the blind rage of anger, the panic of fear, the unmitigated gloom of sadness, the pure ecstasy of joy, the utter rapture of love. These states are boundless; indeed, we speak of "unbounded happiness," or of "anger that knows no limits." And they are complete; beyond them can be only exhaustion and collapse on the one hand, or confusion in which the existing person as such disappears on the other. Moreover, such states of pure emotionality preclude reflectiveness and, therefore, any vantage point which is definable apart from the state itself. The person who can even for an instant be reflective about his own anger thereby degrades it, and he experiences the degradation as his own foolishness—that is, if he is at all capable of a vantage point from which he can make such an estimate. The person who reflects on himself, even for an instant, while in the rapture of love, is thereby cursed with a lack of fulfillment.

In many moments of action, whether impelled by our own needs or by the felt demands of the world, the same nonreflective character is paramount. The vigorous exercise of the body for its own sake, or the pure appreciation of sensual pleasure, as in lolling in a hammock or skiing swiftly, preclude reflectiveness both at the moment and in retrospect. Again, we remember these as experiences, not as sequences of facts or details. It is, in fact, only when we lose some of the richness and the immediate "feel" of the event that we are able to reflect upon it, to differentiate its details, perhaps even to savor its nuances and shadings. Out of this loss and out of this gain arises all the possibility of human knowledge.

The process of reflectiveness, then, is the beginning out of which man becomes something other than a pure experiencer whose momentary state is bounded completely by the given limits of his body. Prior to reflectiveness, or in its absence, change is possible only if *outside of his experience* a change occurs in the person's bodily state. Given reflectiveness, change may occur within experience, to be experienced as choice. Then the person can learn, because he can change his position in relation to a known and limited object. He can construct a stable world in which things repeat themselves—and there open to him the alternatives of either facing the novel as a challenge or fearing the unfamiliar as a threat. Out of reflectiveness comes experienced time; and finally, out of the passage of time into one's history comes memory.

It is in reflectiveness that a person knows himself—not as an object of nonsocial perception (as though he were simply one other thing), but in the same way that, through social perception, he comes to know any person. The data of reflectiveness and of social perception are of the same order; and he who can apprehend the one, in the form of truly knowing himself, can apprehend the other when he meets another person as person. This, then, is why the person who can be reflective seems to infer the experience of others on the basis of his own experience. We can now see that he is not tracing out a logical chain but only shifting the center of his regard. Thus we can understand why it is that self-awareness, that process which is supposed to distinguish man from all other creatures, turns out to be imitated by the simplest feedback mechanism, for it is not at all the mark of being human. The latter requires not merely that apprehension be directed back toward its own source—for this occurs in every feedback loop —but that there supervene what can never occur in a machine: a personal history, a reflective sense of it, and the biography of decision that accords with it.

It does not occur very frequently in clinical testing, nor in the clinical setting in general, that the situation is arranged to call for reflectiveness. It may happen when, in psychotherapy, the therapist continually turns the patient's thinking back upon himself—although even the gain in this way may easily be cancelled out when the understanding gives way to explanation, and a joint exploration of origins and consequences becomes a catechism in causes and results. But only when it does occur is it possible for the mutual struggle between therapist and patient, or examiner and subject, to be replaced by a course of events in which the subject shares his situation with the examiner. As it happens, there is just such a device built into every clinical test, yet the consequences for the investigation of reflectiveness have seemingly never been examined. This device is, of course, the inquiry which, in one form or another, is part of every test instrument when it is used clinically rather than in limited and objective fashion.

In the Rorschach in particular, the procedure of the inquiry makes explicit the basic demand that is made on S by the test instructions. He is asked to agree that two persons may not see the same thing, and then he is required to justify to E the way in which his perception may differ. The structured question contains no such requirement. Rather, the reverse is true, for with such questions as "When is Washington's birthday?" the whole point of asking is to determine whether examiner and subject see eye to eye. A question of the "projective" type, on the contrary, offers more than one possible answer and therefore calls forth each subject's justification for his choice. The ambiguous stimulus demands the reflective subject.

The inquiry is both a test requirement and an approach in testing. It provides an added dimension in the setting where the subject and the examiner meet—for only the reflective subject can share his situation with the examiner, and therefore only with the reflective subject can the examiner change a position of resistance to one in which understanding of some sort is possible. This must be related to the all-important fact that, of all the conceptions which may be used to help us understand the events taking place in the clinical setting, reflectiveness is the only one which rests on a dimension of temporality rather than public time. Here is our clue, that whereas theories of learning and habit, or mechanical systems based on feedback and quanta of information, are at home in a reality with its dimension of public time—an endless line marked off by equally spaced counters—any theory which attempts to encompass the phenomenon of reflectiveness must make room for temporality as the human dimension. For the person is reflective only insofar as he knowingly places himself and his own actions within a human reality. His own present must appear to him, not as a disconnected locus in isolation from its past and future, but as the origin of his memories and the result of his hopes, thereby reversing the scientist's irreversible arrow of time. Like every person who stands recognizably at some point in a history of which he sees himself a part, he *has* a future and *has* a past; they belong to him in a way that cannot be true of the entity or organism whose place is merely at some point on a changeless line.

Turned inward or out, toward the significance of one's own history or the import of another's, reflectiveness repeats each time the relation called by Buber (1958) the *I-Thou.* "If I face a human being as my *Thou,* and say the primary word *I-Thou* to him, he is not a thing among things, and does not consist of things. . . . Thus human being is not *He* or *She,* bounded from every other *He* and *She,* a specific point in space and time within the net of the world; nor is he a nature able to be experienced and described, a loose bundle of named qualities. But with no neighbour, and whole in himself, he is *Thou* and fills the heavens. This does not mean that nothing exists except himself. But all else lives in *his* light" (p. 8). Thus, full perception of another person as person occupies the same place in experience as reflective awareness of oneself; both reach toward knowledge of the person as Thou.

The data of social perception, we have said, are all that there are for a clinical science. In the form of the test subject's attempts to make sense out of his total perceived situation, these data will determine how he goes about taking, or interfering with, the examiner's test. As the consequence of reflective awareness, they will provide the center around which he and the clinician circle in their mutual attempts at understanding, in the projective test as well as in the psychotherapy session. Finally, they will furnish the starting point and the final goal for the endeavors of the clinician as experimenter and examiner. If so, the subject may then be accepted in his full worth as a person who is as marked by intention and caught by history as is the examiner himself. But one final warning must be

added: nothing we can ever do in the clinical situation, or in any
other human setting, will assure our capturing all of a subject as
a person. For a moment we will have him completely in our confident
grasp—and then he will astonish us with a novel delusion, commit
an unheard of crime, or write a poem. By these acts we will be
reminded again of his special glory, that because of what he is, there
is no way at all to take the full measure of that maverick of existence,
man.

BIBLIOGRAPHY

ADAMS, J. K. Laboratory studies of behavior without awareness. *Psychol. Bull.*, 1957, 54: 383–405.

ADORNO, T. W., E. FRENKEL-BRUNSWIK, D. J. LEVINSON, and R. N. SANFORD. *The Authoritarian Personality.* New York, Harper. 1950.

ALLPORT, G. W. The use of personal documents in psychological science. *Soc. Sci. Res. Counc. Bull.*, 1942, no. 49.

ALLPORT, G. W. The trend in motivational theory. *Amer. J. Orthopsychiat.*, 1953, 23: 107–119.

ALLPORT, G. W., and P. E. VERNON. *Studies in Expressive Movement.* New York, Macmillan. 1933.

ASCH, S. E. Studies in the principles of judgments and attitudes: II,

291

Determination of judgments by groups and by ego standards. *J. soc. Psychol.*, 1940, 12: 433–465.

ASCH, S. E. *Social Psychology*. New York, Prentice-Hall. 1952.

AUERBACH, E. *Mimesis*. New York, Doubleday Anchor Books. 1957.

BACK, K. W. Influence through social communication. *J. abn. soc. Psychol.*, 1951, 46: 9–23.

BAKAN, D. Learning and the scientific enterprise. *Psychol. Rev.*, 1953, 60: 45–49.

BAKAN, D. Clinical psychology and logic. *Amer. Psychol.*, 1956, 11: 655–662.

BARRETT, W. Homer and Greek reality. *Chi. Rev.*, 1959, 13: 39–48.

BARTLETT, F. C. Fifty years of psychology. *Occup. Psychol.*, 1955, 29: 203–216.

BASS, B. M. Authoritarianism or acquiescence? *J. abn. soc. Psychol.*, 1955, 51: 616–623.

BECK, S. J. *Rorschach's Test. Vol. II: A Variety of Personality Pictures*. New York, Grune & Stratton. 1945.

BECKETT, S. *Endgame*. New York, Grove Press. 1958.

BEERLING, R. F. Power and human nature. *Phil. Phenom. Res.*, 1955, 16: 214–222.

BELL, J. E. The case of Gregor: Psychological test data. *Ror. Res. Exch.* and *J. proj. Tech.*, 1949 (a), 13: 1–51.

BELL, J. E. The case of Gregor: Interpretation of test data. *Ror. Res. Exch.* and *J. proj. Tech.*, 1949 (b), 13: 433–468.

BENDER, L. *A Visual Motor Gestalt Test and Its Clinical Use*. Amer. Orthopsychiat. Assn., 1938, Res. Monogr. No. 3.

BENTON, A. L. Rorschach performances of suspected malingerers. *J. abn. soc. Psychol.*, 1945, 40: 94–96.

BERG, I. A. Response bias and personality: the deviation hypothesis. *J. Psychol.*, 1955, 40: 61–72.

BERGMANN, G., and K. W. SPENCE. The logic of psychophysical measurement. *Psychol. Rev.*, 1944, 51: 1–24.

BINSWANGER, L. *Schizophrenie*. Pfullingen, Neske. 1957.

BORING, E. G. *A History of Experimental Psychology*. New York, Appleton-Century-Crofts. 1929.

BORING, E. G., and E. B. TITCHENER. A model for the demonstration of facial expression. *Amer. J. Psychol.*, 1923, 34: 471–485.

BROZEK, J., H. GUETZKOW, M. V. BALDWIN, and R. CRANSTON. A quantitative study of perception and association in experimental semi-starvation. *J. Pers.*, 1951, 19:245–264.

BRUNER, J. S. Personality dynamics and the process of perceiving. In R. R. Blake, and G. Ramsey (Eds.). *Perception, An Approach to Personality.* New York, Ronald. 1951. Pp. 121–147.

BRUNER, J. S., and C. D. GOODMAN. Value and need as organizing factors in perception. *J. abn. soc. Psychol.,* 1947, 42: 33–44.

BRUNER, J. S., and L. POSTMAN. Emotional selectivity in perception and reaction. *J. Pers.,* 1947, 16: 69–77.

BRUNER, J. S., and L. POSTMAN. Perception, cognition, and behavior. *J. Pers.,* 1949, 18: 14–31.

BUBER, MARTIN. *Between Man and Man.* Boston, Beacon Press. 1955.

BUBER, MARTIN. *I and Thou* (2nd ed.). New York, Scribner. 1958.

BURKE, C. J. Further remarks on one-tailed tests. *Psychol. Bull.,* 1954, 51: 587–590.

CARTER, L. F., and K. SCHOOLER. Value, need, and other factors in perception. *Psychol. Rev.,* 1949, 56: 200–207.

CHAPMAN, L. J., and D. T. CAMPBELL. Response set in the F scale. *J. abn. soc. Psychol.,* 1957, 54: 129–132.

CLARK, W. E. L. The crucial evidence for human evolution. *Amer. Scientist,* 1959, 47: 299–313.

COHEN, J. *Humanistic Psychology.* London, Allen & Unwin. 1958.

COHN, T. S. Is the F scale indirect? *J. abn. soc. Psychol.,* 1952, 47: 732.

COLE, D. Communication and rapport in clinical testing. *J. consult. Psychol.,* 1953, 17: 132–134.

COMBS, A. W., and D. SNYGG. *Individual Behavior: A Perceptual Approach to Behavior* (rev. ed.). New York, Harper. 1959.

COPLIN, H. The measurement of subjects' orientation toward a Sentence Completion test. Unpubl. Ph.D. dissertation, Univ. of Michigan, 1951. Ann Arbor, Univ. Microfilms, Publ. No. 3482.

COUNTS, R. M., and I. N. MENSH. Personality characteristics in hypnotically-induced hostility. *J. clin. Psychol.,* 1950, 6: 325–330.

CRONBACH, L. J. Studies of acquiescence as a factor in the true-false test. *J. educ. Psychol.,* 1942, 33: 401–415.

CRONBACH, L. J. Response sets and test validity. *Educ. psychol. Measmt.,* 1946, 6: 475–494.

CRONBACH, L. J. Further evidence on response sets and test design. *Educ. psychol. Measmt.,* 1950, 10: 3–31.

CRUTCHFIELD, R. S. Conformity and character. *Amer. Psychol.,* 1955, 10: 191–198.

DEWEY, J. The reflex arc concept in psychology. *Psychol. Rev.,* 1896, 3: 357–370.

ELKISCH, P. The "Scribbling Game"—a projective method. *Nerv. Child,* 1948, 7: 247–256.

ERIKSEN, C. W. Discrimination and learning without awareness: A methodological survey and evaluation. *Psychol. Rev.,* 1960, 67: 279–300.

FALK, J. L. Issues distinguishing idiographic from nomothetic approaches to personality theory. *Psychol. Rev.,* 1956, 63: 53–62.

FERNBERGER, S. W. The APA: a historical summary, 1892–1930. *Psychol. Bull.,* 1932, 29: 1–89.

FOOTE, N. N. Love. *Psychiatry,* 1953, 16: 245–251.

FOSBERG, I. A. Rorschach reactions under varied instructions. *Ror. Res. Exch.,* 1938, 3: 12–30.

FOSBERG, I. A. An experimental study of the reliability of the Rorschach psychodiagnostic technique. *Ror. Res. Exch.,* 1941, 5: 72–84.

FRANK, L. K. *Projective Methods.* Springfield, Ill., Thomas. 1948.

GIBSON, J. J. A critical review of the concept of set in contemporary experimental psychology. *Psychol. Bull.,* 1941, 38: 781–817.

GODDARD, H. H. The Binet tests and the inexperienced teacher. *Trng. Sch. Bull.,* 1913 (March), 9–11.

GOLDSTEIN, H. A malingering key for mental tests. *Psychol. Bull.,* 1945, 42: 104–118.

GOODENOUGH, F. L. *Mental Testing, Its History, Principles, and Applications.* New York, Rinehart. 1949.

GORDON, L. V., and E. S. STAPLETON. Fakability of a forced-choice personality test under realistic high school employment conditions. *J. appl. Psychol.,* 1956, 40: 258–262.

GOUGH, H. G. Simulated patterns on the Minnesota Multiphasic Personality Inventory. *J. abn. soc. Psychol.,* 1947, 42: 215–225.

GOUGH, H. G. The frame of reference of the Thematic Apperception Test. *J. clin. Psychol.,* 1948, 4: 90–92.

GURWITSCH, A. The phenomenological and the psychological approach to consciousness. *Phil. Phenom. Res.,* 1955, 15: 303–319.

GUTTMAN, L. What lies ahead for factor analysis? *Educ. psychol. Measmt.*, 1958, 18: 497–515.

HACKER, A. A political scientist looks at psychotherapy. *Int. J. soc. Psychiat.*, 1956, 2: 23–33.

HALEY, J. The art of psychoanalysis. *ETC: A Rev. of Gen. Sem.*, 1958, 15: 190–200.

HARRIMAN, P. L. *The New Dictionary of Psychology.* New York, Philos. Libr. 1947.

HEALEY, E. Psycho-analysis finally explained. *Punch,* 1934 (Aug. 8), 187: 162.

HEGEL, G. W. F. *The Phenomenology of Mind* (2nd ed.). New York, Macmillan. 1931.

HEIDEGGER, M. *Being and Time* (transl. J. Macquarrie and E. Robinson). London, SCM Press. 1962.

HELLERSBERG, E. F. The Horn-Hellersberg test and adjustment to reality. *Amer. J. Orthopsychiat.*, 1945, 15: 690–710.

HERON, A. The effects of real-life motivation on questionnaire response. *J. appl. Psychol.*, 1956, 40: 65–68.

HEYERDAHL, T. *Kon-tiki: Across the Pacific by Raft.* Chicago, Rand McNally. 1950.

HUNT, H. F. The effect of deliberate deception on Minnesota Multiphasic Personality Inventory performance. *J. cons. Psychol.*, 1948, 12: 396–402.

HUNT, W. A. The detection of malingering: A further study. *US Nav. Med. Bull.,* 1946, 46:249–254.

HUNT, W. A., and H. J. OLDER. Detection of malingering through psychometric tests. *US Nav. Med. Bull.,* 1943, 41: 1318–1323.

JACKSON, D. N. A further examination of the role of autism in a visual figure-ground relationship. *J. Psychol.,* 1954, 38: 339–357.

JACKSON, D. N., and S. J. MESSICK. A note on "ethnocentrism" and acquiescent response sets. *J. abn. soc. Psychol.,* 1957, 54: 132–134.

JACKSON, D. N., and S. J. MESSICK. Content and style in personality assessment. *Psychol. Bull.,* 1958, 55: 243–252.

JAMES, W. *Principles of Psychology* (2 vols.). New York, Dover. 1950.

JONES, E. *The Life and Work of Sigmund Freud,* Vol. 1. New York, Basic Books. 1953.

KELLY, E. L., and D. W. FISKE. *The Prediction of Performance in Clinical Psychology.* Ann Arbor, U. of Mich. Press. 1951.

LAIRD, D. A. Detecting abnormal behavior. *J. abn. soc. Psychol.,* 1925, 20: 128–141.

LAMMING, GEORGE. *Season of Adventure.* London, Michael Joseph. 1960.

LAZARUS, R. S., and R. A. MCCLEARY. Autonomic discrimination without awareness: A study of subception. *Psychol. Rev.,* 1951, 58: 113–122.

LEWIN, K. The conflict between Aristotelian and Galileian modes of thought in contemporary psychology. *J. gen. Psychol.,* 1931, 5: 141–177.

LUCHINS, A. The stimulus field in social psychology. *Psychol. Rev.,* 1950, 57: 27–30.

LYONS, J. Existential psychotherapy: Fact, hope, fiction. *J. abn. soc. Psychol.,* 1961, 62: 242–249.

LYONS, J. On the psychology of the psychological experiment. In C. Scheerer (Ed.). *Cognition: Theory, Research, Promise.* New York, Harper & Row, Publishers. 1963.

MACDOUGALL, W. *Psychology, the Study of Behavior.* New York, Holt. 1912.

MACDOUGALL, W. *Outline of Psychology.* New York, Scribner. 1926.

MCGILL, V. J. The bearing of phenomenology on psychology. *Phil. Phenom. Res.,* 1947, 7: 357–368.

MACLEISH, A. *Collected Poems, 1924–1933.* Boston, Houghton Mifflin. 1933.

MACLEOD, R. B., The Phenomenological Approach to Social Psychology. *Psychol. Rev.,* 1947, 54: 193–210.

MACLEOD, R. B. Teleology and theory of human behavior. *Science,* 1957 (Mar. 15), 125: 477–480.

MALLER, J. B. The effect of signing one's name. *Sch. & Soc.,* 1930, 31: 882–884.

MARGOLIS, B. D. The problem of "facade" in the counselling of low scholarship students. *J. cons. Psychol.,* 1945, 9: 138–141.

MAY, R., E. ANGEL, and H. F. ELLENBERGER (Eds.). *Existence: A New Dimension in Psychiatry and Psychology.* New York, Basic Books. 1958.

MAYO, G. D., and I. GUTTMAN. Faking in a vocational classification situation. *J. appl. Psychol.,* 1959, 43:117–121.

MEEHL, P. E. The dynamics of "structured" personality tests. *J. clin. Psychol.,* 1945, 1: 296–303.

MEEHL, P. E., and S. R. HATHAWAY. The K factor as a suppressor variable in the Minnesota Multiphasic Personality Inventory. *J. appl. Psychol.,* 1946, 30: 525–564.

MELTZER, M. M. Countermanipulation through malingering. In A. D. Biderman, and H. Zimmer (Eds.). *The Manipulation of Human Behavior.* New York, Wiley. 1960. Pp. 277–304.

MELTZOFF, J. The effect of mental set and item structure upon response to a projective test. *J. abn. soc. Psychol.,* 1951, 46: 177–189.

MERLEAU-PONTY, M. *La Structure du Comportement* (4th ed.). Paris, Presses Universitaires de France. 1960.

MEYER, M. F. *The Psychology of the Other One* (2nd ed.). Columbia, Mo., Missouri Book Co. 1922.

MILLER, J. G. Discrimination without awareness. *Amer. J. Psychol.,* 1939, 52: 562–578.

MILLS, E. S. Personality adjustment and the study of abnormal psychology. *J. appl. Psychol.,* 1955, 39: 358–361.

MOWRER, O. H. "Sin," the lesser of two evils. *Amer. Psychol.,* 1960, 15: 301–304.

MURRAY, H. A. The effect of fear upon estimates of the maliciousness of other personalities. *J. soc. Psychol.,* 1933, 4: 310–329.

MURRAY, H. A. *et al. Explorations in Personality.* New York, Oxford Univ. Press. 1938.

MURRAY, H. A. *Thematic Apperception Test Manual.* Cambridge, Mass., Harvard Univ. Printing Office. 1943.

NELSON, B. Phenomenological psychiatry, *Daseinsanalyse,* and Existential Analysis: A "Progress Report." *Psychoanal. & Psychoanalyt. Rev.,* 1961, 48: 3–23.

OLSON, W. C. The waiver of signature in personal reports. *J. appl. Psychol.,* 1936, 20: 442–450.

OSSIPOV, V. P. Malingering; The simulation of psychosis. *Bull. Menn. Clin.,* 1944, 8: 39–42.

PASTORE, N., and M. W. HOROWITZ. The influence of attributed motive on the acceptance of a statement. *J. abn. soc. Psychol.,* 1955, 51: 331–332.

298   BIBLIOGRAPHY

PETERSON, J. *Early Conceptions and Tests of Intelligence.* Yonkers, N.Y., World. 1925.

POLANYI, M. *The Study of Man.* Chicago, Univ. of Chicago Press. 1959.

POLLACZEK, P. P. A study of malingering on the CVS abbreviated individual intelligence scale. *J. clin. Psychol.,* 1952, 8: 75–81.

PROSHANSKY, H. M., and G. MURPHY. The effects of reward and punishment on perception. *J. Psychol.,* 1942, 13: 295–305.

RAPAPORT, D., M. GILL, and R. SCHAFER. *Diagnostic psychological testing* (2 vols.). Chicago, Yearbook Publishers. 1946.

ROCK, I., and F. S. FLECK. A re-examination of the effect of monetary reward and punishment on figure-ground perception. *J. exp. Psychol.,* 1950, 40: 766–776.

ROGERS, C. R. Where are we going in clinical psychology. *J. consult. Psychol.,* 1951, 15: 171–177.

ROGERS, C. R., and R. F. DYMOND (Eds.). *Psychotherapy and Personality Change.* Chicago, Univ. of Chicago Press. 1954.

ROSENZWEIG, S. The experimental situation as a psychological problem. *Psychol. Rev.,* 1933, 40: 337–354.

ROSENZWEIG, S. A suggestion for making verbal personality tests more valid. *Psychol. Rev.,* 1934, 41: 400–401.

ROSS, B. M., and N. LEVY. Patterned predictions of chance events by children and adults. *Psychol. Rep.,* 1958, 4: 87–124.

RUCH, F. L. A technique for detecting attempts to fake performance on a self-inventory type of personality test. In Q. McNemar, and M. A. Merrill (Eds.). *Studies in Personality.* New York, McGraw-Hill. 1942. Pp. 229–234.

RYCHLAK, J. F. Clinical psychology and the nature of evidence. *Amer. Psychol.,* 1959, 14: 642–648.

RYLE, G. *Dilemmas.* New York, Cambridge Univ. Press. 1954.

SANFORD, E. C. Personal equation. *Amer. J. Psychol.,* 1888, 2: 3–38.

SANFORD, E. C. Personal equation: II. *Amer. J. Psychol.,* 1889(a), 2: 271–298.

SANFORD, E. C. Personal equation: III. *Amer. J. Psychol.,* 1889(b), 2: 403–430.

SARTRE, J–P. *Existential Psychoanalysis.* New York, Philos. Libr. 1953.

SARTRE, J–P. *Existentialism and Human Emotions.* New York, Philos. Libr. 1957.

SCHAFER, R., and G. MURPHY. The role of autism in visual figure-ground relationship. *J. exp. Psychol.*, 1943, 32: 335–343.

SCHMIDT, P. F. Models of scientific thought. *Amer. Scientist*, 1957, 45: 137–149.

SEEMAN, W. "Subtlety" in structured psychological tests. *J. consult. Psychol.*, 1952, 16: 278–283.

SKODAK, M. Children in foster homes: A study of mental development. *Univ. Ia. Studies Child Welf.*, 1939, 16: no. 1, 156.

SMITH, L. P. *All Trivia.* New York, Harcourt, Brace. 1945.

SNYGG, D. The need for a phenomenological system of psychology. *Psychol. Rev.*, 1941, 48: 404–423.

SONNEMAN, U. *Existence and Therapy; An Introduction to Phenomenological Psychology and Existential Analysis.* New York, Grune & Stratton. 1954.

SOSKIN, W. F. Frames of reference in personality assessment. *J. clin. Psychol.*, 1954, 10: 107–114.

SPENCER, D. The frankness of subjects on personality measures. *J. educ. Psychol.*, 1938, 29: 26–35.

SPIEGELBERG, H. *The Phenomenological Movement: A Historical Introduction* (2 vols.). The Hague, Martinus Nijhoff. 1960.

STEINMETZ, H. C. Measuring ability to fake occupational interest. *J. appl. Psychol.*, 1932, 16: 123–130.

STEVENS, S. S. Psychology and the science of science. *Psychol. Bull.*, 1939, 36: 221–263.

STOTSKY, B. A. The authoritarian personality as a stereotype. *J. Psychol.*, 1955, 39: 325–328.

STRASSER, S. Phenomenological trends in European psychology. *Philos. Phenom. Res.*, 1957, 18: 18–34.

STRAUS, E. W. *Psychologie der Menschlichen Welt.* Berlin, Springer. 1960.

SUTTIE, I. D. *Origins of Love and Hate.* London, Kegan Paul. 1948.

THOMPSON, C. *Psychoanalysis: Evolution and Development.* New York, Hermitage House. 1950.

THOMSON, G. The new industrial revolution. *Bull. atom. Sci.*, 1957, 13: 9–12.

TILLICH, P. *Systematic Theology*, Vol. 1. Chicago, Univ. of Chicago Press. 1951.

TILLICH, P. *Love, Power, and Justice—Ontological Analyses and Ethical Applications.* New York, Oxford Univ. Press. 1954.

TOMKINS, S. S. *The Thematic Apperception Test: The Theory and Technique of Interpretation.* New York, Grune & Stratton. 1947.

TOULMIN, S. *The Uses of Argument.* New York, Cambridge Univ. Press. 1958.

VERNON, P. E. The attitude of the subject in personality testing. *J. appl. Psychol.,* 1934, 18: 165–177.

WAHL, J. A short history of existentialism. New York, Philos. Libr. 1949.

WALLIN, J. E. W. *The Odyssey of a Psychologist.* Wilmington, Del., Author. 1955.

WARREN, H. C. (Ed.). *Dictionary of Psychology.* Boston, Houghton Mifflin. 1934.

WATSON, R. I. A brief history of clinical psychology. *Psychol. Bull.,* 1953, 50: 321–346.

WATSON, R. I. The history of psychology: A neglected area. *Amer. Psychol.,* 1960, 15: 251–255.

WEISSKOPF, E. A., and J. J. DIEPPA. Experimentally induced faking of TAT responses. *J. consult. Psychol.,* 1951, 15: 469–474.

WELLEK, A. The phenomenological and experimental approaches to psychology and characterology. In H. P. David and H. von Bracken (Eds.). *Perspectives in Personality Theory.* New York, Basic Books. 1957. Pp. 278–299.

WIENER, D. N. A control factor in social adjustment. *J. abn. soc. Psychol.,* 1951, 46: 3–8.

WILD, J. The new empiricism and human time. *Rev. Metaphys.,* 1954, 7: 537–557.

WILD, J. Is there a world of ordinary language? *Philos. Rev.,* 1958, 67: 460–476.

WILLOUGHBY, R. R., and M. E. MORSE. Spontaneous reactions to a personality inventory. *Amer. J. Orthopsychiat.,* 1936, 6: 562–575.

ZUBIN, J. Recent advances in screening the emotionally maladjusted. *J. clin. Psychol.,* 1948, 4: 56–63.

INDEX

acceptance, knowledge and, 13
act, intentionality of, 225; as performance, 157
activity-passivity behavior, 260
Adams, J. K., 178
Adorno, T. W., 241
affectation, 148
aggressiveness, 18
ahistorical thing, 141–142
Allport, G. W., 18, 38, 136, 146
alternative, concept of, 111
ambiguity, philosophy of, 191; psychology of, 171–197
ambiguous stimulus, 177–196
American Ortho-psychiatric Association, 172
American Psychological Society, 172, 256
American psychology, history of, 172
analogy, reasoning by, 9
analyst, role of, 16; see also patient-therapist relations
anthropological psychology, 52, 58
anticipation, vs. reaction time, 114
anxiety, 192
aptitude tests, 226
Aquinas, St. Thomas, 91, 93
argument, rules of, 9–10
Aristotle, 79, 83, 140, 152
Army Visual Classification Test, 228
art, ambiguous stimulus and, 193; vs. technology, 24
artist, 192–197
Asch, S. E., 221–223
"as-if" behavior, 75
association, speed of, 164
associationism, 162, 165
"atmosphere," 273
Auerbach, Erich, 112
Augustine, St., 119–120
autism, restricted, 174
autochthonous field, 177

Back, K. W., 217
Bacon, Sir Francis, 148
Bakan, D., 53, 279–280
Barrett, W., 106
Bartlett, F. C., 116
Bass, B. M., 241
Beck, S. J., 148, 174
Beerling, R. F., 208
beginning and ending, phenomenon of, 79–89
behavior, clinical tests of, 151–157; de-

fining of, 47–49; "marks" of, 48–49; psychologist's interest in, 31–35; see also clinical psychology
belief, affirmation and, 12
Bell, John E., 256–265
Bender, L., 227, 256
Benton, A. L., 227
Berg, I. A., 240
Bergmann, G., 34–37
Bessel, Friedrich Wilhelm, 98–102
Binet, Alfred, 164–166
Binet-Simon Scale, 166–168, 171
Binswanger, L., 51, 110
biography, data of, 28; as history, 14–20
Blake, William, 95, 159
Boas, Franz, 163
book, publication of, 21–22
Boring, E. G., 101, 168, 281
Brozek, J. H., 147
Bruner, J. S., 143, 175–178
Buber, Martin, 14, 50–52, 289
Buddhist temple, Japan, 90
Burke, C. J., 133
Burns, Robert, 279

Campbell, D. T., 241
Carter, L. F., 176
catatonia, 261
Cattell, James McK., 100, 162–164, 168–170
Chapman, L. J., 241
childhood experience, character and, 15, 18; unconscious perception and, 178; withdrawal and, 136
Christianity, idea of God in, 91
chronograph, first, 102
chronology, 84, 97–99, 106–110, 119–121
Clark, W. E. L., 11
clinical psychology, experiments in, 138–139; "golden decade" of, 171; history of, 173–174; privateness of, 149; two kinds of data in, 147, 153; see also psychological tests
clock, 97–99, 106–108
Cohen, John, 120
Cohn, T. S., 242
Cole, D., 216
"coloring," of TAT stories, 271–273
Combs, A. W., 51
communication, explanation and understanding in, 45; independent schema in, 40–41; invention and, 153
conditioned reflex, 115